JOHN BRANDI

THE SACRED MOUNTAINS
OF ASIA

EDITED BY JOHN EINARSEN

SHAMBHALA
BOSTON & LONDON
1995

SHAMBHALA PUBLICATIONS, INC.
Horticultural Hall
300 Massachusetts Avenue
Boston, Massachusetts 02115

Printed in the United States of America on acid-free paper ∞

Distributed in the United States by Random House, Inc., and
in Canada by Random House of Canada Ltd

Library of Congress Cataloging-in-Publication Data
The sacred mountains of Asia/edited by John Einarsen.—1st ed.
p.   cm.
Originally published as: Kyoto Journal, no. 25, c1993.
ISBN 1-57062-088-1 (pbk.: alk paper)
1. Mountains—Religious aspects. 2. Mountains—Asia. 3. Asia—
Religion. I. Einarsen, John.
BL325.M63S23   1995   94-40384
291.3′5′095—dc20   CIP

C o n t e n t s

Borobudur, Ohki Akira

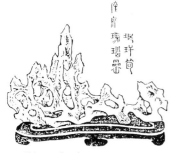

Hsiuo-yü Cave-heaven

*The Womb-cave of Mt. Fuji:
entering the vagina. Sadahide, 1858*

▲ SACRED MAN-MADE MOUNTAINS

Po-shan-lu, Han dynasty
Incense burner with mountains
emerging from water

▲ TRAIL LORE

Mt. Agung, Bali, John Einarsen

THE SOURCE OF
THE PERSONIFICATION OF SHIVA

J O H N   B R A N D I

The mountains work on the psyche of the people.
They are there in the eye.
They penetrate the unconscious.
They lift their folded wings into the sun's mouth,
into the moon's silver cruet.
They begin deep beneath the horizon
and end just before the stars.
The mountains float between children's swings,
between the wooden rungs of village Ferris wheels.
They spread icy wings over timber-stripped folds, over pastures and footpaths,
frangipani and whitewashed shrines.
Over birch, oak, fir, deodar and rhododendron they choreograph storms.
The mountains are makers of clouds, guardians of springs.
They begin the day and make rivers flow.
Their canyons hide yetis and snow leopards.

Mendicants perch before turquoise cascades,
reciting mantras, performing yoga, clicking prayer beads
while ice whiskers form on their legs and chests.
Pilgrims ascend the ice floes, half naked, flagging innumerable shrines.
Traders herd yaks, porters lug merchandise to the feet of bosses
who dwell far behind the mountains, in the shadows of their peaks.
In Europe or North America one may experience
the psychological change, the change in spirit that mountains bring.
But nowhere on the planet is this change more powerful
than when a traveler begins on the immense Indian plateau
and works upward to the Himalayan wall; works through stifling cities,
and parched multitudes, the choking plains whose blistered edges
curl like onionskin into the ruthless horizon.

From thousands of miles south the pilgrims come.
Bending in full body prostrations — meter by meter, kilometer
by kilometer — until the first sight of Langtang or Dorje-Lakpa, framed
with poinsettia flowers, brightens the eye. The Himalayan wall rises
like a ladder into the clouds, mixing mists with snow banners
and snow banners with jet stream cirrus.
The sight immediately reminds the pilgrim that ours
is an imperfect copy of another world.
A world higher up than the flatlands of everyday activities.

Architects of stupas, pagodas, ziggurats, cathedrals —
as well as the builders of Macchu Picchu or the sky villages of the American
Southwest — understood the allegorical aspects of geography;
its metaphor; the primal need to "go up." They matched their architectural
skills with internal quests and stepped closer to heaven. To where
sunlight and rain are born. To where the air is thin, the light rare,
the atmosphere needled with vibrations unencountered below.

All architecture of the sacred resembles the mountain.
The ziggurat spirals upward like smoke into the stars, each tier
representing a celestial cycle, a spiritual plateau.
The stupa rearranges the Elemental Peak into abstract,
three-dimensional mandalas, piled one on top of the other,
to represent earth, water, fire, air, ether.
The pagoda hangs gracefully in mid air like a bell, a mountain flower.
The pyramid represents perpetuity, eternity, the beauty
of precision, the mystery of equations.
The Gothic window shines gloriously into a sanctuary
of prayer, its rarefied wave lengths counterfeiting high-altitude light:
the glacial translucence of solitary ice fields near Ama Dablam's summit,
or the throne of Chomolunga, whose ice-chiseled face spreads
a pinkened aura across Khumbu Glacier.
The sculptured lingam, so important to Hindu ritual,
replicates the lone pinnacle that penetrates heaven's blue.
A reverse cosmology is implied: earth is male; its warm pinnacle thrusts
into the female body of sky, which is cool, all surrounding.
Condensation takes place. A storm is born.

Shiva's power came from the mountains.
On Kailas he meditated, gained sight. Today, as in past generations,
pilgrims trek through rain forests and ice crags to reach
the Tibetan plateau from which pokes the earth's central axis: Mt. Kailas.
Once there, the presence of the mountain is enough.
No need to conquer it. Instead, the pilgrim hunkers down to boil
a pot of tea then packs bedroll on shoulder and sets out
to circumnavigate the mountain. The trek is as much metaphysical
as it is physical. Rounding Kailas, the pilgrim realizes that the mountain
is a snow-covered lingam, the source of the personification of Shiva.

And what of times before the Hindus,
when the mountain had yet to be abstracted into the lingam?
Rudra, the Howler, the Lightning-spitting One, was Shiva's Vedic predecessor.
Pelting the lowlands with rain and hail, Rudra — whose origins reach
into the Paleolithic — was the terrifying deity of high mountains.
The White-faced One who could unpredictably turn dark with tempest,
brighten with fire. Rudra: the pre-Aryan roarer whose voice
was associated with the bull, symbol of virility and fertility
basic to hunting and planting cults alike.

Shiva, then, as Rudra.
Shiva, with his phallic-humped bull, Nandi.
Shiva, colored blue with wood ash. The blue of fire's aftermath.
The blue of rarefied atmosphere, the metaphysical ocean
upon which all thoughts, all continents float. The blue of unaltered,
pure-stream consciousness. This is the Shiva who the modern
sadhu imitates, personifies, venerates.

The Shiva who, with lightning wand and cosmic drum,
sits perfectly erect over the world in trance meditation, voice thundering
powerfully through valleys of mist and terraced grain.
It is Shiva's dance that turns the cosmos.
A dance of birth, death, regeneration. A dance of volcanic eruption.
Glaciers grinding continents. The torrential flood
that submerges Bangladesh. The tsunami of the Pacific.
The tsunami of the mind.

All across the Indian subcontinent Shiva is worshiped.
His caste-bronze idol is showered with marigolds. His hair reels outward
like sun spokes, fertility snakes, jets of water exploding from a thunderhead.
His dance of destruction and rebirth is painted on scrolls,
carried through cities, pasted on rickshaw buggies, displayed on army
jeeps, smuggled into antique shops, glued to restaurant walls,
made into pastries, earrings, and automobile decals.
His infinite store of reproductive power is replicated in metal,
ivory, jade, alabaster, granite, plastic, tourmaline, and glass.
Smooth, hard, eternally erect, splashed with coconut milk,
oiled with camphor, greased with body sweat, sat on in Tantric rituals,
circled with live snakes, smeared with ashes of the dead,
his stone lingam is the mystical, reproductive symbol of India.

But Shiva's real praise is given unconsciously
everywhere in India and Nepal as people go about their daily tasks.
When the Pokhara knife grinder spins his stone and sparks fly,
Shiva dances. When the children of Dhulikel chant rhyme songs from
the seats of their wooden Ferris wheels, Shiva dances.
When the butter maid in Ahmadabad churns her milk, when oxen
wheels squeak under massive loads of peas and lentils
en route to Kanpur, when mischievous monkeys spin the Swayambhunath
prayer wheels, when bright-aproned women thresh wheat
in circular movements or switch open the water gates to power their
mill wheels — they become participants in Shiva's primal dance.

Nowhere but within sight of the planet's highest
mountains is this cosmic aspect of the universe — the galactic spin
of all living things, the mundane yet sacred rotation
of one human around another; of moon around earth and earth
around sun — more emphasized.
The fulcrum-working peasants, lifting water from one canal
to another in rhythmic dance, the spiraling snow banners
from the summits of Machhapuchhare, the eery coils of pyre smoke
at Pashupatinath, or an infant twisting its newly-grown locks
with a tiny set of fingers: these are the many arms
of the Eternal Dancer who creates and destroys our universe
daily; who floods our senses with light and shadow.
This is Shiva, whose circular steps
keep the world round,
whose cosmic song puts the universe
in perpetual motion.

◆

JOURNEY TO THE CENTER OF THE EARTH

R A L P H   J O H N S T O N E

Nobody can approach the Throne of the Gods,

or penetrate the mandala of Shiva or Demchog,

or whatever name he likes to give the mystery of ultimate reality,

without risking his life — or perhaps even the sanity of his mind.

He who performs the parikrama...

with a perfectly devoted and concentrated mind,

goes through a full cycle of life and death.

— *Lama Anagarika Govinda, 'The Way of the White Clouds'*

TIBET

"See you at the mountain!"

With a casual wave of his stick, the old pilgrim stepped out into the morning sunshine and set off. "We'll be there," I called after him. Actually, I was beginning to have doubts. For the last two days, we'd been stranded in this earth-walled shack beside a river crossing in central Tibet, waiting — praying — for a ride west. During that time, the few passing trucks had all been too fearful of Chinese officials to take us with them. It seemed it would be Beijing's Big Brother, not Mother Nature, forcing our return.

But the faith of the wiry old pilgrim made us think twice. Here was a man in his early 60s, armed only with a sack of barley-flour, some dried yak-dung for lighting his fires, and the shaggy sheepskin on his back, stepping out of the door as if he were going for an afternoon stroll. Ahead of him lay 800 km of high-altitude desert, a parched, empty wilderness battered by the icy winds rolling off the Himalayas. Yet here was this old man trudging off into it without trepidation, with a smiling. He'd already

walked 500 km from his native Amdo in northeastern Tibet; no land, no climate, could be too cruel for this journey. He was on his way to the Center of the Earth.

If any destination continually inspires people to risk their lives, it is Mount Kailas. This remote peak in western Tibet has been a popular goal of pilgrimage for over 2,000 years, and is today perhaps the holiest destination on earth. The mountain's striking, snow-domed summit, which provided the inspiration for such major monuments as Angkor Wat and Borobudur, is revered by more than half a billion Hindus and Buddhists in India, Tibet and Nepal. For them, Kailas represents the earthly manifestation of the mythical Mount Meru, the great bridge linking the spiritual and material worlds.

Like so many remarkable places, however, Kailas demands the toughest of journeys. Perched high above the western flank of the Himalayas, close to the Nepalese border, the Kailas range stands on one of the farthest, bleakest horizons in Asia, a crinkle in the corner of the great white tablecloth over Tibet.

To reach it, one has to cross either the precipitous wastes of the world's highest mountains, or the frozen wastes of its highest desert, the Chang Tang — a 5,000-meter-high moonscape the size of France.

We did eventually get across this bleak wilderness, with a group of young monks bound for the holy mountain. But after we'd spent six days in the back of their supply truck, sandwiched between a skinned sheep's carcass and several boxes of putrid-smelling yak butter, our Chinese driver insisted on dropping us outside Ali, the small, dust-swept capital of western Tibet. Again, it was fear of Chinese officials — more prevalent in the sensitive region bordering India — which proved our undoing.

▲▲

Where the road from Ali curls into the Kailas valley, it enters a different world. Here, the lifeless gray sands of the desert give way to boundless colors, shadows to God-given rainbows. Out of a grainy orange plain, peppered with yak and sheep, sprouted a stark series of purple peaks, tongues of pure white snow coiled around their toothy summits. The unique mix of tertiary conglomerate rock — of which the Kailas range is the world's highest — formed swirling, suggestive shapes, each of them richly painted and full of life. It was clear how people who lived beneath such humbling peaks could become so holy, so awed by their gods.

We arrived at Darchen, the start of the Kailas *parikrama* (circuit) in a hailstorm. The mountain was wrapped in thick cloud, but we knew now that we would see it — when we were ready. The town was little more than a rough camp, a cluster of felt tents scattered beneath a cave-pitted hillside. But it sparkled with the devotion of those who'd passed through it. Bunches of multi-colored prayer-flags flowered between hundreds of small stone shrines and slate slabs and yaks' horns, all painstakingly carved with the Buddhist mantra, "*Om, mani padme hum!*" (Hail, jewel in the lotus!)

Across the golden plain below, the steel-blue waters of two large lakes glinted in the evening sun. The easterly of these was the famous Manasarovar, revered by Indians since time immemorial as a creation of the mind of their greatest god, Brahma. The lake first featured in the early Hindu epics, the Puranas, together with the heaven-piercing Mount Meru — the axis-mundi around which the ancient world was believed to rotate. Through the centuries, the links between Meru and Kailas have gradually grown stronger, and today more than half a billion devotees regard the two mountains as one.

The connections between the physical

and mythical peaks rise above mere speculation. Like Meru, Kailas stands at the very top of the world — although at 6,714 meters, the mountain itself is no giant. An extra nudge from the Himalayas some 50 million years ago pushed the Kailas valley slightly higher than its neighbors. Like Meru, Kailas gives rise to four great rivers — the Sutlej, Indus, Brahmaputra and Karnali (a main tributary of the Ganges) all start within 100 km of the mountain — which leave it from the precise points of the compass. Like Meru, Kailas' stunningly-symmetrical snowcap has inspired some of the greatest legends and monuments of our time. And like Meru, Kailas' image is surely destined for immortality.

For Hindus, the peak represents the throne of Shiva, the great god of destruction and transformation; for Buddhists, it is home to their Tantric equivalent, Chakrasamvara (Tib. Demchog). For all Buddhists, Hindus, Jains and Bons — the indigenous animists of Tibet — it symbolises the place where all life begins and ends, where time and eternity meet. Each time the pilgrim circles Kailas, his soul is spring-cleaned, his sins redeemed, his Wheel of Life turned full-cycle. If he gets around 108 times, he will achieve Nirvana in this life.

On our first night in Darchen, we had the honor of meeting a Tibetan who had circled Kailas 140 times. Choying Dorje, a slight, shy man with a big, warm presence, was born in the shadow of the holy mountain and, after a period of exile in India, has now returned to act as China's official pilgrim guide.

As we thawed out over mugs of cheesy yak-butter tea, Dorje told us a little of the history of his beloved mountain. As long ago as 200-300 BC, the early settlers on the near reaches of the Indus had come to view Kailas as the home of their gods. Word soon traveled downriver into India, where the locals had long worshipped the mythical Meru — a mountain of crystal and precious stones, around which all the continents and oceans rotated. After Kailas was recognised as the earthly Meru, Hindu and Jain pilgrims began to pour into Tibet to see it. For the next 2,000 years, they negotiated the treacherous passes of the western Himalayas to set eyes on the sacred peak and wash away their sins in its life-giving waters.

But in the mid-1960s, everything suddenly changed. Mao's fanatical Red Guards, blindly driven by the ideals of the Cultural Revolution, stormed into the region, smashing up the five *gompa* (monasteries) at Kailas and a further eight around Manasarovar. Monks were murdered, pilgrims banned, and the local populace brought to its spiritual knees. For the next decade, there was spiritual darkness in this bright land, until Mao's successors admitted their

COLIN GALLOWAY

great leader may have made a mistake.

Today, new shrines have begun to rise slowly from the remains of the old, and a handful of monks have been allowed back to practice at Kailas. While the local culture is still stifled and strictly controlled, Beijing has begun to allow a few well-heeled, tour-controlled foreigners back into the sacred region. Since 1981, 200 Indians — chosen in a giant national lottery — have visited Kailas annually. Although a handful of hardy travelers have managed to sneak in since the mid-1980s, individual visitors are still barred because, Dorje explained, "they don't bring in any revenue and are often only interested in getting secret information out of Tibet." (If you were only interested in seeing the holy mountain, you had to dig deep — Dorje had heard a figure of US$8,000 quoted by a recent Japanese visitor).

▲▲

A young Tibetan pilgrim squatted beside me, an encouraging smile creasing his smooth, burnished cheeks. In one hand he held a small, bone-handled dagger; in

the other, a clump — rather bigger than I'd expected — of my matted hair. Then, with a short, triumphant whoop, he leapt to his feet and launched the lock ceremoniously into the sea of wilted pigtails and raggedy clothes which lay around us.

Anywhere else, this crude chop would have been nothing more, another ethnic custom to observe and tick off on the traveler's checklist. But here, in this holiest of places, I felt the presence of something greater, something everlasting. We were sitting on a giant ledge of pitted red rock, strewn with tattered old clothes and shoes and slices of slate intricately carved with thousands of tiny prayers. Buddha himself was said to have taught on this very spot, and through the centuries it had become an altar for rebirthing rituals — a rubbish heap of old lives and regenerator of new. Here, if you believed it, a quick haircut could change your life.

In such humbling surroundings, it was hard not to believe. Above us rose a sheer wall of swirling black rock, on whose foreboding face melting snows had carved row upon row of strange symmetrical shapes — lumpy cones and jagged teeth, and swirling spires of ice-tinged rock. And riding above these surreal ramparts, dominating the landscape for miles around, was the striking summit of Kailas — a perfect, pointed dome of brilliant white snow.

For months, while planning this trip, I'd wondered how any peak could be as awe-inspiring, as clearly holy, as people had described this one. But the moment we came face to face, I understood immediately. The mountain possesses an indescribable power to dominate not just its surroundings but the senses of all who draw near. The summit sits on its pedestal like the domed roof of a giant church or temple, rising above a wall of naturally-crafted stupas or Buddha statues.

Beside its remarkable symmetry and setting in a giant conglomerate amphitheatre, there is the uncanny gouge running down its south face which, banded by horizontal striations, forms a giant cross in the ice. Buddhists worship this as a swastika, their symbol of spiritual strength, which they say was created during a duel between the Tibetan yogi Milarepa and a Bon magician for possession of Kailas in the 11th century. (Milarepa won a race to the summit by boarding the first ray of the sun, knocking the priest from his ritual drum, which crashed down the mountain side and caused the great gouge). For Hindus, the laddered gash is Shiva's route to the summit, a literal stairway to heaven. As for us, we decided (somewhat self-righteously) that it could equally represent our own Christian cross. The energy of Mount Kailas was surely too strong, too universal, to discriminate between earthly faiths.

▲▲

Thanks to its pristine isolation Kailas continues to this day to inspire unparalleled devotion, austerity and self-sacrifice. Among the thousands of Tibetans who flock here annually, many follow up epic journeys on foot or horseback by circling the mountain on their stomachs, prostrating themselves over mud and ice for nearly three weeks. Our circuit — on foot — took a more leisurely three days, during which we hooked up with several bands of local pilgrims, all keen to show us the right ways and places of worship.

My impromptu barber was traveling with a dozen young pilgrims who had walked the full 1,200 km from Amdo. They were classic nomads, heavily wrapped in sheepskins and felt hats, their ears studded with big nuggets of turquoise and amber and "mountain coral." They had nothing with them — just their portable shrines, a few sacks of *tsampa* (Tibetans' barley-flour staple) and a blackened kettle — and they insisted on carrying some of our load. In return, we

The Cosmic Mountain:
Mt. Sumeru
between the world below
and the palace of the gods,
Tun-huang Manuscript

gave them pictures of the Dalai Lama, which they gratefully touched to their heads and hearts.

As we walked, they twirled prayer-wheels and muttered mantras in a soft, droning hum. At various spots, they would bow and prostrate themselves to the mountain or to a rock formation dedicated to one of their many deities. The 51-kilometer track is replete with powerful symbolism: foot and head prints made by the Buddha or some prominent saint, caves where famous yogis lived and meditated, rocks for testing your karma, pools of sin-cleansing water. On the ledge where Buddha taught 500 of his disciples, our companions

took time to sink something special into the sea of relics on the ground — a strand of hair, a tooth, a strip of old cloth, perhaps something given to them by another pilgrim on their journey.

One produced a small, rounded rock engraved with the plump, mustachioed figure of Guru Rinpoche, the Indian teacher credited with bringing Buddhism to Tibet. He'd carried it with him for nearly two months, and now he was laying it to rest in this distant, wind-swept place — another dozen hours of carving, another piece of an old life, to add to the tens of thousands already on display.

▲▲

On our two nights at Kailas, we camped outside the monasteries on the frosty ground. The monks offered us warm hospitality, providing welcome tea and tsampa, and showed us around the simple, candle-lit chapels they were in the process of rebuilding. "I started six years ago," one monk told us of his single-handed rebuilding project. "Before then, things were very bad, but now they leave us alone. We can do as we want."

Times have changed since the horrors of the 1960s but, as with all Chinese concessions, there's another side to the story. On our return to Hong Kong, we learned that the authorities had just

given permission to the famous climber Reinhold Messner to scale Kailas' virgin summit — a move sure to anger and upset millions of people. If Messner succeeds, he will join an elite fellowship with Shiva and Milarepa. But most devotees doubt the gods will let him. ▲

THE MARCHMOUNT SYSTEM 五嶽
CHINESE GEOLOGICS

J A M E S   R O B S O N

The Holy Places were the tutelary guardians of rural harmony, so the holy rivers, mounts and woods were considered by the lords as the Ancestral Centers from which they drew the specific Virtue to provide them with the authority to govern their territories.

— *Marcel Granet,* The Religion of the Chinese People

China dwells in geometry. A simple uniform law takes possession of the horizon, its universal rule overruns without any exception the entire plain. A second law, probably the same one, draws a vertical line on this horizon. All orginates from this norm.... It compromises China's apparent addiction to the last universalizing ideology.

— *Michel Serres, "China Loam" in* Detachment

In ancient China mountains were believed to be divinities and were considered symbols of stability and durability.[1] Thus, it is not surprising that this symbolism was taken over by the imperial cult and that certain mountains were integrated into rituals performed by the state.

A dominant mountain cultic system developed by the classical Chinese imperium is referred to by scholars as the Five Marchmount (*wuyue* 五嶽) system. I follow Edward Schafer's translation of the term *yue* 嶽 as 'marchmount,' which he defines as a cosmic and symbolic mountain marking "the marches of man's proper domain, the limits of the ritual tour of the Son of Heaven."[2] The term 'marchmount' is derived from the old French word 'marche': a border region, or frontier.

Some scholars have recently shown on the basis of ancient texts, such as the *Erya* 爾雅, that prior to the Han dynasty the marchmount system did not always consist of five mountains (there had been competing systems of four, nine and twelve mountains), and the mountains associated with the cardinal directions were not always consistent.[3] By the Han dynasty (206 BCE-220 CE), however, the Five Marchmounts were systematized and identified under the name *wuyue*: Mt. Heng 恒 in the North, Mt. Tai 泰 in the East, Mt. Heng 衡 in the South, Mt. Hua 華 in the West, and Mt. Song 嵩 in the Center.

The mountains of the Five Marchmount system should not be confused with the Four Famous Mountain (*sida mingshan*) system, the mountain cultic system established by incoming Buddhists. The Buddhist system of four directional mountains (Mt. Wutai in the North, Mt. Puto in the East, Mt. Jiuhua in the South, and Mt. Omei in the West) mimicked the native Chinese mountain cultic system of the imperial cult, and may have aided the Buddhists in their acculturation on Chinese soil. These two categories used to classify Chinese sacred mountains should not be considered from a sectarian perspective, however, since the marchmounts became influenced by Buddhist cults (the Shaolin Monastery on the Central Marchmount Mt. Song), and the Buddhist mountains of the Four Famous Mountains became influenced by Daoists (particularly Mt. Wutai and Mt. Omei).

Returning to the Five Marchmounts, we find that each was identified as a feudal lord or thearch (*wudi* 五帝) and their status was confirmed in the imperial cult as overseers of morality and the guarantors of covenants. These mountains were then put on the itinerary of the Emperor's ritual progress, in the course of which he would offer the *feng* 封 and *shan* 禪 sacrifices at the base and summit of each of the peaks in order to reinforce his claims to legitimacy. The *wuyue* system thus functioned to delineate an expanding imperial territory, and was used symbolically to aid in governing the imperium. It was thought by the imperium that harnessing the powers believed to reside in the marchmounts could increase agricultural production and protect the empire which they delineated. Perhaps Edmund Burke was on the mark when he wrote, "I know nothing sublime which is not some modification of power."[4]

Of the many ways in which the symbolic modalities evident in the marchmount system might be interpreted, one might be called 'syntactical,' and the other 'associative.' In this reading, each mountain within the sacred mountain system was a 'sign' which provided access to vertical, or metaphoric associations, as well as horizontal, or metynomic structures.[5] Each mountain had symbolic attributes which fit into a template that organized all such 'signs.' These templates changed throughout Chinese history, but by the Han dynasty the five *yue* mountains were conjoined with Chinese five phases theory (*wuxing* 五行), which was based on the template of the "River Chart" (*He Tu* 河圖).[6]

In the *Great Norm (Hongfan)*, an early Coufucian text, the five elements (metal, fire, water, earth, and wood) were each assigned a number. These combinations were arranged according to the *Lo Writ (Lo Shu* 洛書) and the River Chart (*He Tu* 河圖)). These two diagrams were not only magic squares, whereby the addition of any line or column adds up to fifteen, but were spatial diagrams as well. From the Warring States period on philosophers related the five marchmount system to the associations of the five elements and the River Chart (see diagram).

The symbolic correlations provided by the conjunction of the River Chart with the marchmount system was thought to

The esoteric representation of the "True Form of the Southern Marchmount." It is unclear to scholars if these labyrinthine depictions were the product of a birds-eye perspective, or a subterranean perspective. Notes accompanying the charts give directions for coloring in the white areas (signifying water) with either red or yellow. The transmission of these esoteric talismanic diagrams was ritually controlled, since it was thought that they provided access to the control of the deities of the peaks which they represented.

China's Five Marchmounts 五嶽,
aligned with the five elements, and the River Chart associations
(color & number), and the exoteric (popular) representations
of the "Ture Form of the Five Marchmounts."

Northern Marchmount 北嶽

Mt. Heng 恒山

Water 水

Black

1/6

Western Marchmount 西嶽

Mt. Hua 華山

Metal 金

White

4/9

Central Marchmount 中嶽

Mt. Song 嵩山

Earth 土

Yellow

5

Eastern Marchmount 東嶽

Mt. Tai 泰山

Wood 木

Blue/Green

3/8

Southern Marchmount 南嶽

Mt. Heng 衡山

Fire 火

Red

2/7

C H I N A

represent the perceived order, and harmony, evident in the Chinese imperium, and became a prescriptive guide (or template) for literati representations of the different quarters of that realm. The Tang dynasty poet Tu Fu described the Eastern Marchmount Mt. Tai accordingly, "With what can I compare the Great Peak? Over the surrounding provinces, its blue-green hue never dwindles from sight. Infused by the Shaper of Forms with the soaring power of divinity."[7] The Southern Marchmount, on the other hand, is always represented in relation to red, with references to red flowers, usually azaleas, even though those flowers do not grow on the mountain. The south had to be depicted with imagery of red, or fire, and poets writing in the distant capital at Changan (using the system of correlations as their guide) "sensed what they expected to sense and failed to notice what their symbols had not prepared them for."[8] The marchmounts and their symbolic correlations became what Pierre Bourdieu has described as a system of cultural preconditioning, a "system of cognitive and motivating structures, a world of already realized ends."[9]

▲▲

The coherent system depicted in the final version of the Five Marchmount system was the result of a process that had evolved for several centuries. At this point, however, it is difficult to determine why certain mountains were chosen over others for inclusion in the system of five *yue*. It seems, though, that the moun-

tains composing the completed version of the marchmount system were chosen due to their geographic locations as demarcators of the 'marches' of the imperium. Later, for Daoists, the Five Marchmounts were also considered to play an integral role in the maintenance of order within the Chinese empire. By providing order and governing the harmony at the terrestrial level, the Five Marchmounts were the earthly counterparts to other combinations of five that resided in the stars, ensuring celestial harmony, and in the human body, regulating the organs.

The true talismans of the Five Emperors,
    their superior essence forms
    the five planets in heaven,
    their middle essence forms
    the five viscera in the body,
    their inferior essence forms
    the five marchmounts on earth.[10]

The Five Marchmounts' positions at the 'marches' of the empire, delineating the imperium, entailed that those mountains were thought to be embued with a certain power to guard against and repel outside (undesirable) influences. The marchmounts' double role as protectors of the realm and guarantors of harmony was later integrated into folk practices (which can still be seen in China today), whereby pilgrims would affix talismans representing the 'true-form' of the marchmounts to their bodies or to a pilgrim's staff, thus protecting them from noxious influences, wild animals, or demons that might be encountered on their ascent of the mountain. ▲

NOTES ....

1. Edouard Chavannes, *Le T'ai Chan: Essai de monographie d'un culte chinois.* (Paris: Ernest Leroux, 1910): 3.
2. Edward H. Schafer, *Pacing the Void: T'ang Approaches to the Stars.* (Berkeley: University of California Press, 1974): 130.
3. Wu Hung, "The Competing *Yue*: Sacred Mountains as Historical and Political Monuments," unpublished paper presented at "Mountains and the Cultures of Landscape in China" conference, University of California Santa Barbara and Santa Barbara Museum of Art, January 14-16, 1993, pp.25.
4. Edmund Burke, *A Philosophical Enquiry Into The Origin of Our Ideas of the Sublime and Beautiful.* (Oxford: Oxford University Press, 1990): 59.
5. These categories are derived from Roman Jacobson, *Fundamentals of Language.* (Janua Linguarum, Series Minor. I, The Hague: Mouton, 1956)
6. Wu Hung 1993: 33.
7. Paul Kroll, "Verses From on High; The Ascent of T'ai Shan." *T'oung Pao* 69, nos. 4-5, (1983): 228-30.
8. Edward Schafer, *The Vermilion Bird: T'ang Images of the South.* (Berkeley: University of California Press, 1967): 261.
9. Pierre Bourdieu, *The Logic of Practice*, Stanford: Stanford University Press, (1990): 53.
10. "Slightly modified version of the poem in Isabelle Robinet, *Taoist Meditation: The Mao-Shan Tradition of Grand Purity.* Trans. by Julian F. Pas and Norman J. Girardot. (New York: State University of New York Press, 1993): 180.

MOUNTAINS OF THE MOON

B I L L   P O R T E R

Now people apply the term *Chungnanshan* to the 2,600-meter peak forty kilometers south of Sian as well as to the adjacent mountains a hundred kilometers to the east and west. But three thousand years ago, *Chungnanshan* referred to all the mountains from the south shore of the Yellow River's Sanmen Gorge in Honan Province westward along the Wei River to the river's source on Wushushan or Black Rat Mountain, in Kansu Province, a distance of 800 kilometers.

In China's more distant mythological past, *Chungnanshan* had an even wider application that went far beyond Black Rat Mountain. This greater range included the Kunlun as well as the Chungnan mountains and extended somewhat beyond K2 on China's current border with Pakistan, a distance of 3,500 kilometers.

In explaining the more limited application of *Chungnanshan*, early Chinese historians noted that *chung* means "end," *nan* means "south," and *shan* means "mountain" or "mountains." Thus, *Chungnanshan* was said to refer to the eastern end of the mountains that bordered the southern branch of the Silk Road. This explanation made sense of the component words, though it was, in fact, fortuitous and did nothing to explain the special significance these mountains had for the earliest Chinese, who viewed their peaks and valleys as the home of the most powerful heavenly and earthly spirits.

A more intriguing explanation is offered by Taiwan linguist Tu Erwei, who contends that Chungnan and Kunlun are cognates, both stemming from a common word meaning "mountains of the moon." In his *Kunlun Wenhua yu Puszu Kuannien* (Kunlun Culture and the Concept of Immortality), Professor Tu explains that the Kunlun-Chungnan range represented the mythological focus of China's earliest religion, a religion that bridged the dark river between life and death by means of the concept of immortality as manifested by the waning and waxing of the moon. And since the moon goddess lived in the Kunlun-Chungnan range, this is where certain individuals came to gain access to the moon's divinity and the root of its powers.

They weren't ordinary members of society. Nor did they enter the mountains as ordinary people might. They walked the Walk of Yu, dragging one foot, as a wounded animal might to elicit the pity of mountain spirits. Like Yu the Great, after whom this technique was named, they were shamans. And the Kunlun-Chungnan range was their earliest known home.

In his article on shamanism in the *Encyclopedia of Religion* (New York: Macmillan, 1987), Mircea Eliade notes that "throughout the immense area comprising the central and northern regions of Asia, the magico-religious life of society centers on the shaman." Eliade says that in such societies the ecstatic state is considered the ultimate religious experience, and the shaman is its master. In ecstatic trance, the shaman leaves his body, passes through a series of heavens, and communicates with all manner of spirits, seeking and gaining knowledge for the welfare of his community. By providing a link with the spiritual world and bringing back knowledge gained there, he defends his society against darkness. But at the same time, he lives apart from the society he protects.

A person called to be a shaman, according to Eliade, "seeks solitude, becomes absent-minded, loves to roam in the woods of unfrequented places, has visions, and sings in his sleep." Were it not for the ecstatic trance that initiates the novice shaman, this description could just as easily apply to someone following the hermit tradition. And in ancient China, the two were closely connected.

In tracing their connection, the earliest and most important text is one that describes how Ch'i, shaman emperor of the Hsia dynasty, entered the Chungnan-Kunlun range, flew off on a pair of dragons, and received from heaven the elegaic forms of verse used by later shaman-poets in such works as the *Chutzu*, or Songs of Ch'u.

Ch'i was the successor of another shaman, Yu the Great. When Yu founded the Hsia dynasty around 2200 B.C., he ordered his officials to compile a guide to the realm. The result was the *Shanhaiching* (Guide to Mountains and Seas), to which later emperors added as their knowledge of the realm's mysteries increased. Scholars doubt the book's antiquity and are unwilling to date any of its sections earlier than the fourth century B.C. But regardless of what scholars think about the book's date or its veracity, this geography of the spirit is a mine of shamanistic lore that must have been shared knowledge long before it was written down.

The book's chapter on western mountains begins with those south of Sanmen Gorge and continues along the Chungnan and Kunlun mountains all the way to K2 and beyond. Among their magical peaks are the earthly capital of Ti (the highest of heavenly spirits) and the home of Hsi-wang-mu (goddess of the moon and dispenser of the elixir of immortality). There are also mountains where shamans collect ingredients for their own elixirs and fly up to heaven, where people who die early live 800 years and meanwhile enjoy whatever they desire, where the sun and moon sleep, where anything is possible, and where creatures live that are too strange to believe but not to describe.

Recent archaeological excavations

In 1989 Bill Porter, long-time student of Buddhism in Taiwan, went to mainland China with photographer Steven Johnson to look for holy hermits. Passing through the pro-democracy demonstrations at Tiananmen Square, they made their way to the Chungnan Mountains, in central China. There, despite official advice to the contrary, they found that the hermit tradition, both Buddhist and Taoist, is still surprisingly strong. Road to Heaven, *published mid-1993, is Bill Porter's account of the search, and a remarkable record of conversations with those who have renounced 'the world of red dust' for the clarity of life among the peaks.*

when Ch'u Yuan was banished
be wandered along rivers
be sang on their banks
weak and forlorn
till a fisherman asked
aren't you the Lord of the Gorges
what fate has brought you to this
and Ch'u Yuan answered
the world is muddy
I alone am clean
everyone is drunk
I alone am sober
and so they sent me away
and the fisherman said
a sage isn't bothered by others
he can change with the times
if the world is muddy
splash in the mire
if everyone is drunk
drink up the dregs
why get banished
for deep thought and purpose
and Ch'u Yuan said he had heard
when you clean your hair
you should dust off your hat
when you take a bath
you should shake out your robe
why should I let something so pure
be ruined and wronged by others
I'd rather jump into the Hsiang
and be buried in a fish's gut
than let something so white
be stained by common dirt
the fisherman smiled and rowed away singing
when the Tsanglang is clear I wash my hat
when the Tsanglang is muddy I wash my feet
and once gone he was heard from no more

— *Chutzu*

has been given a radiocarbon date of more than five thousand years ago. At the same site, archaeologists also found a bronze knife apparently used in sacrificial rituals. It not only constitutes the earliest bronze artifact found to date in China but also suggests that shamanism was sufficiently important to demand special materials unavailable for other, more profane, uses.

An even more important discovery regarding the development of shamanism in China was also made near the other end of the Chungnan Mountains. Among the artifacts uncovered at the neolithic settlement of Panpo, six kilometers east of Sian, are China's earliest form of writing as well as its earliest examples of shamanistic art: a shaman's fish-spirit mask and what appears to be an early form of the paired dragons used by Chinese shamans to aid them in their heavenly journeys.

The site at Panpo was occupied fairly continuously throughout the fifth millennium B.C., or seven thousand years ago, and it constitutes one of the best examples of China's Yangshao culture, which was followed by the Lungshan culture of the third millennium B.C. When Yu the Great founded the Hsia dynasty near the end of the third millennium, it could only have been on the basis of these Yangshao-Lungshan cultures that he and his ministers compiled the *Shanhai-ching*, the shaman's guide to the sacred world. Although the remains found at Panpo and other Yangshao-Lungshan sites are little more than suggestive, they at least permit us to conclude that no later than the fifth millennium B.C. someone was leaving this earthly realm to communicate with the world of spirits and was doing so near the Chungnan Mountains.

▲▲

It was the middle of August and the middle of summer rains. After waiting for the sun in Sian for a week, we decided to take a chance. Four hours and 120 kilometers later, we were looking up Huashan's one muddy street into the mountains. We could see blue sky.

We dropped our gear in a cheap hotel and set out to explore. Past a gauntlet of tourist shops, we entered the main gate of Yuchuan-yuan, or Jade Spring Temple. It was built in the middle of the eleventh century as a shrine to Ch'en Tuan, who had lived here as a hermit the century before. Besides inspiring early Neo-Confucian thinkers with his *Wuchitu* (Diagram of the Limitless), Ch'en culti-

provide additional evidence suggesting shamanism was far more important than previously realized and that the foothills and plains north of the Chungnan Mountains were its earliest home in China. Archaeologist Chang Kwang-chih has called the shamanistic connection the most important aspect of early Chinese civilization. Chang notes, though, that shamans often needed a little help to communicate with the spiritual realm. Sex and alcohol were important and so were drugs.

In a neolithic village south of Lanchou and not far from Black Rat Mountain, archaeologists have found a clay pot containing carbonized buds of cultivated hemp, or *Cannabis sativa*. Paleobotanist Li Hui-lin thinks that the cultivation of this plant first occurred in this area, where it was used both as a textile fiber

and as a drug. According to Li in *The Origins of Chinese Civilizations*, edited by David N. Keightley (Berkeley: University of California Press, 1983). "Nomad tribes in the north, practitioners of shamanism, apparently used the plant as a drug and carried it west to central and western Asia and India, where it was used primarily as a hallucinogen and not as a textile fiber." A quatrain from the "Greater Lord of Long Life" in the *Chutzu* makes clear the plant's significance to China's early shamans:

first a yin *then a* yang
no one knows what I do
jade buds of holy hemp
for the one who lives apart

The site where the hemp was found

vated Taoist meditation and was known for his ability to remain in a sleeplike trance for months at a time. His reclining figure can still be seen in a small cave on the west side of the grounds. For a small donation, the old lady in charge of the shrine let us inside. We ran our hands over Ch'en's stone figure. It had been touched by so many hands since it was carved in 1103, it looked and felt like polished black jade.

Nearby was a pavilion that Ch'en had built on top of a boulder. And in front of the boulder grew the lone survivor of four cuttings Ch'en planted from the tree beneath which the Buddha was born. According to one Taoist legend, after Lao-tzu joined the immortals, he was reborn as Shakyamuni. The Red Guards apparently thought they had destroyed the last of the four trees, but its gnarled stump was still sending forth shoots.

Just outside the entrance to the main shrine, a stele carved with a representation of Huashan caught out attention. It was cracked in the middle, but we studied it as best as we could through the protective bars and the dust on its surface. If the mountain was anything like the picture, Steve and I were going to lose some weight.

On the east side of the temple grounds, we stopped again at a stone market next to another boulder. This was one of the many graves of Hua T'uo. China's greatest medical genius, who died in A.D. 200 at the age of ninety-seven. For many years Hua lived in a cave on Huashan and collected herbs for which the mountain is still famous; special varieties of Solomon's seal, ginseng, asaram, and acorus, to name a few. Among his accomplishments was the use of acupuncture and hemp-based anesthetics to perform surgery. He is also credited with devising five forms of exercise that were later developed into the basic styles of Chinese martial arts. Although Hua repeatedly refused official posts, he was forced to treat the chronic headaches of Ts'ao Ts'ao, who had usurped the throne at the end of the Han dynasty. When he refused to continue the treatments, he was ordered killed lest he reveal information about Ts'ao Ts'ao's health to his enemies, who were many.

Beyond Hua T'uo's grave and the eastern wall of Jade Spring Temple were two smaller Taoist monasteries. The first was Shihertung Temple, where most visiting monks stay. We walked past its rusted metal gate and after another hundred meters entered the brick and wooden doorway of Hsienku Temple. A Chinese friend in Sian had told us this was where Master Hsieh lived. We found him propped up in bed treating his arthritic knees with a heat lamp. Once renowned for his skill in martial arts, he now had trouble walking. His room included two plank beds pushed

Taipaishan is every green

encircled above by stars

a hundred miles from court

cut off from the dusty world

here a green-haired ancient

wears a cloud sleeps on snow

doesn't talk doesn't laugh

dwells in silence in a cave

one day I met this perfect man

bowed and asked his secret

his smile revealed teeth of jade

instructions for elixir

on his bones I read the words

then his form was gone

high above I searched in vain

this endless heat of passion

oh to gather cinnabar sand

to leave mankind forever

— Li Pai

together and covered by a mosquito net, an arrangement I found in the rooms of other monks who used their beds for meditation and study as well as sleep. There were two chests containing books and clothes, a desk, two folding chairs, a new color TV (presented by the provincial government for help in cultural preservation), and a scroll with the Chinese character for patience on the wall. After exchanging introductions, I handed Master Hsieh a cigar and lit one myself. While we smoked, he told me about his life. He was born in Anhui Province and became a monk while he was still in his teens. After the standard three-year apprenticeship, he came to Huashan to practice. At the time of our meeting, he had just turned eighty and had been living at Huashan for sixty years. His arthritic knees aside, he was unusually robust, and his mind was as clear as the sky after a long rain. I asked him about Taoism.

Hsieh: Lao-tzu said to cultivate tranquillity and detachment. To be natural. To be natural means not to force things. When you act natural, you get what you need. But to know what's natural, you have to cultivate tranquility. Huashan has long been famous as a center of Taoism because it's quiet. There used to be a lot of hermits here. But now the mountain has been developed for tourism. The tranquillity is gone, and so are the hermits.

Where did they go?

That's hard to say. Hermits want to be left alone, so they're not easy to find. They prefer isolation. Some of them returned to the cities. Others moved deeper into the Chungnan Mountains, where it's still quiet. But even if you found them, they probably wouldn't talk to you. They don't like to be disturbed. They prefer to meditate. They're not interested in conversation. They might say a few words to you then close their door and not come out again.

But they have to eat. Sooner or later they have to come out again, don't they?

That depends. Sometimes they eat once a day, sometimes once every three days, sometimes once a week. As long as they're able to nourish their inner energy, they're fine, they don't need food. They might meditate for one day, two days, a week, even several weeks. You might have to wait a long time before they come out again.

Aren't they interested in teaching others?

Yes. But before you can teach others, you have to cultivate yourself. You have to know something before you can teach something. You can't explain inner cul-

STEVEN JOHNSON

tivation just because you know words in books. You have to discover what they mean first.

If people can't learn Taoism from hermits, can they learn from monks in temples?

You can't learn just by visiting a temple. You have to live there for at least three years and help with the daily work. If you can stand the hardship and privation after three years you can ask one of the monks to be your teacher. It's not easy. You have to have a clear head and a quiet mind. As I said before, it takes at least three years of physical training before your mind is quiet enough to understand the Tao.

In the last twenty or thirty years, the political situation in China has been difficult. What effect has this had on Taoism?

I'd rather not talk about this.

Were Taoist monks and nuns able to continue their practice here at Huashan?

Please, I'd rather not talk about this.

When you were living on the mountain,

you must have needed certain things from down below. How did you get them?

We had to carry everything on our backs. I made quite a few trips when I was younger. Nowadays, visitors sometimes give the monks money, and the monks pay others to carry things up so they can concentrate on their practice.

Has there been much change in the number of Taoists living here?

When I first came here, there were forty or fifty old masters on the mountain, more than two hundred monks and nuns, and too many novices to count. Now, only a few of us are left.

What happened to them all?

Some died. Most left. Most returned to their families.

What about the temples?

They're for tourists. Everything has changed. The tourist officials are in charge now.

I asked Hsieh if I could talk with Master Hsing, Hsienku Temple's ninety-year-old abbot. Suddenly Hsieh turned serious and said it would not be convenient. I felt the forty-year shadow of Liberation. Apparently, Hsing had a problem — and it wasn't his health. On our way out, we saw Master Hsing giving instruction to a youth who had come all the way from Chekiang Province to carve dragons and cranes for the temple. Steve and I bowed in greeting and left.

Later, Master Hsieh joined us for a spartan dinner in our hotel room. He excused himself for not being able to talk freely in the temple. The walls, he said, had ears. He said things were getting worse for Taoists, not better. Religion was being resurrected by the government for the purpose of promoting tourism. He said that Taoism was just about dead, that in all of China there were fewer than a hundred and fifty Taoist monks and nuns who could qualify as masters.

Historians of the Han dynasty say there were thirteen hundred Taoist masters of note during the reign of Emperor Ming two thousand years ago when the country's population was around 50 million. In other words, when the population was one-twentieth its current level, there were ten times as many Taoist masters in China. A sad state, indeed, for what many Chinese still call their national religion. ▲

LITERARY DIVERSIONS ON MOUNT JIUHUA
CULTS, COMMUNITIES & CULTURE

W I L L I A M P O W E L L

In the fall of 1987 I joined the throngs of Chinese pilgrims who, throughout much of the year, make the ascent of Mt. Jiuhua, one of the "four great sacred peaks" of Chinese Buddhism. The experience was exhilarating. The weather, typically misty and rainy in this region of central China, was crisp and clear. Such opportune weather deepened and intensified the varied greens of the bamboo and pine forests, the cobalt blue of the sky and the grey of the peaks.

The pilgrim's path begins at "Five Streams" Bridge in the northwest quadrant of the Jiuhua region. From here, the pilgrim has a spectacular view of the entire range of peaks from which the mountain takes its name, "Nine Florate" (*jiuhua*). The trail then works through a gently terraced valley along the western flank of the range, passing several temples, which invariably enshrine the tutelary bodhisattva of the mountain, Dizang (Jap., *Jizo*). From "Two Sages" Temple, at the head of the long valley, the trail begins its ascent in earnest. Switchbacking through dense groves of giant bamboo, and passing a spectacular series of waterfalls which empty into seven "Dragon Pools," as well as several small temples, the trail finally drops over a small rise into the self-contained *Jiuhua Jie* valley halfway up the mountain. The center of Buddhist activities, Jiuhua Jie offers pilgrims a choice of temples in which to stay while taking in the mountain air, engaging in pious rituals on behalf of some recently deceased family member, or gathering their energy and spirits for the ascent to the temple on Jiuhua's summit, Tiantai Peak (1340 meters). The valley is filled with the fragrance of incense from the many tem-

ples, and constantly echoes with the sound of the "Bell of the Dark Realm," which is tolled from a small temple high up on the east ridge of the valley.

Setting off early the next morning, I joined pilgrims snaking their way over the Eastern Scarp (*dongya*), a small ridge separating Jiuhua Jie from the main ridge of peaks. Dropping down into the adjoining valley, the trail threads its way through a small mountain village, *Min Yuan*, before ascending the final ridge. Villagers have lined the trail with shops offering refreshments, walking sticks, and pilgrim bags. Interspersed among village houses are numerous temples occupied almost entirely by nuns. From many of these comes chanting, and the ever-present fragrance of incense. The last stretch of the trail wends its way up the almost sheer cliff that drops off Taintai Peak. The trail passes around, and in some cases goes through, seven or eight more temples which precariously hug to the trail. The views from these temples are breathtaking in both senses. They offer brief respite from the tortuous ascent. The pilgrim, at long last, emerges onto the "Dragon's Spine," the main ridge, and enters the last temple which clings to the summit of Taintai Peak. A continuous din of firecrackers from its roof announces the success of each pilgrim group to make it this far. Looking back on the two-day ascent, one realizes that almost the entire path, from "Two Sages" Temple at the foot of the mountain to the final peak, is constructed of broad stone steps, an extraordinary expenditure of labor and devotion.

It would be easy at the culmination of such an endeavor to give into the feeling

that one had acquired a direct and indisputable sense of what a sacred mountain is, and to assume that one's own experience partakes of a common reality experienced by thousands of previous pilgrims. The old temples that appear to grow out of naked rock, and the foot-worn steps that take one up the mountain impart a sense of timelessness that many of us associate with sacred space. I would suggest, however, that to take such perceptions seriously, satisfying as they may be, would be mistaken. It prevents us from appreciating the cultural and historical processes at work in such spaces and limits our perception of their multivocality. Sacred mountains speak with many voices.

A POET & A BUDDHIST RECLUSE

In the winter of 754 the Tang poet, Li Bo, joined two friends, Gao Ji, a literati recluse, and Wei Quanyu, an official, for an outing in the mountains just south of the city of Qingyang. While resting at the western foot of what was then known as "Nine-Sons Mountain" (*jiuzi shan*), the three companions gazed at the "nine lotus-shaped peaks" through snow-covered pines, and noted the failure of their literati predecessors to have ever acknowledged the mountain. Agreeing that "Nine Sons" failed to do justice to the peaks, they decided on a more fitting name, "Nine Florate/Flowers." Li Bo immediately immortalized the name in the first and last of four couplets the friends composed on the occasion:

Ethereal Matter spilt into the Two Vital Breaths:

A numenous mountain opened into nine flowers.

In shimmering greens, jade-tree colored.

Faintly appear the homes of the Feathered People.

A year later, in 755, Li Bo caught sight of the mountain again while traveling by boat down the Yangtse, which passes Qingyang and Jiuhua Mountain some thirty miles to the north. Recalling the previous year's outing, he composed the following poem to be presented to his Qingyang friend, Wei:

Recently while on the Jiujiang.

I gazed distantly at the Jiuhua peaks;

Out of jade-blue water
hanging from the River of Heaven,

Flourished forth nine lotuses.

The poem finishes with Li Bo lamenting that he was unable to visit his friend who he characterizes as a mountain recluse. Thus, Jiuhua Mountain entered the public record for the first time through the literary diversions of no less a figure than Li Bo, outlined in images that have left their mark until the present era — nine, distant, lotus-shaped peaks bursting forth from celestial waters, its resident sylphs or Feathered People vaguely seen, its recluses difficult if not impossible to visit. Based on these poetic diversions, Li Bo's name has become indelibly associated with the mountain. The renaming anecdote prefaces almost every subsequent work on the mountain.

Apparently unknown to Li Bo at the time he and his friends were on their outing in the western foothills of Jiuhua, a lone Buddhist monk from the Korean kingdom of Silla, Jin Qiaojue, was leading an ascetic existence in an isolated valley halfway up the mountain. He could not have been more than ten miles from the poets when they were composing their couplets. Jin, a member of the royal house of Silla who had taken his monastic vows in his twenties, had arrived at Jiuhua some ten or fifteen years before Li Bo, sometime in the first half of the eighth century. Living as a recluse, he had not attracted attention until he was "discoverd" by several locals in 756. They found him in a cave seated next to a broken pot of gruel made from millet and white clay. Moved by the monk's austerity, the locals sought out funds and constructed a temple for him. Jin authored no poems or other documents, but his presence in the valley, previously mentioned Jiuhua Jie, influenced later perceptions of the mountain no less than did Li Bo's. The valley was physically and socially transformed by his presence there. Not only did it become marked as a Buddhist site by the construction of a temple complex and a "Release of Life Pool,"[1] but its natural features and economy were altered by the construction of water channels and rice paddies.

Jin's death at the end of the eighth century (c. 792) left one additional mark of major significance on the mountain. His internment produced a mummy (*roushen*), its flesh, after three years in the tomb, "appearing as though that of a living person, its bones rattling as though golden chains." Added to these signs, the ridge where Jin's mummy had been enshrined emitted brightly colored lights, visible as far away as the villages at the foot of the mountain. These phenomena were perceived as indicative of Jin's transcendant status. By the beginning of the ninth century, Jin had become identified by many in the region as the bodhisattva, Dizang.

Li Bo's brushes with the mountain and the activities associated with Jin Qiaojue, mark the emergence of two distinctly different representations of Jiuhua that have persisted into the modern period, one distant and somewhat philosophical, the other intimate and embedded in reclusive practice. My own experience, one that bears resemblance to that of many of my fellow contemporary pilgrims, I would suggest, sets out a third representation, neither distant nor intimate, but highly social. These three representations unquestionably fall into the category of what has currently become known as "sacred space." But if we acknowledge all three as in some sense legitimate, then the appropriateness of claiming a "universal" and "timeless" quality for any one representation is called into question. My experience would appear to have been categorically different from those of Li Bo and Jin Qiaojue, though my first inclination might not have been to recognize that possibility. This would not be much of a problem if such universalizations were confined to unreflective experience and hence not made the basis for serious generalizations. But that is not the case. It is exactly such perceptions that tend to dominate much that is written today about sacred mountains in Asia. Such mountains are most often represented as possessing a more or less united image or essence, and as sharing that with other sacred mountains in Asia and even throughout the world. Most commonly, the image that is presented is the dominant or most

culturally appealing discourse on the mountain. What follows here then is an attempt to suggest a multiplicity of discourses on one Chinese "sacred" mountain. The recognition of such multiplicity forces us to acknowledge that the sacred isn't a given, that it isn't simply there. Perhaps more troublesome, it forces us to consider the possibility that the sacred space of a mountain is a product of culture and the struggles that take place within a culture.

Even the cursory examination of Jiuhua that opened this article reveals something of the different discursive configurations or representations of the same place. Through an examination of materials covering the first several hundred years in which there are records on Jiuhua, it will be suggested that each of the principal communities associated with Jiuhua in that early period produced distinctive representational spaces, that implicit in those spaces were particular social practices or lived spaces, and that each community sought to appropriate the same physical space in a different way. More specifically we will ask how, and in what sense, the landscapes of Jiuhua were "produced" by the literati and the several Buddhist communities of the late Tang and Northern Song (the eighth through the thirteenth centuries).

TANG COMMUNITIES

The literati, by training and by explicitly instilled social expectations, constituted one of China's more extensive communities, both in number and geographic scope. The three literati friends whose poetic outing introduced this essay fortuitously reveal the range and types of associations the literati community have had with Jiuhua and with most Chinese mountains, I suspect. Li Bo's contact with Jiuhua was infrequent and distant. He was one of a group of literati who traveled widely and visited many regions in China, either as an official or simply out of a kind of wanderlust. Gao Ji represents the opposite extreme, though he too is a visitor to Jiuhua. As a recluse, albeit on *Shimen Shan*, a nearby mountain, he would have led a relatively more sedentary, but as we will see, not necessarily more solitary existence, and the mountain would have been a daily, lived presence for him. Wei Quanyu, residing in nearby Qingyang, falls somewhere in between his two companions in his relationship to the mountain. An important source of information on certain local sites, such literati, either because they are native to

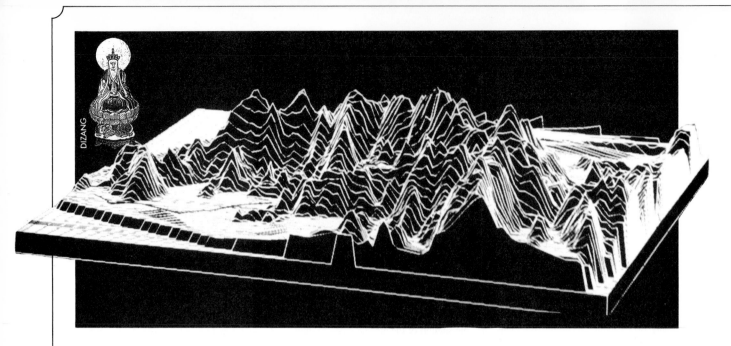

the particular region or because of an official posting, have a relationship to the site that though not transitory, is generally not as intimate as the recluse. In spite of their various relationships to Jiuhua, the three reveal a shared perspective of the place as demonstrated in their companionship and common poetic enterprise. Such bonds were, I think, characteristic of the literati of this and later periods, and were in part what constituted them as a community. It enabled them to have both a very localized presence as well as a pan-China reach.

Whereas the literati provided their own written record of themselves, the other communities on Jiuhua left almost no such records. The primary source of information on these other communities in the late Tang is an essay by an early eighth-century literati recluse, Fei Guanging, who wrote an essay in 813 called, "The Record of Mt. Jiuhua's Temple of the City of Miraculous Transformation" (*Jiuhua shan huacheng si ji*). In this essay we can identfy two different communities with their respective mountain cults.

The first, one lay community with Buddhist inclinations, consisted of villagers and merchants of the surrounding region who combined to finance and build the Buddhist complex in Jiuhua Jie in the middle of the eighth century. When the temple was renovated in 780, Fei notes that "the merchants west of the Yangtse could see the mountain above the clouds, and made offerings of bolts of silk and strings of cash. They burned incense and payed homage, and from a distance prayed for blessings..." We are also told that "wealthy families in nearby towns payed homage whenever they raised their eyes (to the mountain), and without fail saw to the plowing of his fields." These passages suggest two important points about the lay Jiuhua cult. First, by late the Tang Jiuhua Jie was being incorpo-

rated into the local economy not only through offerings, but through the production of rice on temple land. Second, and equally significant, the mountain itself, beyond functioning simply as the site of cult as it had done for the monk, Jin, was becoming a cult of site. Its members need only catch sight of from a distance to be moved to acts of piety. There is no indication at this time of any developed pilgrimage traditions in the lay community.

The other community conspicuous in Fei's essay is the monastic community. What had been the site of Jin's solitary, reclusive practice, had now become the site of a thriving monastic cult. Knowledge of Jiuhua had spread even to Korea, and many came from there to be trained by Jin. But as to what that training might have consisted of, it is difficult to say. There is no indication in any of the literature of what Buddhist affiliations Jin had, or of what kind of influences he may have been subject to. All that is clear is that Jin engaged in sutra copying and meditation, "sitting upright, without thought," often in caves or under cliffs. Thus, if Jin's monks emulated their master in their own practices,[2] the monastic cult would be one of meditation, pious acts such as sutra copying, and austerities.

The events associated with Jin's death at the end of the eighth century and the mummy that resulted had some potentially significant implications for several of these Jiuhua cults. One possible result of Dizang's becoming associated with Jiuhua is that the mountain may have taken on some of the aura of Tai Shan as a netherworld cult. According to sutra accounts, though Dizang had vowed to exert himself in the salvation of beings suffering in any of the six destinies, he took particular interest in beings who had fallen into the lowest of the six destinies, the Indo-Sino Buddhist underworlds or hells. Given Dizang's role in

the underworld courts, to which the newly deceased were directed for reward and retribution, his presence on Jiuhua, even as a mummy, would certainly have opened the possibility for the development of underworld or mortuary cults there. Such cults are clearly present by the Ming.

TANG LANDSCAPES

Having described the general nature of the various communities that were engaged with Jiuhua during the eighth century, we should attempt to determine in what sense its landscape might have been sacred for each of these communities.

Li Bo'a use of the term *ling*, "numenous," to characterize the mountain as it transformed itself into the nine peaks, an event parallel to the cosmogonic division of Ethereal Matter into the yin and yang breaths, is perhaps the earliest literatei characterization of Jiuhua as in some sense sacred. But the most common device used in characterizing Jiuhua as sacred in literati poetry is its representation as a microcosm, a bounded cosmos constituted during the primal era of creation. This cosmogenesis, explicit in Li Bo's opening couplet, is signaled in a number of other ways as well. Most obvious is the name of the mountain. Even before Li Bo's famous couplet, the number nine had been assigned to the jumble of peaks along its central ridge. The auspicious significance of nine in Chinese numerological traditions is manifold, and well-known.

In addition, as in landscape painting, the juxtaposition of rivers and mountains informs much Jiuhua poetry. This, as has been noted by Paul Demieville, was a fundamental structuring device in the representation of microcosmic, hence sacred, space. Jiuhua's proximity to the Yangtse naturally lent itself to such a juxtaposition. Fei specifically notes in an otherwise laconic description of the construction of Jin's temple complex that the lay devotees structured channels to direct water into temple fields, and the Release of Life Pool. Hydraulics would seem to play an essential role in the production of some sacred geography, both as it is represented in painting and poetry, or as it is lived through the physical alteration of nature for social and economic purposes.

What is significant about the Jiuhua literati cult at least through the Northern Song period is not that its images are unique, since similar descriptions of Chinese sacred mountains are to be found throughout their writings, but that the literati vision of Jiuhua is only that, a vision. It is viewed in its totality, as nine peaks, a microcosm, and there is little sense of experience on the mountain or in any of its valleys. Though the nine peaks can be viewed together from several locations, these are in all cases some distance removed from the mountain. Their poetry tends more toward vistas of the mountain than views from it. The predominant literati cult of Jiuhua at this time then was a cult of site, and Jiuhua does not really seem to have functioned as the site or place of that cult.

Though the Buddhist communities left few literary records of their presence on the mountain, they did build temples, and these might suggest some of the ways in which they structured their landscape. Fei's account suggests that it was only the valley of Jiuhua Jie that underwent the monastic transformation described previously, a supposition confirmed by the date of temple constructions as reocorded by the gazetteers. Living within this very isolated part of the mountains, cut off from views of the main ridge with its nine peaks, the monks' *lived space* would potentially be far less inclusive or microcosmic than the literati's *representations* of Jiuhua. The Buddhists appear to have made no attempt to occupy a mountain center, however that might have been construed, or the main ridge with its "nine" peaks.

With the emergence of the Dizang cult at the beginning of the ninth century the scope of Buddhist construction on and around the mountain was significantly extended. Based on gazetteer records of the location and dates of construction, at least twenty new temples and retreats were constructed, some in the surrounding foothills and villages. It is likely that this construction was directly related to the spread of the Dizang cult and indicates that it had become popularized and diffused throughout the rural areas around Jiuhua.

SONG LANDSCAPES

Tendencies only dimly perceptible in the late Tang become more conspicuous in the Northern Song. The number of prominent literati writing about Jiuhua increased significantly, and the spread of Buddhist institutions encompassed not only the entire mountain, but extended into the surrounding countryside. The discursive structures that began to give shape to Jiuhua in the Tang were also carried over into the Song. The literary materials that we have made much use of to characterize Jiuhua in the late Tang, are precisely those that were the most cited in the Song.

Increasingly conspicuous in the gazetteers is the spread of Buddhist sites out of Jiuhua Jie, and into various other regions in the range. Whereas there were just over twenty temples on the mountain at the end of the Tang, there were over forty by the end of the Northern Song. In addition, a temple was built for the first time on the relatively inaccessible summit of the highest peak, Tiantai.

The well-known Linji Chan (Jap., Rinzai Zen) monk, Da Hui (1090-1162), credited with carrying Chan traditions to Jiuhua, wrote a poem entitled "Wandering on Jiuhua Shan, Commenting on Tiantai's Heights" that provides some sense of Buddhist perceptions during the Song.

Rambling about on Tiantai, not making a sound,

One peal of the pure bell
echoes off ten thousand peaks.

Five-needle pines embrace
the canopied Sylph's Terrace,

Nine lotuses open into a Buddha Land.
This southern realm looks down on the
Jiang's white form.

Easterm Scarp sits facing
the evening sun's brilliance,

A single verse of poetry
has already usurped its fame.

Standing on the highest peak in the range, Da Hui invokes Jin Dizang by reference to the Five-Needle Pine supposedly brought to China from Korea by Jin, and the characterization of Jiuhua as a Buddha Land, an accomplishment also attributable to Jin. This view of a Buddhist realm encompassing the entire mountain, and of Jin Dizang's role in producing it, confirms what has been suggested earlier by the spread of temple structures following the advent of the Dizang cult, namely that the Buddhists space was being extended far beyond Jin's small valley. Viewing the nine lotus-shaped peaks as a Buddha Land also parallels the literati vision of the range as a microcosm, an all-encompassing space. Like the literati, some Buddhists were engaging in a discourse that encompassed the entire range of peaks. Also invoked at the end of Da Hui's poem is Li Bo, the author of the verse

that had already usurped the mountain's fame or perhaps its name.

The literati who came into contact with Jiuhua in the Northern Song also continued precedents set in the late Tang. Many literati travelers on the Yangtse emulated Li Bo in producing distant views of Jiuhua. Several literati took up eremitic residence on the mountain. In addition, two other modes of interaction with the mountain became common in this period. Many of the literati travelers began to visit the "recluses." This is reflected in poems praising particular recluses and the reclusive life in general. It also appears to have become more common in this period to engage in mountain wandering, *you shan*, short tours around the important sites on the mountain. The two most prominent literati recluses on Jiuhua during this period were Teng Zongliang (990-1047) and Liu Fang (n.d.). Teng, who was a native of Loyang, took up residence under *Yunwai* ("Beyond the Clouds") Peak, located midway between Qingyang and Jiuhua Jie. His hut was thus considerably more accessible to urban centers and travel routes than Jin's valley. Liu Fang was a native of Qingyang who gained considerable recognition as a scholar, but never entered public service. He constructed a thatched hut under *Shuang* Peak, located even closer to the urban culture of Qingyang than Teng's study. Thus, not as secluded as their writings would suggest, the recluses were not particularly solitary either. Visits to these two recluses became quite common among many of the most prominent literati of the Northern Song. Among those who were associated with Liu Fang and who made excursions to his hut were Wang Anshi, (1021-1086), the dismissed liberal reformer, and Su Je (1039-1112), brother of the conservative, Su Shih.

Mei Yaochen (1002-1060), is said to have been one of Teng Zongliang's many guests. Mei's one poem on Jiuhua is typical of works written for, or about, the Jiuhua recluses. They tend towards stereotyped images of the life of the recluse and contain little in the way of local knowledge of place. Except for a possible reference to the location of Teng's hut, Cloudy Peak, probably an abbreviation of "Beyond the Clouds" Peak, the recluse could be on almost any mountain in China. Following Teng's return to public life Mei wrote:

Making light of fears, you lived in the mountains,

Having previously yearned for a secluded hut.

Wanting to be close to Cloudy Peak

How few were (even) your rustic guests!

Stream vegetables on your chopping board,

And forest birds looking at your books.

How could you make light of these pleasures,

And return to the boarder cars[3]?

There is simply no sense of place here. Also, conspicuously absent from this, as well as from most literati poems on Jiuhua, is any indication whatsoever of the lay or monastic Buddhist presence on Jiuhua. Even a recluse living on Jiuhua in the eleventh century would have been in relatively constant contact with the Buddhists and within sight of their temples. Yet, other than animals, these poems represent the mountain as all but unpopulated.

The one place Buddhist presence appears in literati works is in the *you shan* "wandering the mountain" pieces. It is clear that by this time Jiuhua was fairly replete with temples, which given their general policy of offering accommodation to travelers, must have greatly enhanced the prospect of vising Jiuhua. An elderly and retired Wang Anshi, writes warmly about his stay at Jin's former temples, *Huacheng.* Awakening in the middle of the night Wang looked out on Li Bo's lotus-shaped peaks, proclaimed a monkish, frugal contentment, and acknowledged Jin's culinary contribution to the mountain, *huang jin.* Here, as in most poems incorporating Buddhist spaces on Jiuhua, the sites tend to function primarily as idealized settings for more personal reflections.

Both Su Je and Wang Anshi wrote longer more reflective poems on Jiuhua, again quite devoid of any suggestion of the Buddhist presence. Su Je's poem entitled "Passing Jiuhua Mountain," was written as he was sailing down the Yangtse on his way to a new post following the defeat of his faction in the Song court. The poem is one of the "distant views" genre, and characteristically begins with his surprise when the peaks first come into view:

Suddenly startled by the Jiuhua Peaks

Arching up before me.

Nine dignified sylphs

Appear faintly through misty clouds

Cloaked in the aurora,

Capped by blue stone.

With a wave they announce to mortals

You can gaze, but you can't touch.

The poem proceeds to a description of the life of an anonymous recluse living on the peaks where he seeks out fungi that prolong his life. The poem closes with a lament that the poet is unable to visit the recluse in his stone chamber. Li Bo's nine lotuses have become sylphs, but the mountain remains distant and unattainable.

Wang Anshi's very long poem, "On a Boat with Pingfu, Gazing at Jiuhua," is also framed in the "distant view" mode. For him the peaks that suddenly emerge in the moonlight are likened to the coiffures of the Taoist goddess, Xi Wangmu. Much of the rest of the poem is speculation on the futility of the attention certain emperors have lavished on such mountains as the Marchmounts. Wang notes with approval that Jiuhua, shrouded in mists, has virtuously kept itself hidden from those attentions. It's almost as though the mountain, rather than serving to conceal the recluse, actually takes on the persona of a concealed recluse.

MICROCOSMS & FETISHES

Much that has been written on the religious syncretism and mutual contact between various cults during Northern Song might lead one to expect a high degree of convergence or integration in the social and religious landscapes of this watershed period. This proves to be only partially true in the case of Jiuhua. Whereas there was a clear movement by certain Dizang cults, monastic and lay, to appropriate the representational space of the entire mountain as the literati had done before them, they also succeeded in appropriating most of its lived space as well. Although Da Hui invoked Li Bo in his poem, it is not clear that the Buddhists were any more inclined to include the literati in their representations of that space than the literati were willing to include the Buddhists. Buddhist and literati communities living in close contact on Jiuhua in this post-medieval period, seem, with some exceptions, as mutually incognizant of their respective spatial products as they were during the Tang.

The literati for their part had moved no closer to physical occupation of Jiuhua as a lived space than they had been during the Tang. They continued in their tendency to look from the outside, and to represent the site in an iconic fashion, even in the poetry of the recluse. But this was no less an appropriation of Jiuhua than that of the Buddhist cults. As Henri Lefevbre (*The Production of Space*) has observed, "Property in the sense of possession is at best a necessary precondition, and most often merely an epiphenomenon, of 'appropriative' activity, the highest expression of which is the work of art. An appropriated space resembles a work of art, which is not to say that it is in any sense an imitation work of art." Part of the literati's representation of Jiuhua involved what sometimes appears to be an intentional distancing. And with this distancing came the power of that, which when concealed, can only be imagined. Images of Mt. Jiuhua such as "faintly perceived," or "shrouded in mists" make what is presented as a visibility all but invisible. By fetishizing Jiuhua in this fashion, the literati were empowering Jiuhua while at the same time laying the ground for its appropriation into a state-like system of sacred sites on the order of what had already been achieved through the sacred Marchmounts [see page 16]. Michael Taussig (*The Nervous System*) has written, "In this peeling off of the signifier from its signified, the representation acquires not just the power of the represented, but power over it, as well." Such an event was exactly what overtook Jiuhua in the sixteenth century when it was included in the "Four Great Luminous Mountains" of Buddhism. It was in this period that the pilgrims' path, described at the beginning of this essay, came into existence, producing the space that conditioned my experience of the mountain. It was also in this period that what Wang Anshi had found laudable about Jiuhua, its "humble seclusion," ceased to be true. Jiuhua gained the patronage of the Wan Li Emperor. Ironically it was not the literati vision of Jiuhua that was institutionalized, but a powerful Buddhist microcosm, still only nascent in the Northern Song, the realm of Dizang Budhisattva as experienced by pilgrims over the past 500 years. The literary representations proved to be diversions.

It is clear that there have been many sacred Jiuhuas, not only throughout its history, but often at the same time. More importantly, it is clear in each case that the space constituted as sacred has been a social product, emerging from the lived space of the communities concerned, and at the same time conditioning the way that space was lived. ▲

NOTES ....

1. Fish or eels rescued from local markets were released into these pools in a popular Buddhist ritual of compassion. They constituted an important feature of most Buddhist temples in China.
2. The potential fallacy of such an assumption was revealed to me in a discussion I had with the present abbot and head of the Jiuhua Buddhist Association, Ren De, in 1988. Following a long discussion of Chan Buddhism and its practices, in which it was clear the abbot spoke with much first hand knowledge, I asked him if he trained his monks in such traditions. He sighed, and lamented that it required all his time and effort simply to maintain discipline.
3. The use of "boarder cars," vehicles used on state business, indicated a resumption of official duties.

Falling Flowers Rising to the Threshold of the Eye

TAKEDA YOSHIFUMI

JOHN EINARSEN

On a spring day long ago, as we watched gentle sunbeams playing on the blossoms in her garden, my grandmother told me about the cherries of Yoshino. Ever since, no cherry tree in bloom, not even a weeping cherry, could quite satisfy me deep down in my heart. Each year spring came and went. Each year the cherry blossoms, in their brief season, would bloom and fall away, and faintly in the distance I could hear her words, as she sat on the veranda with the bright sun on her back, her eyes half closed behind old-fashioned spectacles.

Perhaps I was in a kind of youthful revolt against the conventional notion that cherry blossoms are the paragon of beauty. For me it was not that "the flowers are beautiful," but simply "there are some beautiful flowers." The years went by and I became an adult, and I found that as my eyes gazed upon cherry blossoms, somehow they fell into place with the eyes of my grandmother on that sunny day long past.

A grandmother with eyes half closed, hunched on a bench watching the figures of her frolicking grandchildren on the roof of a neighborhood department store... this scene is from an essay "On Rooftops" by Muramatsu Tomomi. For me that brilliant sunshine, playing relentlessly upon the fading frailty of the old woman, splendidly evokes the contrasts of light and dark at the threshold of the sky.

I am certain that as she spoke to me back then, my grandmother was seeing not the cherry blossoms in front of her eyes, but the entire image of Yoshino which welled up inside her. It was a triumphant image, nurtured by the portrayals of kabuki and dance and romanticized by literature and historical tales. No cherry blossoms are more served by the arts and literature than those of Mt. Yoshino. Among the most memorable accounts is Saami's story of a heavenly maiden who descends to the mountain of flowers to perform a celestial dance, and disappears back on high.

Once associated with Mt. Yoshino, the image of cherry blossoms becomes removed from everyday life and takes on a sense of the surreal. This is partly because Mt. Yoshino is steeped in history, and also has much do to with the fact that it has been regarded as a quintessential Mountain. While cherry blossoms in a townscape are seen horizontally, mountain cherries are panoramic and at the same time vertical, placing before our eyes a veil that connects earth and sky. They rise to a space of vacancy and seem to mingle with the mists of heaven. It is at that point, where the blossoms become indiscernible from the mist and the clouds, that celestial maidens tread.

From ancient times, Mt. Yoshino was an image of the ideal locale, having at various times been called Fragrant Mountain, Beloved Fields (Eshinu or Aishino)

and Fields of Good Fortune (Yoshino). Yet it has always been a rarefied locale, a place of seclusion or ritual confinement, with a kind of extraterritorial existence of its own.

Mt. Yoshino has also long been a sanctuary for mountain ascetics, associated with nearby Mt. Omine. The peaks visible in the distance from atop Yoshino are still seen to demark a realm infused with spirituality, of a feminine character. Ascetics go up the hill blowing conch shells and chanting "Confess! Confess!" and "Purify the six senses!" As they embark up the mountain path, they believe they are crossing into the other world: "Placing a hand on Yoshino's copper torii, a joy like entering the paradise of Amida Buddha." Mt. Yoshino and its cherry blossoms were each seen as a portal of two worlds, both entrance and egress.

Sakura, the word for cherry blossom, is said to derive from the idea of the bud where a divine spirit is closeted until the tip (*saki*) bursts (*sake-ru*) and blooms (*saku*). In several ways, then, Mt. Yoshino has been regarded as the edge

of this world. The higher reaches are a ritualistic place, a fitting scene for a climax, aptly decorated by suddenly blooming cherry trees, and subject to no less sudden precipitation.

Several of Japan's noted historical outsiders were attracted to Mt. Yoshino. I am reminded again of rooftop-essayist Muramatsu, who envisions a present-day fugitive taking refuge atop a Ferris wheel, only to fall from its height downward through the air. And with the sound of the rising wind that scatters the petals up the ravines, I hear in the distance my grandmother's voice: "The cherry blossoms of Mt. Yoshino scatter upward from below." Heaven and earth turned upside-down by the reverse energy of Mt. Yoshino. Surely she is not the only one to see the sorrows of the Southern Dynasty in its falling blossoms. ▲

Translated by Stephen Suloway

PILLARS OF THE SKY

S T E P H A N   K Ö H L E R

TAIWAN

"We thank God for bringing you here safely, on this long and dangerous road…" my host intoned in Japanese, then switched to Rukai. "Takitobi toobiki toa omasu…."

Having already aimed my spoon at some steaming millet dumplings in a dented aluminum bowl, I sat chastened as Kaynoan began saying grace. His elbows were on the plastic-laminated table and his forehead rested against the zigzag wall of his short, strong fingers, pointing up at the dim fluorescent bulb that lit his smoky kitchen. Every few seconds he tilted his bald head slightly and raised his voice. I heard him hesitate and fall back on phrases he had already used — a record with old grooves and some blanks for daily variations. Finally, in Japanese, "…and thank you for keeping bacteria from growing on this precious food you have given us, so we will not have indigestion."

He dug in to the cooked bananas with crushed peanuts, putting them in a bowl marked with a Christian cross and the words, World Vision. "The priest keeps telling us to watch out for bacteria," he commented. Indeed, this Rukai village in the foothills looked quite tidy, a far cry from the Chinese towns in the flatlands below. Yet how often I had heard the Chinese referring to the Rukai and the other nine native tribes of Taiwan as dirty, lazy, primitive.

"Which church do you go to?" I asked. I had seen crosses embroidered with light bulbs atop several buildings in the village.

"The big one, on the hill. It's the best church, by far. The other three aren't really serious. The priests are charlatans. You can tell by the people who go there. They don't prosper as much as I do. They drink, and they aren't lucky with their orchards."

Four churches for a village of about 100 permanent residents, and everyone tells me theirs is the best. Typical, I thought, of the fragmentation of the native minorities. After the Kuomintang took over Taiwan for its millions of mainland refugees in 1949, missionaries of all stripes were encouraged to work among the remote tribes, where they made a far higher proportion of converts than among the Chinese majority. The government eventually forced the Rukai and other groups to leave their scattered tiny communities along footpaths high in the mountains, for concrete-block villages along roads near the plains. Today there are 300,000 descendants of the tribes, among 20 million ethnic Chinese with roots on the mainland or in Taiwan. Half or more of the ethnic minorities are in the cities, and there is little political or community linkage among them or even among villages of the same group.

"What attracted the Rukai to Christianity?" I asked my friend as we ate. "The Japanese left in 1945, and you were on your own for a few years before the Kuomintang arrived. You could have restored your old ways…"

"The Japanese were here for a long time," replied Kaynoan, speaking to me in the language he had learned during the half-century of colonial rule. "We were confused and uprooted when they left. They destroyed our original belief system, calling almost everything we did an ignorant superstition. A lot of our men went to war for Japan, and not many came back healthy. But we did learn a lot from them, hygiene, health care, farming, machinery. Some of it worked for us, some did not. The Japanese officers made us move our pigs out of our houses. They made us stop burying our family members under the floor of the house, and carry them to a graveyard. Maybe that was the right thing to do, regarding those bacteria. And they thought our slate houses were too low and too dark, but when we built them higher with more windows, the typhoons damaged them badly.

"The Japanese were like strict fathers. They hit us in the face if we did not greet them. They kept our guns and bows and arrows, which we needed for hunting, and made us go to school every day for four hours. When they left all of a sudden, we had nothing, neither our traditions nor the masters who told us what to do. We welcomed the missionaries, because they were offering us something to believe in, and they treated us with much more respect and understanding than the Kuomintang. In many ways the Chinese were crueler than the Japanese. They never lived with us as the Japanese did, they just sent police and soldiers to control us. The shifts changed all the time, so no relationships could grow.

"The missionaries gave us nice things, plastic bowls, dishes, spoons, clothes with crosses and Jesus faces printed on them. And they promised us that we could hunt in the taboo places without attracting bad luck. Even the Japanese had respected those areas. They did not make us log the forests in sacred places. But everyone went hunting and harvesting when we were told that Jesus protects us wherever we go, if we go to church regularly. Also we were told about the tortures of hell which were waiting for us if we did not attend church services. And another thing, an important thing, is that my church has a savings and loan program with the best interest rates in the whole country."

We had finished the meal and moved to the sitting room for drinks with Kaynoan's 100-year-old mother and his wife, Navay. The bearded Caucasian man watched over us from a print of a 19th-century oil painting, his eyes on a ray of light breaking through dark clouds of sin. Navay joined the conversation. "Walking in the mountains used to be very difficult. We couldn't pass by certain rocks when we were pregnant. Now, since we have Jesus, we don't have to worry about all that. Everyday life is much more practical. Also, the shamans were taking advantage of people, charging them a lot of money and just telling lies, pretending they could heal people with all their hocus-pocus, whereas the Christian hospital is very good. Our son works there and has a steady income."

It all made sense. It would be hard to live in the debris of an animistic system that was shattered by outsiders. Starting over with something new might have been much easier than glueing together the pieces of a broken jar, many of them missing. Yet while their new religion might work for them in their present circumstances, it seems to have brought in still more alienation. Why wear a necktie to church in a native community? Why the mock-Italian church buildings, with glue-on plastic "stained glass" windows? Why is there no acknowledgment of the world that the elders grew up in just a few miles away? Aren't there some things that deserve to be remembered?

"I know you think of yourselves as Christians now. But I am very curious to know how you lived before, with the attitudes and beliefs which are truly your own."

Kaynoan responded, "Our old beliefs are closely connected to places in our original territory. Down here, there is very little that relates to our old way of life. We moved here only 14 years ago. If you want to know about the old life, we should hike up to the old village. I could show you the pillars which held up our sky."

▲▲

The path up to the abandoned village was rarely wider than one foot, with plenty of opportunities to fall freely for hundreds of feet. Even before we came to a shaky bridge across a gorge, I was wondering how they carried their belongings down to the new village, for I had seen quite a few old totems and mortars for crushing millet. The flora changed from tropical to subtropical, and became almost temperate by the time we reached the village, 1100 meters above sea level. Cherry and pear trees were in bloom, mosquitos scarce. We were in a steep bowl of mountains with a generous radius, perhaps two-thirds of the way down from the rim. The view in every direction was superb.

In 1976 there had been 180 homes. Most of them now were heaps of slate. Slate was used for everything: roofs, walls, floors, furniture, stairs, paths, and the lifesize totem figures on the outer walls, flat like gingerbread.

"The Japanese thought this place was founded about 2000 years ago, but recently some Chinese archaeologists did some digging, and they say it has been in use for 4000 years." Kaynoan gave me this information with evident pride, as he began sweeping away a layer of white dust to expose the slate floor of his house. "It's the white ants," he explained, pointing to the ceiling beams. "You can't keep them away without daily smoke, but I only get up here every couple months." He moved on to the roof, closing up holes made when typhoons shifted the slate tiles. I busied myself pulling weeds on the terrace.

"How strong are you?" Kaynoan was standing right in front of me, making me feel like a giant. "I saw a nice camphor log about 10 minutes down the hill. If we can get it up here, we can replace that rotten beam in the center of the roof." My mind pictured us sleeping that night under a slate sword of Damocles, and my strength swelled. Soon my shoulder was accepting the pain of one end of the six-meter log, as I watched the little man in front of me, decades older, maneuver up the remains of a once-splendid slate stairway. When the termite-hollowed beam came down it was as light as white bread, and it broke into three pieces as I threw it out onto the terrace.

By now most of the mountain rim was veiled in clouds, with floating windows that provided alternating views of selected peaks. Out of context, I lost my orientation and sense of scale. That foggy slope, was it one of the high peaks or just a hill? Bother, maybe this time I would not learn much about the old territory.

"Since it is cloudy, I will show you some places we can walk to," said Kaynoan. He handed me a machete, and we set out attacking the thorny bushes that had overgrown the paths. I lacked experience in chopping at the stubborn maze, and my hands bled from scratches. From the ridge above his house, we had a breathtaking view of the gorge we had crossed that morning. The river fell in narrow chutes cut into the naked rock or rested in pools of emerald green. A

solitary stone like a squarish candle, four feet high, marked the high point of our ridge. "The name of this rock is Tamaunalu (**19**). It has protected our village for ages, but once it fell over and the shaman reerected it. However, he put it up facing east instead of west. Afterward a plague spread in the tribe. A couple of healthy families moved and founded a new village, Rumingan (**11**), on the ledge of that slope over there. Eventually, after the mistake was found and corrected, those people rejoined the village."

I touched the reddish surface of the rock. "Do you think it's strong enough to protect your tribe in the new town a few miles from here?"

"Of course! Most of us were born under its eyes. But now we have Jesus Christ, and we don't need this rock anymore."

Kaynoan slashed onward toward the every-louder sound of water, until we stood before a wet stage which was lapped by foam and twigs. This pool (**17**) was the artery of life to the mountain community. "Women came here to get water, the children swam and fished. And that stone over there with the dimple, where the stream is fast, is where the men washed their heads. Of course they stopped taking them after the Japanese came. When I was a kid I was horrified to see our hunters come home carrying bloody heads with staring eyes."

We climbed a rock shoulder along the creek, to a place where we could see a cave from above. "This is where Pali used to live. He was a mighty man with magic eyes. He caused earthslides just by looking at a mountain, and killed people by casting his eyes on them. He saved the village a couple of times when it was attacked by the Paiwan tribe. Pali always wore a giant hat which almost

reached his chin, like an upside-down basket. When he was hungry, he would pull a string that was connected to a little tree in the village. When the tree shook, food was brought up by a girl. She must have been terrified, and she had to be careful all the way up not to spill the soup."

On the way down we passed a regularly segmented building, four halls under one roof. The dirty walls of crumbling concrete radiated melancholy, unlike the strong though lonely surfaces of the timeless slate walls. Each room had a smooth green wall panel, like a minimalist painting. "I enjoyed school," Kaynoan said. "I was one of the smart ones, the others were dull and not serious. Even now I remember my Japanese, and write and read it, too. Nobody else in the village is as able as I am." This was the style in which Kaynoan constantly reminded me how lucky I was to have met him. His boasts always made me smile, because everyone else in the village talked in the same way.

After a dinner of rice and millet with spinach picked on our afternoon walk,

we sat by candlelight on shaky old chairs that seemed to have been built for small children. Kaynoan pulled out his harmonica and recalled several songs young men would play at night in front of girls' houses. Suddenly, he jumped up and let out a bird-like scream, followed by a rough song, almost shouting, which made my blood freeze and my hair stand on end. This piercing tune had nothing to do with mating. My system pumped adrenalin. A new, non-cerebral element of myself was awakened to the journey.

"When my father or grandfather had taken a head, that is how they announced their victory to the other tribe. Our men could shout loudly, to be heard through the jungle and across the valleys, right to the enemy's village. Then those people knew that they had to look for a headless body just where the scream came from."

After a while we talked for a bit. Kaynoan told me that the imports of Chris-

tianity had replaced barbarism. "If we weren't Christian, we would have cut off your head days ago."

He was beginning to nod off. We made up our beds — blankets on foot-high benches of handsawn camphor wood. "Shall I blow out the candles?" I asked the almost-snoring Kaynoan.

"Are you out of your mind?" He sat bolt upright. "All those ghosts! Without candles they creep up on you at night…" I left two tapers burning, and listened to a quirky lullaby of animal voices.

▲ ▲

I was outside in time to see the first pinkish aura above the mountains. Even the blue-black slate seemed to glow with soft light for a minute or two. Purple, blue, orange, yellow, and finally the sun put fingers around the topmost peak, 2500 meters, and pulled himself up. The sound of rolling stones, earthslides of

considerable scale, came intermittently across the broad bowl. Constant change.

"Where is the ink?" Kaynoan came out carrying my roll of oversize drawing paper. Good, he had remembered my request that he draw something of the old ways — at least a map of the old places, surely Jesus would not be offended.

I found brushes and ink, and he immediately began sketching on a small sheet. It looked like a roundish fruit, maybe a papaya. But there were protrusions, and gradually I saw resemblances to the mountain skyline. I had taken it for granted that a panorama was to be drawn in a scroll-like fashion, linear, with a beginning and an end. Kaynoan's vision was circular. He envisioned himself at the center of a sketch that had no starting point. His body turned at a steady pace as he scanned the view and transmitted it to paper, often without looking. He kept going around, scratching his shiny head, reworking the lines until they were smudged and he was frustrated.

"I have looked at these mountains for more than 70 years, and I can't even make a decent map."

"Don't worry, there is plenty of paper," I encouraged him. I went in and made a fire for tea, and as I thought about his

map projection, I had an idea. During breakfast I said: "Since we carried up all this paper, we might as well use it. If we put two big sheets together, you can sit on your map and draw around yourself, instead of just imagining the center." Kaynoan dived into a process which took him three hours. He never talked or took a break. A highly paid surveyor could not have matched his concentration. Finally he put down the brush and the lecture began.

"The mountain behind this village, north, is Aluan (**18**). It is behind the trees, but I drew it from memory. There are two ponds near its peak, Palugnuru below and Kadagilan above (**17**). In periods of drought, we made spears with many oranaments tied to them, leaves, feathers, flowers. Two of our fastest runners, I was chosen many times, went up the path, about an hour's sprint, and threw a spear into each of the ponds with a loud prayer, and ran back without taking a single break. If they stopped, the rain would come only as far as that point, no further, and our fields would stay dry. I never stopped, of course.

"The road to Adilu, built by the Japanese, is in that fold (**16**). It was wide enough for two horses, but now it is all weeds, nobody tends it. On the peaks above the road there should still be big chunks of camphor wood, left over from when we had to log all the old trees for the Japanese. Actually, we could take a stroll up there this afternoon and bring some down for carving.

"That peak is Talalakichanu (**14**). It means Swallows' Peak. We saw thousands of swallows when we hunted and logged there. Below it is a taboo area called Daibulu (**15**), where we could not kill an animal or harvest fruit. Fortunately we never had to log trees there. Can you see the steep place? That is where Grandmother lives. We say Lakaingut (**13**). She is a rock 30 meters high, and she often has a veil of mist and drizzling rain around her. Our grandmother distributes game to Rukai villages. Since she faces the village of Adilu, it was those hunters who almost always came home with as much game as they could carry. The peak to the right of grandmother is Parathudanu, the second highest in this area (**12**). [Wutohsan, about 2600m]

"This is an old taboo area called Tatalilioro (**10**). When we became Christian, all taboo areas became open for hunting deer and gathering fruit. The priest said Jesus would protect us if we believed in him. Right after I became Christian, I hiked in there and climbed a huge tree to pick ogyo fruit from a vine that grew on it. When my basket was full, I lost my balance and fell. It felt like I would never land, the tree was so high. My head hit a rock. I woke up bleeding and crawled home, because I knew I would die if I stayed overnight out there. My skull was cracked slightly, right here." He pointed to a scar on top of his head.

"If I had died I might have gone to Balukuan (**9**). The flat saddle area is our sanctuary for the spirits of the dead. Only brave and honest people are let in. Of course no hunting was permitted in Balukuan. Only deformed fir trees grow in its cold climate. At dusk they look like dancing snakes. Anyone who stayed there overnight almost went insane, from seeing the dead in their dreams and hearing all their whispering voices.

"Whenever we leave the village and enter a mountain path, we give presents to the gods and spirits. usually pork skin and alcoholic drink. We put a portion

for each god on a separate leaf and sprinkle alcohol in all directions. You must never speak loudly, or sing in the mountains like Chinese tourists do. Last year Auvini guided a group of students to Balukuan and they played guitars and were noisy all night. Then on their way back they were caught in a storm, during the dry season, mind you, and a Japanese anthropologist slipped off a rock and was injured. So you better behave in Balukuan!

"We call this mountain Dakulusan (**8**). It is named after Navay's grandfather, who broke down crying when he was a little boy because he was so tired from carrying a boar they had caught. 'Dakulu' means to cry. But only our family uses this name. There are many names used by various families, which they pass down in tales about their ancestors.

"This is Mau Alu Alun (**7**), which means pine peak, because of the trees at the top. The next one up is the single tooth, Rigai (**6**), which is very hard to pass, and then we come to Rigarigalanu (**5**), many teeth, which also means a saw.

Dakalaus (**4**) is the highest peak [3190m]. It is the home of the sky god,

Yabulun. Once or twice each year, when the monsoons go on day after day to try to steal our crops, we pray to Dakalaus and Yabulun sends a mighty thunderstorm to chase away the rain. But Kaburugan (**3**) used to be much higher than Dakalaus. On the earliest Dutch maps of Formosa, you can see it. Dakalaus

was just a little shorter, and he was constantly jealous. One day, the two mountains were having a chat at sunrise. Dakalaus said to his neighbor, 'Do you know the crumble game? Not every mountain can do it, but if we try hard, we could play crumble today. We have plenty of rocks to spare, so it won't hurt

little sermon. Sometimes the priest invites people with brains to do part of the service."

And so we left the old gods behind to meet the schedule of the new, but not without a score of stories about medicinal plants and water spirits and hunting incidents on the path down.

▲ ▲

Navay welcomed us with joy, and pineapples fresh from the orchard. The glare of Jesus' gaze in the framed prints on the walls jabbed my eyes, after all that nature. Kaynoan noticed my frown and said, "Those pictures are exotic to us, something new from far away. Maybe you put pictures of our totem carvings on your wall and think they are special." Touché. But the Rukai are Christians without history. Do they know about the headhunters of Europe, the armies who joined the churches in crusades and unholy alliances?

After only about 35 years of going to church, an elder like Kaynoan, at least, has not lost his aboriginal relationship to nature. Having heard his tales shift perspective back and forth again and again, I realized that he operates from a dual consciousness. As faithful as he is to the Christian patterns, he is not half as Christian at heart as the European who has cut his ties with the church to become a Buddhist monk in Munich.

I suppose I will not be so quick to remind that monk of the sanctity of his native traditions. But then, his native traditions are not poised to disappear from the surface of the earth. Even so, my hope for the Rukai to believe in their own gods is largely a projection of my own longing for a point of unity and simplicity, a place without confusion. Such a unity can only be created for myself. I could not ask Kaynoan to "Be Rukai for me," I had to be it myself.

Dinner was on the table, and this time I remembered to pray along with Kaynoan.

to send a few downhill. And since you, Kaburugan, are higher, older and wiser, please go first and show me a fine example.' Kaburugan was flattered, and he began to huff and puff and made a little landslide. 'That's the stuff!' said Dakalaus. 'But I think you can make some bigger rocks fall, so even Alisan, the tallest peak on this island, will hear of you.' Well, that was the end of Kaburugan being the higher mountain. And when he said, 'Now it's your turn,' Dakalaus just laughed and laughed, and since then they haven't said another word to each other.

"The rocks and earth of Kaburugan filled the valley and we had a huge flood. We lost all of our fire. An antelope called Chikipalici visited a fly on the peak of Dakalaus who could make fire by rubbing her front legs together, and brought some burning twigs back to us. The lower village of Badain (**2**) had even worse trouble. Thirty men died, and the flood finally ended there when the shaman sacrificed a baby pig to the river. Badain is the home of Laban, the goddess of fertility who comes next after Yabulun, the sky god.

The demon Mauto Tokoro is Laban's opponent, and when he is able to spy on her while she is working, a child is born dead.

"This nose-shaped mountain is Piuma (**1**). It is in the Paiwan land, and we often had territorial fights about it. All that headhunting, an endless chain of revenge. I am so glad it's over."

"And where is hell?" I finally asked.

"We call it Korunguru (**0**), and we believe it is somewhere in the west, toward the flatlands. That is where hell is, isn't it?"

The sun had grown strong, and we moved into the cool stone house. Kaynoan kept looking at the drawing and scratching his head, still not satisfied that everything was precise. I suggested that we celebrate with some of his favorite Chinese medicine brandy, with a deer on the label to show that it contains antler shavings.

"*Kampai* to Dakalaus!" I said. "What a wonderful trip. Since the weather is so nice, why don't we stay another day and look for camphor wood?"

"No, I have to go to church in the morning, and tonight I must prepare a

Dear Jesus, *thank you for protecting us on our trip up and down the mountain, keeping snakes from our path and providing good food. Please help me to give a good speech in church tomorrow, so that everyone will be impressed with my brightness....*

Dear Dakalaus, *thank you for having me around you and inspiring Kaynoan to tell me so much about you and your brothers and sisters. Please be strong and pull your children back into the mountains, so they will not rot in the cities and will make use of their own resources....*

▲

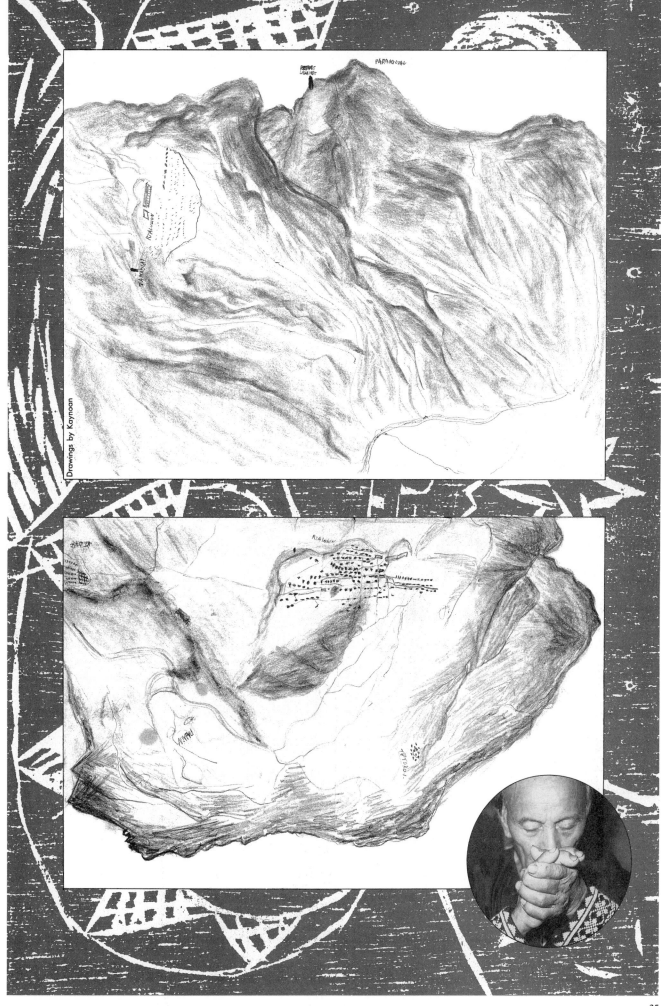

Drawings by Kaynoan

PARAGOPAL

FLYING MOUNTAINS
& WALKERS OF EMPTINESS

SACRED SPACE IN JAPANESE RELIGIONS

Shintai is one aspect of Shinto that still remains shrouded in darkness, partly for an obvious reason: it usually remains hidden in the shrine. The word *shintai* itself appears in religious literature only from the middle of the Heian period; today most priests prefer the word *mitamashiro*. A *shintai* may be a knot, a *tama*, a mirror, a sword, or any object of striking appearance. It can also be a mountain. In some cases the *shintai* is nothing more than the support or *yorishiro*; in other cases the *shintai* is perceived as being the divinity itself — tradition tells us which is which. Since the case of the mountain, however, is particularly important in the development of Japanese concepts of sacred space, it should be examined in more detail.

The task of describing how mountains came to be defined as sacred space by the Japanese presents some difficult problems because of the lack of sufficient historical information. From what period on, and for what reason, were some mountains treated differently? We cannot fully answer these questions. At any rate, we can say that the notion of the sacred mountain appears in such early texts as the *Kojiki* and the *Fudoki*. The generic term *shintaizan* (mountain as *shintai*) first appears in the *Shoku-Nihongi*, book 10. It is clear that the religious significance of mountains continued to grow in Japan from the Heian period on, possibly with some influence from Daoism. A *shintaizan* was a mountain which in its entirety was regarded as the support or site of residence for the divine or as the actual body of a divinity or group of divinities. In the case of the *shintaizan*, there is no main shrine on or near the mountain, only a veneration hall. We can see examples in the Ōmiwa Shrine south of Nara, the Suwa Shrine in Nagano, and the Kanasana Shrine in Saitama.

In studying the deification of mountains in Shinto, it is helpful to refer to Haruki Kageyama's classification of sites of residence of Shinto divinities into three types: distant sites (*oku* or *kuma*) on a mountain, or consisting of the mountain itself; central sites (*naka*) lying at the entrance to valleys; and close sites (*hotori*) located on the plains.[1] These three types are generally related: they delimit the influence of a divinity and allow communication between distant villages. The distant shrine receives the name of *oku no miya* in Shinto and *oku no in* in Buddhism. Famous examples are the *oku no miya* of the Kibune Shrine in Kyoto and the *oku no in* of Kōyasan.

Perhaps the most simple explanation for the deification

of mountains in Japan is that early attitudes of reverence were inspired not so much by the special qualities of any particular mountain but by characteristics of mountains in general as opposed to plains. Human activity belonged to the plains, where people lived; mountains were untouched and were areas of nonactivity. Corpses were abandoned or buried on mountains; hence the mountain was seen as a space whose nature was Other (not belonging to common categories of experience within the profane).

Probing further, we may describe three different categories of mountains which have been deified in Shinto. The first category comprises mountains revered for their importance in agriculture. The welfare of an entire community may depend on them. The shrines on these mountains are usually called *mikumari* ("water distribution") and are situated near sources of water or at the foot of mountains from which rivers flow. The most famous *mikumari* shrine is that of Yoshino, which developed, under various Buddhist influences, to become an extremely important shrine. Rituals aimed at smoothing the passage of divinities of fertility from the mountains to the plains in spring and vice versa in autumn are performed in such shrines, which may be the most ancient indication of why mountains were regarded as sacred: clouds accumulate on peaks, and rains fall on the slopes, enlarging these streams which provide water for agriculture. The divinity or divinities act as regulators of the flow and oversee the entire process of the agricultural cycle.

A second type of sacred mountain, possessing a main hall or *honden*, may be seen simply as a contact place of the divine. Daoism may have played an important role here, especially in the formation of cults and rituals in the Kansai area at such places as Mount Katsuragi. The divinities revered there are not necessarily linked to agriculture.

Yet there is a third, crucial factor in the formation of early mountain creeds: the notion of the mountain as the realm of death. In Shinto, just as the nature of time-in-life

This study was originally presented at the Seminar on Time and Space in Japanese Culture in Maui, Hawaii, January 1977, sponsored by the Social Science Research Council and the American Council of Learned Societies. All translations are by Allan G. Grapard, unless otherwise indicated. Excerpts from the original essay are reprinted here with the kind permission of the Department of the History of Religions, University of Chicago, © 1982.

is seen as being different from the nature of time-in-death, so a distinction is made between the space-of-life and the space-of-death. This is precisely the same distinction that is made between the plains and the mountains. The essentially Other world of death (*takai*) is referred to by several names: the Land of Constant Darkness (*tokoyo no kuni*); the Land of Roots (*ne no kuni*); and the Land of Yellow Springs (*yomi no kuni*).

Probably the first thing to come to mind when relating mountains to death is the burial mound or *kofun*. There is ample evidence for a theory which links the presence of divinities in the mountains with the souls of the departed. After death, souls are seen as undergoing a process of purification, at the end of which they become gods (*kami*). They then have the power to decide upon crops and other human affairs. Some rituals performed on mountains today show definite traces of ancient funeral ceremonies. The sacred mountain Hachiōji at the foot of Mount Hiei illustrates some of these points. The mountain is surrounded by tumuli. Haruki Kageyama has made a comprehensive study of the process through which Mount Hachiōji emerged as sacred space, showing the importance of the tombs as well as of agricultural rituals that are performed there. The mountain possesses all the elements we have mentioned so far: the two shrines (male and female) at the top are built in front of a huge rock (*iwasaka*); trees are used as supports (*yorishiro*) at the time of the descent of the divinities (and are then called *himorogi*); and, finally, there are shrines both at the foot of the mountain and at a distance from it. Rituals aimed at calling the divinities down in spring and at sending them back in autumn stress the distinction between the elevated area and the plain and serve as markers for the agricultural timetable. This mountain was to become central to the formation of Tendai Shinto-Buddhist syncretism during the Kamakura period, when a systematic expression of syncretism that was to become the substance of Japanese religiosity appeared.

There remains one last item to add to this necessarily superficial description of sacred space in early Shinto, that is, the early Chinese influence. It can be recapitulated in these terms: sacred space was organized by priests according to the theory of the five elements and chosen according to the theories of divination which were accepted by the Bureau of Religious Affairs and the Buddhists. Here is a text from the Heian period which clearly shows Chinese and Buddhist influences in the definitions of space. It is called the *Tōnomine ryakki*: "Mount Tan [Tōnomine] where Fujiwara no Kamatari is enshrined is a space without equal. To the east is located the great mountain of Ise, from which the great divinity Amaterasu protects the country; to the west is Mount Kongō, where the Budhisattva Hokki, expounding the Law, benefits all human beings; to the south is Mount Kimpu [Yoshino], where the Great Avatar is waiting for the coming of Maitreya; to the north is Mount Ōmiwa where the avatar of the Tathāgata is leading the people to release."[2] This short excerpt indicates that the mountain in question is seen as an axis mundi, the center of the universe, but with a mention of the four directions, which is a Chinese element.

BEGINNINGS

As soon as Esoteric Buddhism was introduced to Japan in the early ninth century, a complex interaction began between Shinto and Buddhism which eventually resulted in the emergence of a second category of sacred space, that of the sacred area. According to early Esoteric Buddhism, sacred space was the "site of the realization of Buddhahood." By contrast to other schools of Buddhism, which maintained that Buddhahood could only be realized in a space that was *not* of this world, Esoteric Buddhism proposed that Buddhahood could be realized in this body, in this life, and in this world. The result was a sacralization of this body, this life, and this world. The practice of Buddhism was seen as enhancing the quality of the world in which it was carried out and ultimately provoking a change of perspective on the universe.

A highly significant factor in the evolution of the sacred area in Esoteric Buddhism was the choice of mountain areas of Japan as the favorite training ground of early practitioners. We find this happening as early as the Nara period, when only mixed esoteric Buddhism had been introduced. The *Nihon Ryōiki* (820) gives several examples of this, the most famous being in the text on En no Ubasoku, later regarded as the patriarch of Shugendō (the religion of mountain ascetics), who practiced on Katsuragi and Yoshino.[3]

The importation of Shingon Buddhism by Kūkai (774-835) at the beginning of the ninth century was the start of a tremendous change. Kūkai, a mountain practitioner since his youth, chose as the center for Shingon practice a mountain located not too far from Yoshino, Mount Kōya (Kōyasan) in the Kii peninsula, just as Saichō, founder of the Japanese Tendai school, had chosen Mount Hiei. There is little doubt that Kūkai was able to utilize the concept of sacred mountains in early Shinto to his own advantage. If in Shinto the mountains were seen as sites of the residence of the divine and, consequently, as protectors of the community, Kūkai saw them as sites for the realization of Buddhahood and also as areas protecting the state. The role of Shingon in protecting the state (*chingokokka*), as envisioned by Kūkai, is very similar to the role played by mountains and early Shinto shrines at the village level.

Rituals used to sacralize a particular area in Esoteric Buddhism reveal interesting parallels with Shinto rituals. Kūkai wrote two texts to be read (as the *norito* were read in Shinto) as part of these rituals. The first was written for the ceremony consecrating Mount Kōya as the site of practice leading to the realization of Buddhahood. Here is an excerpt:

I, the sramana Henjō Kongō, hereby address respectfully all the Buddhas of the ten directions, the deities of the great mandalas of the two realms, the divinities of the five classes, the deities of Heaven and Earth of this country, all the demons inhabiting this very mountain, spirits of the earth, water, fire, air, and ether. All beings possessing form or mind necessarily have the Buddha-Nature. Buddha-Nature and Essence pervade the entire Realm of Essence and are not separate.... Those who awaken to this Truth may enjoy themselves eternally on the calyx of the five wisdoms, whereas those who fail to recognize this will be submerged for a long time by the mud of the three worlds.... The Emperor, deciding to spread this teaching, granted this space, which was deemed correct after careful divination at the four directions. Consequently a temple shall be built on this parcel granted by His Majesty.... All spirits and demons, retire! Withdraw seven leagues from this center, in all directions, zenith and nadir included! All good demons and spirits who can draw some benefit from the Law, reside here as it pleases you. May this center for practice be patronized... by the venerable spirits of all Emperors and Empresses of this Country, as well as by all divinities of Heaven and Earth. All spirits of the dead, protect this space day and night, and help fulfill this wish![4]

In this text, we find striking parallels with Shinto on the following points: (1) A mountain has been chosen as the holy site of practice. (2) No differentiation is made between the realm of the Buddha and the realm of humans. (3) The holy site is ritually purified by chasing away all enemies of the Law and inviting in all friends. (4) Protection for the living is offered by the spirits of the rulers of the past and all the spirits of the dead.

In Kūkai's second text, written to dedicate an altar which would be used for the rituals in front of the two mandalas, we find the following passage: "This space is our own property, and we intend to perform a service for seven days and seven nights to all divinities of the mandalas. We will set up an altar for this purpose.... Therefore, made strong by our faith in the efficacy of the law, we wish to perform the rites of space binding and protection of the body.... Enter this space and altar! Help realize this ritual, accept my request, and respond to this invocation!"[5] As a ritual definition of sacred space, this prayer, too, is highly reminiscent of Shinto practice. As in Shinto, divinities are invoked and their presence is visualized. In the case of Shingon, a further attempt is made to actually identify with the divinities. These two brief excerpts suggest, however, to what extent sacred space in early Esoteric Buddhism was ritually defined, purified, and entered in a syncretic manner. Correct practice could be performed only in a space sacralized in this manner.

Kūkai thought that the Buddhas could best be visualized after a quest leading to the top of the mountains. In 814 he wrote a remarkable text describing the ascent of Mount Futara by the monk Shōdō, who attained Buddhahood. The story of the ascent is followed by a description of the mountaintop scenery as if it were the Pure Land, the sacred space where a Buddha resides.[6] As we read this text, it is impossible to doubt that we are in the presence of an attitude structured by the earlier beliefs described in the preceding section. At the same time, a new perspective has been opened up which is distinctive to Esoteric Buddhism. For in Kūkai's text it is *not only by ritual* that profane space is made sacred. An *internal process* leading to Awakening, by allowing the subject to see the world in entirely different terms, can also transform profane space to sacred. This interior experience, whereby the transcendent nature of phenomena is recognized, is central to Esoteric Buddhist doctrine.

The stories surrounding the "death" of Kūkai on Mount Kōya provide further examples of the syncretic process. Despite the historical records of Kūkai's cremation, a belief existed that he had not died but had instead entered a trance (*nyūjō*) within the mountain and was awaiting the appearance of Maitreya, the Buddha of the Future. This event was also called *nyūzan* ("entering the

mountain"). [7] Here again we can see that mountains are linked to death in a manner that is in origin not at all Buddhist. The belief that Kūkai was still meditating there became one more reason to see Kōyasan as sacred, and the mountain is today one of the largest and most impressive graveyards in the world.[8]

Thus, we can see that, by the middle of the Heian period, a sacred geography had evolved in Japan according to which a clear distinction was made between the plains (the world of the secular) and the mountains (the world of the holy). In both Shinto and Buddhism, only those sites which had been ritually defined possessed the characteristics of metaphysical realms. In the earliest Shinto, sacred sites had not necessarily always been seen as cosmic centers. It was probably under Chinese influence that they gradually became defined as such. When Buddhism became prevalent, Esoteric Buddhism proved to be the religious system which was best suited to preexisting conditions. Esoteric Buddhism did not dramatically alter these conditions. Rather, it used them in a highly creative manner by developing a complex syncretism, one result of which we will now describe.

THE SACRED AREA

The emergence of the notion of the sacred area in Esoteric Buddhism during the Heian period (793-1185) marked the culmination of the second stage in the evolution of Japan's sacred geography. The concept of the sacred area had two important features of medieval Japanese Buddhism: the pilgrimage and the mandala.

Let us begin by considering the medieval pilgrimage as an expression, in spatial and temporal terms, of a specific Buddhist vision of the religious experience. Although a pilgrimage is generally regarded as a visit to a sacred space, in Esoteric Buddhism it is much more than that. The practice of pilgrimage is intimately related to the Buddhist notion that the religious experience was a process (ongoing practice) rather than simply the final goal of practice. Through practice, a larger consciousness was opened up, and consequently, a larger spatial realm of human experience could be discovered. Gradually, a network of roads was mapped out for believers, leading to various sacred spaces (which, as we shall see, came increasingly to be defined in a syncretic manner). The quality of the religious experience was such that the entirety of the path followed by the pilgrim was seen to be sacred. The processes involved in the pilgrimage were complex and had to become the basis for a complete change in the pilgrim's consciousness and perspective on the universe. The pilgrimage was an exercise in rebirth and magical transformation.

To understand the notion of pilgrimage more fully, we must first discuss the distinction posited in Esoteric Buddhism between the "lower world" of the profane (the realm of the ordinary experience), and the "higher world" of the sacred, which is the site of the manifestation of the divine or the chosen site of practice leading to Buddhahood. When pilgrims went from one world to the other, they were actually going to meet the Other. This experience in Otherness began with the first step out of the house; as soon as the pilgrims set out on the road, they became foreigners: the pilgrims were and were not themselves as soon as they moved into a realm which transcended their former knowledge of the world. We are told over and over again that this process is of a therapeutic nature: the actual physical effort is good; the rivers crossed purify the pilgrims and may even rejuvenate them; and the pilgrims may realize their own true nature. This exrcise is fundamental; it is a prerequisite to the ultimate change. The farther pilgrims move from their common world, the closer they come to the realm of the divine. We might mention that in Japanese the word for "walk" is the same word which is used to refer to Buddhist practice; the practitioner (*gyōja*) is then also the walker, one who does not reside anywhere, who abides in emptiness. All this is of course related to the notion of Buddhism as a path: practice is a concrete approach to Buddhahood.

When the pilgrim-practitioners arrived at the mountain, their general attitude had already changed: they had become nomads avoiding all bonds of time and space, freed from the attachments of common life, from inferior time which corrupts. They had reached an experience made up of moments which are totally different from whatever had been known within the realm of cause and effect. This experience was crystallized by the contact with the sacred site: a discovery of the sacred landscape which made possible a direct vision of the metaphysical realm in which the divine resides. It was essential, however, that this space, the essence of which was its stability, no longer be seen as "different." Through participation in religious practice, a fusion had to occur between man and the sacred environment, with the practitioner becoming an "eternal human being" dwelling in the divine. Or was it that the divine dwelled within the human? The ecstasy felt at the summit of a mountain was said to eliminate all pain and all existential malaise, and to introduce the awareness of another order of existence which the pilgrims could bring back into everyday life. Seeing the sacred center should reorder the pilgrims' perspective on the world; death could be conquered by attributing eternity, not to the moment of perfection, but to the process of perfecting. In Buddhist terms, the pilgrims realized that "transmigration is Nirvāna."

While the practice of pilgrimage flourished in medieval Japan, another form of sacralization of time and space was developing among mountain ascetics (*yamabushi*). Rituals of Esoteric Buddhism (both Tendai and Shingon) practiced by these priests aimed at an interiorization of the Buddha within the practitioner which led, in turn, to an identification of the realm of the Buddha with the realm of man. The mandala, or representation of the residence of the Buddha, could therefore be none other than this natural world. A new perspective was opened up on the world: it could be seen, not as a world of suffering, but as an "actualization of the mandala." The site of practice became a natural mandala, a large geographical area endowed with all the qualities of a metaphysical space.

Mandalization, an ultimate exercise in magical manipulation, is one of the most remarkable phenomena of medieval Japan. Once again it was Kūkai, the mountain-oriented practitioner, who developed the philosophical system underlying mandalization. In Esoteric Buddhism, as in most religions, the aim of religious practice may be seen as a return to the source. As Kūkai wrote: "All beings who dwell in illusion ignore their original residence; they sink into the three directions and migrate through the four types of birth. It is because they do not know the cause of their suffering that they fail to wish to return to the origin of all things. This is why the Tathāgata felt compassion for them and showed the way back home."[9]

While Esoteric Buddhism may not differ much from other religions in seeking a return to the source, it does differ in its choice of symbols and in the attitudes and practices which are required to effect this return. "So that all beings may suddenly awaken to the heart-mind of the Buddha, and so that they may swiftly go back to the original source, I shall explain the teachings of Shingon and show the way to those who are lost."[10] Where, for example, is man's original residence and home? Esoteric Buddhism is quite clear on this point: the original residence, the abode of the Buddha, is *within one's own*

Kozanji, Jingoji Kyoto

heart-mind. Home is at the heart of our being, originally pure and endowed with all the qualities of the Buddha, but hidden under the flux of passions and delusions created by the belief that the ego does really exist independent from everything else. As Kūkai also said: "Since beyond the beginnings and up to now, the fundamental residence of the heart-mind is emptiness; however, it is covered by false opinions and is fettered by passions."[11] He further wrote: "Who is within illusion resides in a polluted space; he who awakens resides in a pure space, which is also called Pure Land."[12]

It is clear from this that in Kūkai's thought Awakening could bring about the transformation of polluted profane space into pure space, a Pure Land, the original residence of the Buddha's heart-mind. Kūkai defined the process as one of interiorization, since the Buddha's residence is originally within us. It is an illusion that the Pure Land of the Buddha is exterior to man, so totally transcendent that going beyond the realm of forms is necessary. But Kūkai warned: "In the middle of my mind, there is the principle of the mind of the pure Bodhi."[13] This amounts to saying that we have always been there before entering the sacred space, that the transmutation is not really a change but is merely becoming what one already was.

As we have said, a mandala is a representation of the residence of the Buddha. Since the Buddha was seen as transcending all characteristics and dualisms, the mandala was a metaphysical space which provided an insight into what Buddhism called the Realm of Essence (*hokkai*). Distinctions between the absolute and the relative, transmigration and Nirvāna, and passions and Awakening were seen as arbitrarily imposed by man. By contrast, a mandala described the organization and mysteries of the universe from the perspective of things as they are in their fundamental "suchness." Kūkai held that suchness could be apprehended by the practitioner through a realization of the Three Mysteries, that is, by ritual identification of man's basic functions (body, speech, and mind) with the triple aspect of the Buddha's world. This identification is what led Kūkai to talk of the "mandala of my mind."[14]

Thus we know that the mandala is a representation of the original nature of our heart-mind, free of illusions and passions. Correct positions and mūdras (body), correct utterance of the mantras (speech), and correct meditation

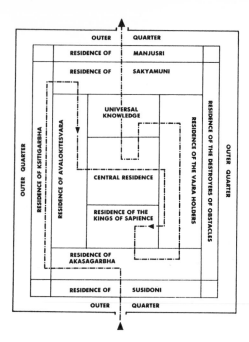

```
                    OUTER    QUARTER

              RESIDENCE OF    MANJUSRI

              RESIDENCE OF    SAKYAMUNI


                    UNIVERSAL
                    KNOWLEDGE



                   CENTRAL RESIDENCE


              RESIDENCE OF THE
              KINGS OF SAPIENCE


       RESIDENCE OF
       AKASAGARBHA



       RESIDENCE OF    SUSIDONI

                    OUTER    QUARTER
```

FIG. 1 — General movement of the mountain ascetics through the Womb mandala of mountains, according to the Shozan engi.

(mind) are the substance of practice and the keys which open the residence of the Buddha within the practitioner. The mandala drawings in front of which these practices are performed can be seen as supports to meditation perhaps comparable to the circular drawings Jakob Boehme proposed when he spoke about the possibility of representing God: "Even though such a representation may not be sufficiently elaborate, it is nevertheless a meditation. One could make of it an excellent drawing inscribed within a circle, in order to support the meditation of those whose understanding is not advanced. Please note that desire turns within, right down into this heart, which is God."[15]

A practitioner of Esoteric Buddhism "enters" a mandala through its gate, invokes the divinities which are represented, and identifies with them one after the other until reaching the center, in which there is a representation of the cosmic Buddha from which all other Buddhas and their lands emanate. The practitioner goes from the manifestation to the source, from the form to the essence, and finally reaches the realization that form and essence are two-but-two.

It was this realization that "form and essence are two-but-not-two" which was reflected in the practice of "mandalizing" geographical areas — naming certain locations or broad areas as mandalas. As Kūkai said: "The Body of the Buddha is the body of all living beings, which in turn is that of the Buddha. Different, yet not different. Not different, yet different."[16] We might say that the entire experience of meditating on the mandala was one of integrating the absolute into the relative, the metaphysical into the physical. Once this integration had been realized, it was natural to compare the structure of the mandala with that of the universe, to see one in the other. This is exactly what was done. Over time, the two main mandalas of the Shingon school were projected over geographical areas to produce natural mandalas, sacred spaces for practice and the realization of Buddhahood. Moreover, this practice led inevitably to a dramatic expansion of the concept of sacred space. Gradually and systematically, a sacralization of different areas took place, until finally Japan itself, in its entirety, came to be viewed as a sacred space.

To trace the entire process through which space was mandalized in medieval Japan is a complex task, but we can point out at least a few of the important steps. We know that Kūkai considered Mount Futara to be a cosmic center. Soon afterward, the real founder of Shugendō, Shōbō (832-905), founded the Shingon monastery Daigo-ji and probably started to develop the Shugendō doctrine while residing in the Yoshino area. In 1007, Michinaga made a pilgrimage to Yoshino, from the accounts of which it is clear that the mountainous area was regarded as the site of the appearance of Maitreya, the Buddha of the Future. Dating of texts concerning Yoshino is extremely difficult; we must jump to 1180, the supposed date of compilation of the Shozan engi, a remarkable text describing the Yoshino-Ōmine-Kumano area as the Vajradhātu ("Realm of Diamond") and Garbhadhātu ("Womb") mandalas. This is the first example of the mandalization of space done on a large scale. The Yoshina/Kimpusen area was seen as the Diamond mandala. The Kumano area was seen as the Womb mandala. The Ōmine mountain was the center in which it was possible to realize that the two mandalas were in fact not two — the not-twoness of fact and principle was to be acknowledged at the summit of that mountain. Once the mandalas were projected onto these mountains, the practice of the mountain ascetics was to go from peak to peak, venerating the Bodhisattvas and Buddhas residing on them, performing the services, rituals, and meditation as they would in front of graphic representations on an altar in the temple. Just as one entered a painted mandala, performing the same rituals, they would enter the mountains, thereby penetrating the Realm of the Buddha. Their walk in those pure spaces was regarded as a process along the Middle Path, that of Emptiness. As the Shozan engi states: "The peaks are the residence of the Buddhas and Bodhisattvas... and the sacred places on the mountains are the dwelling sites of the divinities and of the Immortals."[17] And later in the same text: "Alongside the peaks of the Buddhas, they tread Emptiness."[18] These practitioners established connections not only between each summit and each divinity, but also between each site's natural virtues (water, hot springs, medicinal herbs) and each divinity's qualities:

Bathing in the salt of creeks, valleys, beaches and ponds allows one to wash away the suffering of this triple world. Such is the Ocean of virtues and powers required to push one away from bad deeds in this very life. There, one practices purification with constant seriousness.... The river to the right is the water upon which one meditates on Avalokitesvara; the river to the left has the miraculous power to cure diseases: it is in fact the river which flows from beneath the seat of Aksobhya. Those who tread those spaces and cross these rivers must think that each drop of water, each tree of these mountains is a drug of immortality, even if they suffer from a heavy past of misdeeds.[19]

It is evident from this short passage that the pilgrimages of these mountain practitioners were spatial moves aimed at the eradication of time: not only are we told that immortality can be attained but we are shown by some of the rituals concerning the penetration of the Womb mandala that we are in the presence of a rebirth. Who could wish for more in terms of the destruction of the law of cause and effect, that great mother of time?

Figures 1 and 2 are drawings of the Womb mandala showing the general movement of the practitioners and the exact order of progress in the Ōmine pilgrimage as described in the Shozan engi. Most of the places named in the text actually exist, although we do not know to what modern places some of them correspond. Only a few of these names are to be found in a detailed map of the area. The number of actual peaks in the area is probably larger than the 100 listed in the text; that number is suspiciously symbolic.

Be that as it may, the point is that the Diamond mandala (*kongō kai*) corresponds to the Yoshino area, in the north of the Kii peninsula; the Womb mandala (*taizō kai*) corresponds to the Kumano area, in the south of the peninsula, which is the abode of Avalokitesvara, the Great Bodhisattva of Compassion; and Ōmine is the transcending center. As the *Buchū shōkanjō keihaku* aptly puts it:

This peak is the pure temple of the two realms: it is the original, noncreated mandala; the summits covered with trees are the perfect altars of the nine parts of the Diamond mandala, and the caverns filled with fragrant herbs are the eight petals of the lotus in the Womb mandala. Mountains and rivers, trees and plants are the true body of the Buddha Mahāvairocana; the wind over the crests, the peals of thunder ascending from the depths of the valleys all proclaim the Law of the Body of Essence. The Venerated Ones of the three sections are well aligned; the innumerable saints are magnificently seated. There, colors and sounds are perceived in their original state; the natural knowledge of the world as it is not empty any more. The natural mandala is made up of the many mountains where one practices the Three Mysteries.[20]

It is clear that, by this time, the qualities of sacred space were being attributed to a large part of the Kii peninsula; each mountain has become a kind of *iwasaka* on which many aspects of the realm of essence manifest themselves in a constant metaphysical rain as the summits are draped with mists through which the practitioners pass in their search for the Way.

Another fascinating text which reveals the ongoing process of the mandalization of the country is the *Hachiman Gudōkun*, written between 1301 and 1304. As a syncretic text, it reveals once again how closely Buddhist and Shinto elements were interwoven in defining sacred space in Japan. The role of Hachiman, the Shinto deity who is the protector of the nation, is described in the text. As in the following excerpt, however, Shinto mythology and Buddhist concepts are employed side by side in describing the nation.

This Land Akitsushima [Japan] is the noble space of the manifestation of more than three thousand divinities; it is the superior space of the spreading of the saintly teachings of the greater and lesser vehicles, true and temporary alike.... Since this country is by nature the Original Country of the Great Sun [Mahāvairocana, or Dainichi no honkoku/Dai nipponkoku], the eight Provinces of Bando correspond to the eight petals of the lotus in the Womb mandala, and the Nine Regions [Kyūshū] of the Western Sea correspond to the nine parts of the Diamond mandala; the yin and yang aspects correspond to the mandalas in their aspect of Principle and Wisdom. Those who inhabit this country are the descendants of Izanami and Izanagi, and are the heirs of the original nature, the Tathāgata in its body of essence.[21]

We can say that by the Muromachi period the phenomenon of mandalization had become well entrenched in Japan. Perhaps the most dramatic manifestation of the syncretic aspect of mandalization was the habit of designating certain Shinto shrines as mandalas. In the case of the Ise shrine, of great importance because of its status as the shrine directly linked to the imperial family and to the state, this occurred fairly early. We find the Ise shrine mentioned in the *Shasekishū* [A Collection of Small Pebbles], written between 1261 and 1262, and also in the *Daijingū sankeiki* [Pilgrimage to Ise] of Tsūkai in 1286. By the Kamakura period, we know that the two shrines at Ise were regarded as two mandalas. Another example of mandalization was the building in 1484 of the cosmic temple of Kyoto's Kagura-oka by a leading figure in syncretism, Yoshida Kanetomo (1435-1511). Other examples of how pervasive mandalization eventually became are Zeami's reference, in the *Kintōshō*, to Awaji Island as the Diamond mandala and to Sado Island as the Womb man-

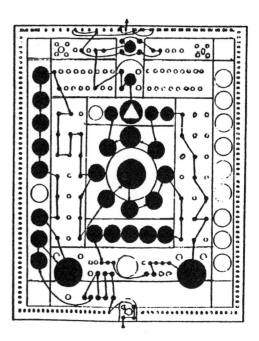

FIG. 2 — *Exact movement through the Womb mandala, according to the Shozan engi.*

dala. The *Jinteki mondō*, written by the middle of the Edo period, divides all of Japan into two mandalas, one in the east and one in the west.[22] Such a perception might be regarded as a culmination of the process of mandalization.

MANIPULATION OF SPACE

We are told in many texts that the Buddhas and Bodhisattvas, having come to Japan, remained there in the form of Shinto divinities, and that this was possible only because they had brought with them their residences, the mountains. Thus, some Japanese mountains were considered to be parts of the continent which had come flying in and landed with all the pomp that one can imagine accompanying such an event. Here are some examples: "Ōmine is in fact the southwestern area of the Diamond Cavern (=Vulture's Peak) located in the southeast of the country of birth of the Buddha. How did it arrive here in Japan? Suddenly, in the middle of the night of the nineteenth day, eighth moon of the third year, Sōchō era [538, time of the introduction of Buddhism to Japan], repeated peals of thunder and tremendous noises filled the air, and the earth shook as if moved by a great earthquake."[23] And, further in the same text: "On the fourteenth of the second moon of the second year, Shōhei era [933], the Master of Contemplation Teisū, writing down the sacred spaces of Kimpusen, wrote this statement which he said had been handed down to him from master to master: 'A long time ago, there was in China a mountain called Kimpusen, residence of the Bodhisattva Zaō [Vajragarbha]. However, this mountain came flying [to Japan]; it approached as if floating over the ocean...'"[24] It was not only Kimpusen, site of the coming of Maitreya, which arrived in Japan from the continent. Kumano, the Pure Land of Avalokitesvara (Kannon), flew in from India, making stops in China, Kyūshū (at Hikosan), and Shikoku, before reaching the Kii peninsula, where it landed and remained.[25]

An even more impressive account of such fantastic events is given in the *Jinteki mondō*, already mentioned above. The title of this work could be translated "a dialogue on drops and dust," but it also could be called "a dialogue on creation," because the text begins with a quote from Kūkai's text on the ascent of Mount Futara by Shōdō: "Dust and drops accumulate and mix, decorating the residence divine."[26] A further possible translation is "pregnant dialogue," since a whole mountain is said to exist within one single particle of dust and an entire ocean within a single drop of water. But let us read the text:

Our country Japan is originally Mount Mitra, located in the northeastern part of Vulture's Peak in India.... The earth shook six times; mountains, crumbling down, created oceans, while turbulent oceans brought mountains down. Trees were swept away by floods, while stones floated, and living creatures lost their homes. For seven days and seven nights the sun and the moon were uncertain in their course. During that time, this Mount Mitra came to be missing; it had entered the waters where it received protection from the Dragon-King. Then, the divine beings Izanami and Izanagi, manifestations of Mahāvairocana of the Two Realms, desired to make our country out of this mountain. Using their divine superpowers, they pushed the mountain out of the ocean, causing islands to appear. The first of these islands was Awaji.[27]

It is fascinating to see that even in the Edo period efforts were still being made to establish cosmogonies to show the sacred nature of Japan from a syncretic perspective. This is an aspect of the mythical vision mentioned at the beginning of this study. Another good example is the Nō play *Kasuga Ryūjin*, in which the holy man Myōe Shōnin is told by an oracle of the Shinto divinities that it is not necessary to travel all the way to China and India, since most of the sacred sites at Kasuga *are* those famous places in *Japan*.[28]

Yet another way to sacralize space was to make some edifying connections. I shall offer one quite clear case, which is not unusual. The excerpt describes the very large religious complex surrounding *Usa*, the original site of Hachiman in Kyūshū at Mount Rokugō:

In the district of Kunisaki, Province of Toyokuni, is a place called Rokugō. There, twenty-eight temples have been erected, on the basis of the twenty-eight chapters of the Lotus sutra. Symbolically expressing the threefold composition of the scriptures, these temples are divided into three groups: the fundamental (eight temples), the middle (ten temples), and the final (ten temples). In the more than 100 pavilions of this last group, there are as many representations of the Buddha as there are words in the Lotus sutra. Expressing the desire to place these 69,380 statues within the sacred space of the twenty-eight mountains, in the ninety-nine caverns, and in the 100 and some pavilions, the three pilgrims unified their hearts and started work on each mountain. Choosing the correct days and orientations, they invited carpenters, sculptors, artists, painters and had them create the effigies of the Buddha.[29]

A huge enterprise indeed! "The mountains are the Lotus sutra; they are the body of the Buddha; the world is the realm of Awakening." Such statements are at the basis of Japan's sacred geography and architecture.

To summarize, we have seen that the mandalization of space was a vast historical process which aimed at making all Japan a sacred site: that of the manifestation of the divine in its many forms and the site of the practices leading to the realization of Buddhahood. Evidence for this is to be found in much religious literature (I have uncovered here only one corner of the box). One category of this literature is made of the *engi* texts, in which the origins of temples and shrines are traced. The written texts were often accompanied by paintings, forming some of the most beautiful painted scrolls Japan has produced. Many of the famous sites of Japan continue to be defined through mandalization, which has become one of the most distinctive expressions of the Japanese perception of time, space, and man's activities. This perception has been decisively influenced by the syncretic tradition including Shinto, Daoist, Esoteric Buddhist (both Tendai and Shingon), and Pure Land elements. In this sense, mandalization represents a rich facet of Japan's cultural development.

The concept of sacred space has found many different expressions in the history of Japanese religions. Underlying the appearance of these expressions has been a historical process whereby the definition of sacred space was gradually expanded from the sacred site to the sacred nation, and which ultimately resulted in a sacralization of the total human environment and all of human activity. It may be shown, indeed, that, as the centuries passed, more and more emphasis was laid in Japanese religion on everyday behavior as the tool of the Way.

By the end of the Edo period, Japan was ready to accept its own sacredness. The combined influence of the ritual view of Esoteric Buddhism, the anti-ritual view of Zen, and the more "secular" view of Confucianism, with its emphasis on everyday ritual, had prepared the way for this. In conclusion, we may comment that sacred space in Japan was originally seen as determined by a spontaneous manifestation of the divine (through external power) yet gradually came to be seen as determined through experience (internal power). This might be seen as determined through experience (internal power). This might be seen as a process of integration of the divine and human realms. Hayashi Razan, a Shinto and Confucian thinker of the beginning of the Edo period, came to this conclusion: "The divine is located within the heart-mind of human beings."[30] He might have hit the nail right on its head. ▲

NOTES ···

1. See Haruki Kageyama, Shintaizan (Tokyo: Gakuseisha, 1971). p.226. Mountains which were considered to be the abode of divinities received, during the Nara period, the name *Kannabi*. 2. *Tōmomine ryakkai*, in zoku gunsho ruijū 24, no. 43, p. 424. 3. See Y. Endō and K. Kasuga, eds., *Nihon ryōiki* (Tokyo: Iwanami, 1967), p. 134. 4. See S. Watanabe and Y. Miyasaka, eds., *Shōryōshū* (Tokyo: Iwanami, 1965). P. 408. 5. Ibid., p. 410. 6. Ibid., p. 182. See my translation of the text in A. Tobias and H. Drasdo, eds., *The Mountain Spirit* (New York: Overlook Press, 1979). P. 51. 7. See Seishin Moriyama, *Bunka shijō yori mitaru Kōbō Daishi den* (Tokyo, 1933). p. 865. 8. See Ryushin Katsuno, *Hieizan to Kōyasan* (Tokyo, 1966), p. 225. 9. Kūkai, "Himitsu mandara jūjushinron," in *Kōbō daishi zenshū* (Tokyo: Sankibō, 1968), 3:210. Hereafter referred to as *Zenshū*. 10. Kūkai, "Heizei Tennō Kanjō bun," *Zenshū*, 2:119. 11. Kūkai, "Unjigi," *Zenshū*, 1:90. 12. Kūkai, "Issaikyō kaidai," *Zenshū*, 2-446. 13. Kūkai, "Hiz&ki," *Zenshū*, 2:621. 14. Ibid., p. 628. 15. Cited in C. G. Jung, *Psychologie et alchimie* (Pairs: Buchet/Chastel, 1970), p. 216. 16. Kūkai, "Sokushin jōbutsu-gi," *Zenshū*, 1:56. 17. *Shozan engi*, in *Jisha engi* (Tokyo: Iwanami, 1976), p. 91. 18. Ibid., p. 100. 19. Cited by Gaston Renondeau, *Le Shugendo: Histoire, doctrine et rites des Yamabushi* (Paris: Imprimerie Nationale, 1965), p. 110. 20. Ibid., pp. 110-11. 21. In *Jisha engi*, p. 209. 22. *Jinteki mondō*, in *Zoku gunsho ruijū* 32, 202. 23. In *Jisha engi*, p. 90. 24. Ibid. 25. Y. Kondō, ed., *Shintō-shū: "Shintō yūrai no koto"* (Tokyo: Kadokawa, 1964). 26. See Grapard, "Kūkai: Stone Inscription...." in *Mountain Spirit* (New York: Overlook Press, 1979), p. 58. 27. *Jinteki mondō*, p. 202. 28. "Kasuga ryūjin," *Hōshōryū-Koe no hyakubanshū* 80 (1972): 10. 29. "Rokugō Kaizan Ninmon daibosatsu hongi," in *Jisha engi*, p. 316. 30. Hayashi Razan, "Shintō denjū," in *Kinsei Shintōron*, ed. S. Taira and A. Abe (Tokyo: Iwanami, 1972), p. 12.

Young Man after Prostrations, Tibet, 1993

H I M A L A Y A

Photographs by Linda Connor

Vajra, Zanskar, Ladakh India, 1985

God's joy moves from unmarked box to unmarked box,
from cell to cell. As rainwater, down into flowerbed.
As roses, up from ground.
Now it looks like a plate of rice and fish,
now a cliff covered with vines,
now a horse being saddled.
It hides within these,
till one day it cracks them open.

— Rumi, 12th century

The Patient One, Lamayuru Monastery, Ladakh India, 1988

Prayer Flag and Chörtens, Ladakh India, 1988

Monks, Phiyang Monastery, Ladakh India, 1985

Prostrations, Gandon Monastery, Tibet, 1993

Sand Mandala, Mindroling Monastery, Tibet, 1993

They are incomprehensible, the things of this earth.

The lure of waters. The lure of fruits.

Lure of the two breasts and long hair of a maiden.

In rouge, in vermillion, in that color of ponds

Found only in the Green Lakes near Wilno.

And ungraspable multitudes swarm, come together

In the crinkles of tree bark, in the telescope's eye,

For an endless wedding,

For the kindling of the eyes, for a sweet dance

In the elements of the air, sea, earth and subterranean caves,

So that for a short moment there is no death

And time does not unreel like a skein of yarn

Thrown into an abyss.

— C. Milosz

Masked Monk, Phiyang Monastery, Ladakh India, 1985

"Remember that under the skin you fondle lie the bones
waiting to reveal themselves."
— *Ikkyu*

HUANG SHAN

Photographs by Wang Wu-sheng

Huang Shan: The Cult of Site (Sight) & Representation

James Robson

A mountain has water as blood, foliage as hair, haze and clouds as its spirit and character. Thus, a mountain gains life through water, its external beauty through vegetation and its elegant charm through haze and clouds.

> Guoxi (11th century landscape painter)[1]

Paintings of Huang Shan, the range of bare, precipitous, pine-clad and mist-hung peaks in southern Anhui province, are seen everywhere in China today; climbing the mountain is nearly obligatory for Chinese landscapists, most of whom have done pictures of it, some of them virtually devoting careers to it.[2]

For hundreds of years mountains in China have been the objects of widely divergent practices, ranging from religion to art and politics; in short, mountains were one of the places where nature and culture met. The earliest dictionary in China, from the second century, tells us that mountains were believed to "exhale vital breath [Ch. *qi* 氣 Jpn. *ki* 気], giving birth to the myriad of things." This understanding of mountains was most likely inspired by those local communities that lived at the foot of various mountains and who saw clouds coalesce on their peaks and drop rain that collected in rivers that in turn flowed down to irrigate their fields. Mountains, rising up solidly from flat surrounding plains, also became symbols of stability and durability and were integrated into imperial rituals as delineators and protectors of the imperium. These mountains, located at the cardinal directions, came to be known as the Five Marchmounts (*wuyue* 五嶽).

During the third and fourth centuries CE Daoists began to frequent mountains which they considered the abodes of immortals and as repositories of the necessary ingredients for their alchemical endeavors. As Buddhism took root in China it copied the native Chinese classificatory scheme and developed its own mountain cultic system that considered four mountains as the abodes of *bodhisattvas*, these mountains came to be known collectively as the Four Famous Mountains (*sida mingshan*). In addition to these nine mountains, classified by their religious affiliation (Imperial, Daoist or Buddhist), there is one mountain in China that has become the most well known solely on the basis of its sublime beauty: Huang Shan.

Huang Shan, located in Huizhou prefecture of Anhui province in southeastern China, is often referred to as a single mountain but is actually comprised of thirty-six peaks, the highest being 1800 meters. Among these peaks, four stand out as the main peaks: Lotus Flower Peak, Old Man Peak, Start-to-Believe Peak, and Heavenly Citadel Peak. All of these highly suggestive toponyms were meant to reflect the unique shapes of Huang Shan's peaks, and they preserved hints of its prior religious affiliations.

Huang Shan's religious history stretches back into China's hazy mythical past, when it is believed that the legendary Yellow Emperor went there in search of the elixir of immortality; upon completing his quest he established that this mountain was to be a dwelling place for Daoist immortals. Huang Shan also became inhabited by Buddhists who built their first temple at the base of the mountain in the eighth century. The Buddhist presence on the mountain was memorialized in the toponomy of the mountain, with the prominent Manjusri Terrace, and Lotus Flower Peak.

In spite of these vestiges of religion, Huang Shan, in contradistinction to the Five Marchmounts and Four Famous Mountains, did not achieve its renown on the basis of pious pilgrims, but primarily through the works of Chinese artists who were captivated by the sublimity of the mountain's natural topography.[3] Indeed, Huang Shan became a cult of site that inspired a cult of sight.

Xu Xiako's (1588-1641) record of his visit to Huang Shan in 1618 is an example of how a traveler experienced the mountain with an aesthetic sentiment rather than a religious piousness: "There I looked down the vale where peaks and rocks enfolded each other in all kinds of postures and feasted my eyes on their many tints."[4] Those who came to Huang Shan were drawn by its natural features, not its religious associations. Huang Shan was the product of a more secular piety, attracting pilgrims, poets, artists and essayists to explore and gaze upon its craggy pine scattered peaks, rather than strive for ecstatic visions of Buddhas and Bodhisattvas.

The two main aspects of Huang Shan's unique landscape which attracted these artists were the mountains propensity for the coalescence of clouds and cliffs and its combination of scabrous rocks and gnarled pines. In response to these images, later generations came to refer to the four main peaks of the Huang Shan massif as the "Huang Sea," referring to the sea of clouds floating and surging about the midriff of the craggy peaks that jut up out of the clouds as if islands in the sea.[5] Huang Shan's rocky cliffs, interspersed with pines that seem to be clinging tenuously to its vertical faces, were the models for works that became famous throught China (and the world for that matter) as the epitome of Chinese landscape painting of the seventeenth and eighteenth centuries.

James Cahill, the noted art historian of Chinese landscape paintings, has noted that the landscape paintings of Huang Shan are indicative of a shift from the religiously inspired monumental landscapes of the Song dynasty (960-1278) to the predominantly secular, even literati, landscape renditions of seventeenth century artists like Shitao, Meiqing, Hungren, and Chengmin.[6] Under the influence of these painters a new movement in Chinese painting was born. This new school, which took its name Tiandu (Heavenly Citadel) from one of the main peaks of Huang Shan, painted in a style that Cahill suggests, "reflects a shift of emotional commitment from the world of human affairs to the natural world."[7]

Those artists who later came to Huang Shan were often in a quandary, it seems, as to how they might be able to represent the vast magnificence of the mountains unique topography. The Ming dynasty poet and critic Yuan Zhongdao (1570-1623) commented from his perch on the Refining Cinnabar Terrace on Huang Shan, "even Wu Tao-tzu or Ku K'ai-chih [great painters of the eighth and fifth centuries respectively] couldn't describe one ten-thousandth of this."[8]

Despite this admonition, Huang Shan still continues to capture the attention of artists, and essayists, who try in their own unique ways to express the mountain's unparalleled natural grandeur. Wu-sheng, a contemporary Chinese landscape photographer, is heir to the long tradition of artists inspired by the landscape of Huang Shan. Although Wu-sheng captures images of Huang Shan with a different medium than his ancient predecessors, his large-format black and white photographs evoke scenes reminiscent of landscape paintings from the seventeenth century. The cult of site, and sight, continues. ▲

1. Trans. by Susan Bush and Hsiao-yen Shih, "The Landscape Texts," in *Early Chinese Texts on Painting.* (Cambridge: Harvard University Press, 1985), pp. 167. 2. James Cahill, "Huang Shan Paintings as Pilgrimage Pictures," in Susan Naquin and Chün-Fang Yü eds., *Pilgrims and Sacred Sites in China.* (Berkeley: University of California Press, 1992), pp. 246. 3. See Joseph McDemott, "The Making of a Chinese Mountain, Huangshan: Politics and Wealth in Chinese Art," in *Asian Cultural Studies,* (Tokyo, 1989). 4. Quoted in Cahill 1992: 252-253. 5. Harriet T. Zurndorfer, *Change and Continuity in Chinese Local History: The Development of Hui-chou Prefecture 800-1800.* (Leiden: E. J. Brill, 1989), pp.220. 6. Cahill 1992. 7. Zurndorfer 1989: 219. 8. Cahill 1992: 252.

The path to Han-shan's place is laughable,

A path, but no sign of cart or horse.

Converging gorges — hard to to trace their twists

Jumbled cliffs — unbelievably rugged.

A thousand grasses bend with dew,

A hill of pines hums in the wind.

And now I've lost the shortcut home,

Body asking shadow, how do you keep up?

— Han-Shan (Jp. Kanzan; trans. by Gary Snyder)

THE PATH OF THE SPIRITUAL ATHLETE

The Marathon Monks of Mt. Hiei

A *gyōja* (Skt. *ācārin*) is a spiritual athlete who practices (*gyō*) with a mind set on the Path of Buddha. In Tendai Buddhism there is an appropriate practice for everyone: "Those who cannot be saved through insight meditation should take up the esoteric teachings; those who cannot be saved by the esoteric teachings should undergo some sort of religious practice." Of all the disciplines practiced on Hiei, the mountain marathon — *kaihōgyō* — has had the greatest appeal over the centuries, for it encompasses the entire spectrum of Tendai Buddhism — meditation, esotericism, precepts, devotion, nature worship, and work for the salvation of sentient beings.

In principle, all Tendai priests and nuns* must do kaihōgyō at least one day during their training at Gyō-in. Men who wish to become abbots of one of the subtemples on Hiei frequently opt for a 100-day term of kaihōgyō. The requirements for the 100-day term are: to be a Tendai ordinand in good standing, sponsorship by a senior Tendai cleric, and permission of the Council of Elder Gyōja.

If permission is granted, there is one week of preparatory training (*maegyō*) before the term begins. The candidate is given a secret handbook (*tebumi*) to copy which gives directions for the course, describes the stations to visit, lists the proper prayers and chants, and contains other essential information. Because this handwritten manual is often damaged by rain and constant handling, the gyōja makes two copies.

Also during this week, all the marathon monks of that particular term clear the route of debris, especially glass, sharp rocks, sticks, and branches, and piles of leaves in which vipers like to hide. While the new gyōja are rather lax about such clearing of the path, the senior marathon monks — who know what it is like to have their feet slashed or punctured by pointed objects or to step on a poisonous snake — cover every inch of ground thoroughly.

* Theoretically, a woman could undertake the 100-day kaihōgyō, *but formal permission is not likely to be granted anytime soon owing to the recent failure of a young Japanese Jōdō sect nun to finish a preliminary 21-day term because of exhaustion.*

On day one, the gyōja suits up in the unique Hiei uniform and visits Sō-ō's tomb to ask for spiritual guidance. The pure-white outfit — made of white cotton only, for animal hair, skin, and silk are prohibited — consists of a short kimono undershirt, *nobakama* pants, hand and leg covers, a long outer robe, and priest's surplice. Around the waist goes the "cord of death" (*shide no himo*), with a sheathed knife (*goma no ken*) tucked inside; these two accessories remind the gyōja of his duty to take his life — by either hanging or self-disembowelment — if he fails to complete any part of the practice. This is the reason the gyōja is dressed in white — the color of death — rather than basic Buddhist black. A small bag to hold the handbook, a sutra book, two candles, and matches is hung over the right shoulder; on occasion a flower bag to hold *shikimi* branches or food (offered at spots along the way) is draped over the left shoulder. The gyōja carries his rosary in his left hand.

Inside the *higasa*, the distinctive woven "trademark" hat of the Hiei gyōja, a small coin is placed; if the monk dies on pilgrimage he will need the money to pay the boatman on the Oriental equivalent of the river Styx. Except for rain, the Great Kyoto Marathon (*kirimawari*), and the Katsuragawa Retreat, the higasa must be carried, not worn, by all gyōja with fewer than 300 days of training; it is always held in the left hand, and if put down it must be placed on the *hisen*, a special type of fan. The higasa is covered with oiled paper when it rains. Since Buddhist monks and other religious pilgrims customarily wear large round straw hats, the reason for the peculiar elongated shape of the Hiei gyōja hat is uncertain, especially because it appears to afford less protection against sun, rain, and wind. On the other hand, one marathon monk believes that the length of the hat keeps branches away from the gyōja's face and provides a clear view, two important considerations for those who walk along pitch-black mountain paths. The shape of the hat is also said to represent a lotus leaf breaking the surface of the water, signifying the emergence of Buddhist enlightenment in the midst of the world of illusion.

Eighty pairs of straw sandals are allotted for the 100-

day term in Mudō-ji. For the longer Imuro Valley Course, gyōja are allowed the use of one pair per day. During the Great Marathon, the monk can use as many straw sandals as necessary, usually going through five pairs a day. This style of straw sandal is, like the hat, lotus-shaped and is thought to have originated in India. Most gyōja have their sandals made by a pious old grandma who lives in Sakamoto — her sandals are treasured as being both comfortable and good luck. In sunny, dry weather, one pair can last three or even four days, but in heavy rains the sandals disintegrate in a few hours. Thus the gyōja carries one or two spares.

The old-fashioned straw raincoat and the paper lantern, the other two permitted articles, are on occasion replaced in stormy weather by their modern counterparts — a vinyl raincoat and an electric flashlight. Rain — and in early spring, snow — is the bane of the marathon monks. It destroys their sandals, extinguishes their lanterns, slows their pace, washes away their paths, and soaks them to the bone. In years when the rainy season is especially bad, a marathon monk's robe never dries out completely.

The basic rules of kaihōgyō are as follows:

> During the run the robe and hat may not be removed.
> No deviation from the appointed course.
> No stopping for rest or refreshment.
> All required services, prayers, and chants must be correctly performed.
> No smoking or drinking.

On the first day of the term, which begins at the end of March or the beginning of April, the new gyōja is accompanied by his master, who takes him through the entire course, giving his disciple various instructions and pointers. Thereafter the marathon monk is on his own. Since the gyōja is supposed to train alone, when there is more than one candidate (as has been the case every year recently), both the initial day of the run and daily starting times are staggered.

The day begins at midnight. After conducting (or attending) an hour-long service in the Buddha Hall, the gyōja munches on one or two rice balls or drinks a bowl of miso soup and then dresses. At Mudō-ji, the 30-kilometer (18.8-mile) journey commences at around 1:30 a.m. From Mudō-ji the marathon monk proceeds to Kompon Chū-dō and from there through the rest of the Eastern Precinct, then on to the Western Precinct, Yokawa, down to Sakamoto and back to Mudō-ji, stopping at 255 stations of worship and negotiating thousands of stairs and several very steep slopes along the way. At Imuro Valley, the course is longer, 40 kilometers (25 miles), with a few more stations of worship, and runs from Sakamoto up to the Eastern Precinct, Western Precinct, Yokawa and then back down to Imuro.

The stations include stops at temples and shrines housing just about every Vedic, Buddhist, Taoist, and Shintō deity that exists in the pantheons of those creeds; at the tombs of the Tendai patriarchs and great saints; before outdoor stone Buddha images; at sacred peaks, hills, stones, forests, bamboo groves, cedar and pine trees, waterfalls, ponds, springs; even a stop at one or two places to placate the gremlins or hungry ghosts residing there. At each station the gyōja forms the appropriate

mudra (ritual hand gesture) and chants the necessary mantra; the stops range from a brief ten seconds to several minutes. During the entire course the monk sits down only once — on a stone bench beneath the sacred giant cedar at the Gyokutaisugi, to chant a two-minute prayer for the protection of the Imperial family while facing the direction of Kyoto Palace.

Depending on the weather and the pace, the gyōja returns to the starting point between 7:30 and 9:30 a.m. The course can be conquered in six hours or even five and a half, but that is likely to draw criticism from senior monks, who disapprove of youngsters racing through the pilgrimage, hastily rattling off the chants and prayers. Most gyōja take between six and a half and seven and a half hours to complete the circuit.

Following an hour-long service in the main hall, the monk goes to his quarters to bathe and then to prepare the midday meal. After a simple, high-calorie lunch of noodles, potatoes, tofu, miso soup, and rice or bread, there is an hour's rest and time to attend to chores. At 3:00 p.m. there is another temple service. The second and last meal is taken around 6:00. By 8:00 or 9:00 p.m. the gyōja should be sleeping.

This routine is repeated daily without fail, one hundred times, with the exception of kirimawari, the 54-kilometer (33-mile) run through Kyoto. It occurs between the 63rd and 75th days of the term, depending on the gyōja's starting date. In kirimawari, a senior marathon monk accompanies the new gyōja as they visit the holy sites of Kyoto and call on parishioners in the city. The new gyōja are thereby introduced to "practicing for the sake of others in the world." The freshmen receive more refreshment than usual during kirimawari, but they lose a day of sleep — kirimawari takes nearly twenty-four hours to complete, and almost as soon as they return to Hiei they must be out on the road again.

The freshman marathon monks have a very rough time. It takes two or three weeks to memorize the exact location of each station and the appropriate chants and mudrās. Before then, gyōja unfamiliar with the route sometimes get lost in the heavy fog that frequently blankets Hiei and go miles out of their way. Despite the cleaning of the pathways during the pre-training period, there are still plenty of sharp edges or points to cut tender feet to the quick. By the third day the legs and Achilles tendons begin to throb, and after a week they are painfully swollen. Cuts and sores become infected, and monks who were raised in the southern part of Japan often develop frostbite. Most monks run a slight fever the first few weeks, suffer from diarrhea and hemorrhoids, and experience terrible pains in their backs and hips. By the 30th day, however, the worst of the discomfort is over, and around the 70th day the gyōja has acquired the marathon monk's stride: eyes focused about 100 feet ahead while moving along in a steady rhythm, keeping the head level, the shoulders relaxed, the back straight, and the nose and navel aligned. The monk also runs in time with the Fudō Myō-ō mantra he continually chants.

Following successful completion of a 100-day term and participation in the Katsuragawa Summer Retreat, a gyōja may petition the Hiei Headquarters to be allowed to undertake the 1,000-day challenge (sennichi kaihōgyō). This involves being free of family ties, willingness to observe a twelve-year retreat, and careful screening by the Council of Elder Gyōja. If accepted, the marathon monk follows the program as outlined in the table.

The first three hundred days are the basic training, the "boot camp" of the marathon monks. From the fourth year, the monks are allowed to wear *tabi*, Japanese-style socks, which considerably lessen the wear and tear on their feet. In the fourth and fifth year, though, the pace quickens to 200 consecutive days of running from the end of March to mid-October. Upon completion of the 500th day, the monk earns the title "White-Belted Ascetic" (Byakutai Gyōja) and may use a walking stick for the rest of the runs. He is also qualified to perform *kaji*, "merit transference" prayer services. Upon completion of the 700th day, the gyōja faces the greatest trial of all: *dōiri*, nine days without food, water, sleep, or rest.

A few weeks prior to dōiri, the monk sends out this invitation to the other Tendai priests: "I cannot express my joy at being allowed to attempt dōiri. This foolish monk vows to commit himself wholeheartedly to the nine-day fast, purifying body and mind, hoping to become one with the Great Holy One Fudō Myō-ō. Please join me for a farewell dinner." The *saijiki-gi*, the symbolic "last meal," is attended by all the senior priests on the mountain — a goodbye party to a gyōja who might not survive. This point is underscored by having the screens in the room reversed, just as they would be for a funeral.

Following the meal, a bell is struck at 1:00 p.m., and the senior marathon monks and other high-ranking Tendai prelates accompany the gyōja into Myō-ō-dō. The gyōja begins by making 330 full prostrations; after this, the guests depart, the doors are sealed, and the gyōja is left to his nine-day prayer fast.

At 3:00 a.m., 10:00 a.m., and 5:00 p.m. the gyōja chants the Lotus Sūtra before the altar. (During the course of the fast, the entire text is recited). At 2:00 a.m. he performs the *shusui* (water-taking) ritual. Chanting the Heart Sūtra, he walks to the Aka Well, about 200 meters from the temple, and scoops up a bucketful of water, carries it back to the main hall, and offers it to the image of Fudō Myō-ō. The remaining hours are spent sitting in the lotus position silently reciting the Fudō Myō-ō *mantra* — *"namaku samanda bazaranan sendan makaroshana sowataya untarata kanman"* — 100,000 times in all. It takes about 45 minutes to recite the mantra 1,000 times. Working in twenty-four-hour shifts, two monks, holding incense and candles, are always in attendance to make sure the gyōja remains awake and erect, touching his shoulders whenever he appears to be dozing off.

For several weeks prior to dōiri, the gyōja tapers down on his intake of food and water to prepare for the fast, usually limiting himself to one simple meal of noodles, potatoes and soup during this time. (He would usually not eat anything at the farewell dinner.) The first day is no problem, but there is some nausea the second and third day. By the fourth day the pangs of hunger usually cease. By day five, however, the gyōja is so dehydrated that the saliva in his mouth is dried up and he begins to taste blood. To prevent the sides of the mouth from adhering permanently, the gyōja is allowed, from the fifth day, to rinse his mouth with water, but every drop must be spat back into the cup. Unbelievably, the amount of liquid returned is often greater than the original amount. The

drops that remain on the gyōja's tongue are compared to the sweetest nectar. Defecation usually disappears from the third or fourth day, but very weak urination generally continues right to the end. Also from day five, the gyōja is given an arm rest when he recites the Lotus Sūtra.

The 2:00 a.m. water-taking ritual helps revive the gyōja. As he steps out of the hall made stuffy by incense smoke and poor circulation, the pure, bracing mountain air helps clear his head. Gyōja claim further that they absorb moisture from the rain and dew through their skin during this walk outdoors. The round trip to the well takes fifteen minutes the first day, but near the end it requires an hour, as the gyōja seems to move in a state of suspended animation.

The dōiri — the actual period without food, water, rest, or sleep is seven and a half days (182 hours) — is designed to bring the gyōja face-to-face with death. Hiei legend has it that the original period of dōiri was ten days; when almost all of the monks died it was shortened just a bit. It was further discovered that the humid months of summer were too dangerous;— the deaths of the two dōiri monks mentioned in the modern chronicles both occurred in August — they rotted internally.

All the gyōja agree that the greatest ordeal of dōiri is not starvation or thirst but keeping the head erect and not being able to rest. It is interesting to note that the hardest part of making a Buddha image is the carving of the head. If the head is not perfectly balanced between the shoulders and on top of the body, sooner or later, it will fall off due to improper stress. Maintaining the correct posture at all times is the ultimate challenge.

During dōiri, the gyōja develop extraordinary sensitivity. They can hear ashes fall from the incense sticks and other normally inaudible sounds from all over the mountain. Not surprisingly, they can smell and identify food being prepared miles away, and they see beams of sun and moonlight that seep into the dark interior of the temple. At 3:00 a.m. on the ninth and concluding day, the gyōja makes his final trip to the Aka Well. A large crowd of upward of three hundred Tendai priests and lay believers gathers to attend the grand finale. The trip to the well, which only required twenty minutes the first few days of dōiri, now takes the weakened gyōja an hour to complete. He returns to the hall, sits before the altar, and bows his head as an official document from the Enryaku-ji Headquarters is read, proclaiming the end of the fast. The gyōja is then given *Hō-no-yū*, a special medicinal drink, to revive him. The final barrier is three circumambulations around the hall. When that is done, the gyōja emerges from the "living death" as a radiant *Tōgyōman Ajari*, "Saintly Master of the Severe Practice."

Most gyōja report that they pass out for a second or two when they emerge from the temple out onto the veranda, in what is evidently a sudden transition from death back to life — for the gyōja, according to physiologists, who have examined them at the conclusion of the rite, manifest many of the symptoms of a "dead" person at the end of the dōiri. As dōiri nears conclusion, the gyōja experience a feeling of transparency. Nothing is retained; everything — good, bad, neutral — has come out of them, and existence is revealed in crystal clarity.

Some may condemn this type of severe training as a violation of Śākyamuni's Middle Way, but such death-

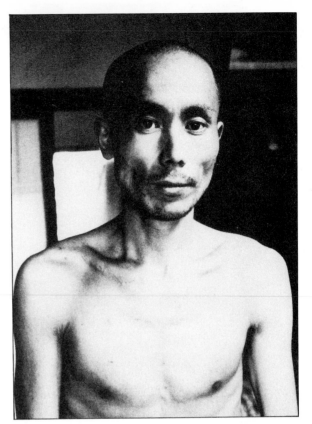

One of the most recent gyōja, Utsumi Shunshō, born in Shikoku in 1943, completed the full 1,000-day term in 1979, and succeeded his master as abbot of Myō-ō-dō soon after fulfilling the 100,000-prayer, eight-day fast and fire ceremony in 1981. Upper left: a new Buddhist saint is born as Utsumi emerges from Myō-ō-dō upon completion of the dōiri. Upper right: Skeleton-thin, but triumphant; Ustumi just after the dōiri. Bottom: Utsumi leads a procession over Gyōja Bridge, a famous Kyoto landmark, during the Great Marathon and the Kyoto One-Day Run, kirimawari. Photographs by Namba Tadashi.

FIRST YEAR	100 days		*Shingyōja* (freshman)
		30 (40) km each day	No tabi; hat carried
SECOND YEAR	100 days	one-day *kirimawari*, 54 km	No tabi; hat carried
THIRD YEAR	100 days		No tabi; hat carried
FOURTH YEAR	100 days		Tabi permitted; hat worn from 301st day
	100 days		Upon completion, *Byakutai Gyōja*
		30 (40) km, kirimawari	
FIFTH YEAR	100 days		Wooden staff permitted from 501st day;
	100 days		on 700th day *dōiri*; 9 days without food, water, sleep, or rest
			Upon completion, *Tōgyōman Ajari*
SIXTH YEAR	100 days	60 km each day	*Sekisan Kugyō* (Sekisan Marathon)
SEVENTH YEAR	100 days	84 km each day	*Kyoto Omawari* (Great Marathon)
	100 days	30 (40) km, kirimawari	Upon completion *(mangyō)*, *Daigyōman Ajari*
	1,000 days	38,632 (46,572) km	

NOTE: The numbers in parentheses are for the Imuro Valley course; all distances are approximate. From the second year, all monks participate in the Katsuragawa Summer Retreat, July 16-20. A secret rite known as the *Ichigassui* is usually performed once during the 100 day term.

defying exercises lie at the heart of Buddhist practice. There would be no doctrine of the Middle Way if Śākyamuni had not nearly fasted to death, subjecting himself to the most rigorous austerities to win enlightenment. Asceticism did not get him enlightenment, but it did lead to his transformation into a Buddha. This is why the emergence of a marathon monk from dōiri is compared to Śākyamuni Buddha's descent from the Himalayas following his Great Awakening. As one of the gyōja's relatives remarked, "I always dismissed Buddhism as superstitious nonsense until I saw my brother step out of Myō-ō-dō after dōiri. He was really a living Buddha."

Around 3:30 a.m. the gyōja, twenty to thirty pounds lighter, returns to his room, where he is greeted by his family and other well-wishers, receives a *shiatsu* massage, and sucks on chunks of ice made out of water taken from a miraculous spring on Mount Hira. The gyōja will then lie down for a few hours but only sleep about twenty or thirty minutes. It takes two weeks or so before he can take solid food; until then he lives on ice shavings, water, thin soup, *sake* or *amasake* (sweet, lightly fermented rice wine), and pudding. Nor does he sleep much the next several weeks, averaging two or three hours a night.

Following successful completion of the "seven hundred days of moving and the nine days of stillness," the gyōja are indeed men transformed. Grateful to be alive, full of energy, fortified by a vision of the Ultimate, constantly moving toward the light, and eager to work for the benefit of all, the monks head into the final stages of the marathon.

In the sixth year, the route lengthens to include a round trip to Sekisan-in at the base of Hiei (*Sekisan Kugyō*). The Sekisan Marathon along the extremely steep Kirara Slope — the slope used by Hiei warrior-monks of old to swoop down on Kyoto — increases the course to 60 kilometers (37.5 miles), requiring fourteen to fifteen hours for stopping at all 260 stations of worship.

The seventh and final year again has two 100-day terms. The first — perhaps the supreme athletic challenge of all times — consists of a *daily* 84-kilometer (52.5 mile) run through the environs of Kyoto. The run encompasses the 30-kilometer walk around Hiei, the 10 kilometers of Kirara Slope, and the 44-kilometer circling of Kyoto. This is the equivalent of two Olympic marathons, and it is not run once every four years but performed 100 days in a row. During the aptly named Great Marathon (*Ō-mawari*), the monk sets out from Hiei at 12:30 a.m., covers the 84 kilometers over the next sixteen to eighteen hours, and then arrives, sometime between 4:00 and 6:00 in the afternoon, at a temple in the center of Kyoto to rest for a few hours. The following day, beginning at 1:00 a.m., the monk reverses the course. The course was originally the city limits of Kyoto; the gyōja was thus circling the capital as he prayed for the protection of all its inhabitants, wise and foolish, saints and sinners, rich and poor, young and old alike. Nowadays part of the course cuts through the pleasure quarters of the city, past hostess bars, love hotels, strip joints, mah-jong parlors, and pornographic theaters. The denizens of that world, too, receive the prayers of the marathon monk.

In addition to the three hundred or so stations of worship, the gyōja blesses hundreds of people each day (thousands on weekends and holidays). People of all ages sit bowing along the road to be blessed by the touch of the gyōja's rosary on their heads, diseased portions of their bodies, crippled limbs, hospital robes, or even on photographs of their loved ones. The gyōja is considered to be a vehicle, if not an incarnation, of the great saint Fudō Myō-ō, with the capability of transferring his merit to others. The Great Marathon is truly the practice of bestowing merit on others; while the monk's previous runs were solitary pursuits deep in the mountains, this marathon is for the benefit of all those struggling to survive in the midst of a big city, a silent turning of the Wheel of the Dharma, preaching by example rather than with empty words. Since the Great Marathon takes place in summer, the colorful procession of Tendai priests, lay believers, photographers and filmmakers, interested observers, joggers, and other assorted hangers-on literally stops traffic in the busy tourist season.

Negotiation of the 84-kilometer course is made somewhat easier by the use of a "pusher" on straightaways. A padded pole is placed at the small of the monk's back while the pusher applies a gentle force. If the pusher (a different person every day) has a lot of experience, he can supply as much as half the locomotion needed by the marathon monk on long stretches. If, on the other hand, the pusher is a novice or a young parishioner who cannot keep up with the monk, the extra assistance is nil. (Some marathon monks dispense with the pusher for part or all of the course.) Another attendant carries a small folding chair along, placing it down the instant the monk is held up by traffic lights or crowd control. Perhaps because of the constant encouragement and excitement of being welcomed by crowds of admirers, the gyōja come through the Great Marathon in surprisingly good shape despite the almost total lack of sleep. Such sleep as they do get is deep, sound, and refreshing. An old saying goes: "Ten minutes of sleep for a marathon monk is worth five hours of ordinary rest."

During the Great Marathon the monk is supported by dozens of sokuhō-kō parishioners. This special group of supporters accompanies the monk on his rounds, directing traffic and carrying equipment, preparing his meals, washing his clothes, and attending to his other needs. Some of the sokuhō-kō — the position is inherited from generation to generation — have been serving in this way for decades, covering nearly as much ground as the gyōja themselves.

The final 100-day term on the regular course is a snap; on day 1,000 the gyōja, who has run enough to have circled the globe, is declared to be a Daigyōman Ajari, "Saintly Master of the Highest Practice." Several weeks later the marathon monk vists the Kyoto Imperial Palace to conduct a special thanksgiving service known as dosoku sandai. When the emperor maintained his court in Kyoto, everyone had to remove his or her footwear before entering the grounds. A Hiei marathon monk was the sole exemption from this custom — he alone could enter the palace clad in straw sandals. The ceremony evidently originated with the kaihōgyō patriarch Sō-ō's visits to the palace centuries ago to cure the Imperial family's ailments.

There are two other practices integral to the 1,000-day marathon. The first is the annual Katsuragawa Retreat (Katsuragawa Geango) held from July 16 to 20. Gyōja who have completed at least one 100-day kaihōgyo term gather on Hiei on July 16. (Some gyōja from outlying districts walk hundreds of miles to get there.) Lining up in order of seniority (according to the number of retreats attended), the gyōja set out from Hiei at 4:00 a.m.A.M. for Mount Hira, 30 kilometers (18.8 miles) distant. The impressive body of gyōja — in certain years they can number as many as fifty — descend en masse from the mountain and pass through Otsu City on their way to Katsuragawa, arriving in the valley about twelve hours later.

During the retreat, the gyōja fast and conduct various rites. The highlights of the retreat are, first, the taikomawashi festival, in which the new gyōja, in imitation of Sō-ō's leap into the waterfall to embrace Fudō Myō-ō, bound off a large rotating drum and into a crowd of excited spectators; and, second, the secret rite at Katsuragawa in which the gyōja, firmly anchored by a lifeline, actually throw themselves into the cascading falls.

Since the Katsuragawa Retreat is devoted to the memory of Sō-ō, it takes precedence over all else, and marathon monks doing 200 days a year interrupt their running to attend. Thus the actual number of days on the road is more like 980 than an even 1,000, although recently the monks have been adding on the extra days after formal completion.

The final rite of the initiation for the marathon monks is the 100,000-prayer fast and fire ceremony, the jumanmai daigoma. One hundred days before the ceremony, the gyōja embarks on a stringent fast. All grains — rice, wheat, soy beans, and the like — plus salt and most leafy vegetables are prohibited. Consequently, the monk is obliged to live on potatoes and other root vegetables, boiled pine needles, nuts, and water. The fast dries the gyōja out, almost mummifying him, so that he will not expire of excessive perspiration during the eight-day fire ceremony in which he will sit in front of a roaring fire, casting in prayer stick after prayer stick. On each stick a supplicant has written a petition, which the gyōja "relays" to Fudō Myō-ō. Usually the number of prayer sticks exceeds 100,000, going as high in some cases as 150,000. Although this fast is one day shorter than that of dōiri and a few hours of sitting-up sleep is permitted, most gyōja feel that this is the greater trial — it is, in the early stages, "like being roasted alive in hell."

Here again, the gyōja eventually becomes one with the fiery presence of Fudō Myō-ō, consuming all evil and purifying the world. The Great 100,000-Prayer Fire Ceremony takes place two or three years after completion of the 1,000-day marathon. It is not obligatory, but most of the modern marathon monks undergo it, partly to raise money for new construction projects — people donate money for each prayer stick that they write. Sakai Yūsai is the most recent monk to have done the ceremony, the sixth since the end of World War II.

Altogether there have been forty-six 1,000-day marathon monks since 1885. Two monks completed two full terms, one died (on purpose) on the 2,500th day of practice, and one, Okuno Genjun, did three full terms but without actually running each day during the third term. The majority of the marathon monks were in their vigorous thirties, while the oldest, Sakai, completed day 2,000 when he was sixty-one years old. The number of monks who died or committed suicide on route is not known, but the path is lined with unmarked graves of gyōja who have been killed in action. No one has expired in recent memory during the 1,000-day marathon, but at least three monks perished in the nineteenth century. ▲

MOUNTAINS & WATERS SŪTRA
Sansui-kyo

1

Mountains and waters right now are the actualization of the ancient buddha way. Each, abiding in its phenomenal expression, realizes completeness. Because mountains and waters have been active since before the Empty Eon, they are alive at this moment. Because they have been the self since before form arose they are emancipation-realization.

2

Because mountains are high and broad, the way of riding the clouds is always reached in the mountains; the inconceivable power of soaring in the wind comes freely from the mountains.

3

Priest Daokai of Mt. Furong said to the assembly, "The green mountains are always walking; a stone woman gives birth to a child at night."

Mountains do not lack the qualities of mountains. Therefore they always abide in ease and always walk. You should examine in detail this quality of the mountains' walking.

Mountains' walking is just like human walking. Accordingly, do not doubt mountains' walking even though it does not look the same as human walking. The buddha ancestors' words point to walking. This is fundamental understanding. You should penetrate these words.

4

Because green mountains walk, they are permanent. Although they walk more swiftly than the wind, someone in the mountains does not realize or understand it. "In the mountains" means the blossoming of the entire world. People outside the mountains do not realize or understand the mountains walking. Those without eyes to see mountains cannot realize, understand, see, or hear this as it is.

If you doubt mountains' walking, you do not know your own walking; it is not that you do not walk, but that you do not know or understand your own walking. Since you do know your own walking, you should fully know the green mountains' walking.

Green mountains are neither sentient nor insentient. You are neither sentient nor insentient. At this moment, you cannot doubt the green mountains' walking.

5

You should study the green mountains, using numerous worlds as your standards. You should clearly examine the green mountains' walking and your own walking. You should also examine walking backward and backward walking and investigate the fact that walking forward and backward has never stopped since the very moment before form arose, since the time of the King of the Empty Eon.

If walking stops, buddha ancestors do not appear. If walking ends, the buddha-dharma cannot reach the present. Walking forward does not cease; walking backward does not cease. Walking forward does not obstruct walking backward. Walking backward does not obstruct walking forward. This is called the mountains' flow and the flowing mountains.

6

Green mountains master walking and eastern mountains master traveling on water. Accordingly, these activities are a mountain's practice. Keeping its own form, without changing body and mind, a mountain always practices in every place.

Don't slander by saying that a green mountain cannot walk and an eastern mountain cannot travel on water. When your understanding is shallow, you doubt the phrase, "Green mountains are walking." When your learning is immature, you are shocked by the words "flowing water," you drown in small views and narrow understanding.

Yet the characteristics of mountains manifest their form and life-force. There is walking, there is flowing, and there is a moment when a mountain gives birth to a mountain child. Because mountains are buddha ancestors, buddha ancestors appear in this way.

Even if you see mountains as grass, trees, earth, rocks, or walls, do not take this seriously or worry about it; it is not complete realization. Even if there is a moment when you view mountains as the seven treasures shining, this is not returning to the source. Even if you understand mountains as the realm where all buddhas practice, this understanding is not something to be attached to. Even if you have the highest understanding of mountains as all buddhas' inconceivable qualities, the truth is not only this. These are conditioned views. This is not the understanding of buddha ancestors, but just looking through a bamboo tube at a corner of the sky.

Turning an object and turning the mind is rejected by the great sage. Explaining the mind and explaining true nature is not agreeable to buddha ancestors. Seeing into mind and seeing into true nature is the activity of people outside the way. Set words and phrases are not the words of liberation. There is something free from all of these understandings: "Green mountains are always walking," and "Eastern mountains travel on water." You should study this in detail.

7

"A stone woman gives birth to a child at night" means that the moment when a barren woman gives birth to a child is called "night."

There are male stones, female stones, and nonmale nonfemale stones. They are placed in the sky and in the earth and are called heavenly stones and earthly stones. These are explained in the ordinary world, but not many people actually know about it.

You should understand the meaning of giving birth to a child. At the moment of giving birth to a child, is the mother separate from the child? You should study not only that you become a mother when your child is born, but also that you become a child. This is the actualization of giving birth in practice-realization. You should study and investigate this thoroughly.

8

Great Master Kuangzhen of Yunmen said, "Eastern mountains travel on water."

The reason these words were brought forth is that all mountains are eastern mountains, and all eastern mountains travel on water. Because of this, Nine Mountains, Mt. Sumeru, and other mountains appear and have practice-realization. These are called "eastern mountains." But could Yunmen penetrate the skin, flesh, bones, and marrow of the eastern mountains and their vital practice-realization?

10

You should know that "eastern mountains traveling on water" is the bones and marrow of the buddha ancestors. All waters appear at the foot of the eastern mountains. Accordingly, all mountains ride on clouds and walk in the sky. Above all waters are all mountains. Walking beyond and walking within are both done on water. All mountains walk with their toes on all waters and splash there. Thus in walking there are seven paths vertical and eight paths horizontal. This is practice-realization.

11

Water is neither strong nor weak, neither wet nor dry, neither moving nor still, neither cold nor hot, neither existent nor nonexistent, neither deluded nor enlightened. When water solidifies, it is harder than a diamond. Who can crack it? When water melts, it is gentler than milk. Who can destroy it? Do not doubt that these are the characteristics water manifests. You should reflect on the moment when you see the water of the ten directions as the water of the ten directions. This is not just studying the moment when human and heavenly beings see water; this is studying the moment when water sees water. Because water has practice-realization of water, water speaks of water. This is a complete understanding. You should go forward and backward and leap beyond the vital path where other fathoms other.

17

Mountains have been the abode of great sages from the limitless past to the limitless present. Wise people and sages all have mountains as their inner chamber, as their body and mind. Because of wise people and sages, mountains appear.

You may think that in mountains many wise people and great sages are assembled. But after entering the mountains, not a single person meets another. There is just the activity of the mountains. there is no trace of anyone having entered the mountains.

When you see mountains from the ordinary world, and when you meet mountains while in mountains, the mountains' head and eye are viewed quite differently. Your idea or view of mountains not flowing is not the same as the view of dragons and fish. Human and heavenly beings have attained a position concerning their own worlds which other beings either doubt or do not doubt.

You should not just remain bewildered and skeptical when you hear the words, "Mountains flow"; but together with buddha ancestors you should study these words. When you take one view you see mountains flowing, and when you take another view, mountains are not flowing. One time mountains are flowing, another time they are not flowing. If you do not fully understand this, you do not understand the true dharma wheel of the Tathāgata.

An ancient buddha said, "If you do not wish to incur the cause for Unceasing Hell, do not slander the true dharma wheel of the Tathāgata." You should carve these words on your skin, flesh, bones, and marrow; on your body, mind, and environs; on emptiness and on form. They are already carved on trees and rocks, on fields and villages.

18

Although mountains belong to the nation, mountains belong to people who love them. When mountains love their master, such a virtuous sage or wise person enters the mountains. Since mountains belong to the sages and wise people living there, trees and rocks become abundant and birds and animals are inspired. This is so because the sages and wise people extend their virtue.

You should know it as a fact that mountains are fond of wise people and sages. Many rulers have visited mountains to pay homage to wise people or to ask for instructions from great sages. These have been important events in the past and present. At such times these rulers treat the sages as teachers, disregarding the protocol of the usual world. The imperial power has no authority over the wise people in the mountains. Mountains are apart from the human world. At the time the Yellow

Emperor visited Mt. Kongdong to pay homage to Guangcheng, he walked on his knees, touched his forehead to the ground, and asked for instruction.

When Shākyamuni Buddha left his father's palace and entered the mountains, his father the king did not resent the mountains, nor was he suspicious of those who taught the prince in the mountains. The twelve years of Shākyamuni Buddha's practice of the way were mostly spent in the mountains, and his attainment of the way occurred in the mountains. Thus even his father, a wheel-turning king, did not wield authority in the mountains.

You should know that mountains are not the realm of human beings nor the realm of heavenly beings. Do not view mountains from the scale of human thought. If you do not judge mountains' flowing by the human understanding of flowing, you will not doubt mountains' flowing and not-flowing.

20

It is not only that there is water in the world, but there is a world in water. It is not just in water. There is also a world of sentient beings in clouds. There is a world of sentient beings in the air. There is a world of sentient beings in fire. There is a world of sentient beings on earth. There is a world of sentient beings in the phenomenal world. There is a world of sentient beings in a blade of grass. There is a world of sentient beings in one staff.

Wherever there is a world of sentient beings, there is a world of buddha ancestors. You should thoroughly examine the meaning of this.

21

Therefore water is the true dragon's palace. It is not flowing downward. To consider water as only flowing is to slander water with the word "flowing." This would be the same as insisting that water does not flow.

Water is only the true thusness of water. Water is water's complete virtue; it is not flowing. When you investigate the flowing of a handful of water and the not-flowing of it, full mastery of all things is immediately present.

22

There are mountains hidden in treasures. There are mountains hidden in swamps. there are mountains hidden in the sky. There are mountains hidden in mountains. There are mountains hidden in hiddenness. This is complete understanding.

An ancient buddha said, "Mountains are mountains, waters are waters." These words do not mean mountains are mountains; they mean mountains are mountains.

Therefore investigate mountains thoroughly. When you investigate mountains thoroughly, this is the work of the mountains.

Such mountains and waters of themselves become wise persons and sages.

At the hour of the Rat, eighteenth day, tenth month, first year of Ninji [1240], this was taught to the assembly at Kannondōri Kōshō Hōrin Monastery.

Translated by Arnold Kotler and Kazuaki Tanahashi from *Moon in a Dewdrop: Writings of Zen Master Dōgen* edited by Kazuaki Tanahashi. Copyright © 1985 by the San Francisco Zen Center. Reprinted by permission of North Point Press, a division of Farrar, Strauss & Giroux, Inc.

WALKING THE GREAT RIDGE OMINE ON THE WOMB-DIAMOND TRAIL

I started climbing snowpeaks in the Pacific Northwest when I was fifteen. My first ascent was on Mt. St. Helens, a mountain which I honestly thought would last forever. After I turned eighteen I worked on ships, trail crews, fire lookouts, or in logging camps for a number of seasons. I got into the habit of hiking up a local hill when I first arrived in a new place, to scan the scene. For the Bay Area, that meant a walk up Mt. Tamalpais.

I first arrived in Kyoto in May, 1956. Because the map showed Mt. Atago to be the highest mountain on the edge of the Kitano River watershed, I set out to climb it within two or three days of my arrival. I aimed for the highest point on the western horizon, a dark forested ridge. It took several trains and buses to get me to a complex of *ryokan* in a gorge right by a rushing little river. The map had a shrine icon on the summit, so I knew there had to be a trail going up there, and I found it. Dense *sugi* groves, and only one other person the whole way, who was live-trapping small songbirds. Up the last slope, wide stone steps, and a bark-roofed shrine on top. Through an opening in the sugi trees, a long view north over hills and villages, the Tamba country. A few weeks later I described this hike to a Buddhist priest-scholar at Daitokuji, who was amused ("I've never been up there") and mischievous enough to set me up with a friend who had Yamabushi connections. I was eventually invited to join a ritual climb of the northern summit of Omine, the "Great Ridge." As it turned out I was inducted as a novice Yamabushi (*sentachi*) and introduced to the deity of the range, Zaō Gogen, and to Fudō Myō-ō.

After that experience on Mt. Omine I took up informal mountain walking meditations as a complement to my Zen practice at Daitoku-ji. I spent what little free time I had walking up, across, and down Hieizan or out the ridge to Yokkawa, or on other trails in the hills north of Kyoto. I did several backpacking trips in the Northern Japan Alps. I investigated Kyoto on foot or by bike and found an occasional Fudō Myō-ō — with his gathered intensity — in temples both tiny and huge, both old and new. (Fierce as he looks, he's somehow comforting. There is clearly a deep affection for this fellow from a wide range of Japanese people.) I studied what I could on the Yamabushi tradition. What follows, by way of prelude to a description of a pilgrimage down the length of the Great Ridge, barely touches the complexity and richness of this rich and deeply indigenous teaching. My own knowledge of it is, needless to say, rudimentary.

It must have started as prehistoric mountain-spirit folk religion. The Yamabushi ("those who stay in the mountains") are back country Shaman-Buddhists with strong Shinto connections, who make walking and climbing in deep mountain ranges a large part of their practice. The tradition was founded in the 7th or 8th centuries C E by En-no-Gyōja, "En the ascetic," who was the son of a Shinto priest from Shikoku. The tradition is also known as Shugendō, "the way of hard practice." The Yamabushi do not constitute a sect, but rather a society with special initiations and rites whose members may be lay or priesthood, of any Buddhist sect, or also of Shinto affiliation. The main Buddhist affinity is with the Shingon sect, which is the Sino-Japanese version of Vajrayana, esoteric Buddhism, the Buddhism we often call "Tibetan." My mountain friends told me that the Yamabushi have for centuries "borrowed" certain temples from the Shingon sect to use as temporary headquarters. In theory they own nothing and feel that the whole universe is their temple, the mountain ranges their worship halls and zendos, the mountain valleys their guest-rooms, and the great mountain peaks are each seen as boddhisattvas, allies, and teachers.

The original Yamabushi were of folk origin, uneducated but highly spiritually motivated people. Shugendō is one of the few [quasi] Buddhist groups other than Zen that make praxis primary. Zen, with its virtual requirement of literacy and its upper class patrons, has had little crossover with the Yamabushi. The wandering Zen monk and the travelling Yamabushi are two common and essential figures in *No* dramas, appearing as bearers of plot and resolvers of karma. Both types have become Japanese folk figures, with the Yamabushi the more fearful for they have a reputation as sorcerers. Except that the Zen people have always had a fondness for Fudō, and like to draw mountains even if they don't climb them.

Photographs by Yano Takehiko

Yamabushi outfits make even Japanese people stop and stare. They wear a medieval combination of straw *waraji* sandals, a kind of knicker, the deer or *kamoshika* (a serow or "goat-antelope" that is now endangered) pelt hanging down in back over the seat, an underkimono, a hemp cloth over-robe, and a conch shell in a net bag across the shoulder. They carry the *shakujo* staff with its loose jangling bronze rings on top, a type of sistrum. A small black lacquered cap is tied onto the head. (I have a hemp over-robe with the complete text of the Hannya Shingyo brush-written on it, as well as black block-printed images of Fudō Myō-ō, En-no-Gyōja, some little imps, and other characters. The large faint red seals randomly impressed on it are proof of pilgrimages completed. The robe was a gift from an elder Yamabushi who had done these trips over his lifetime. He had received it from someone else and thought it might be at least a century old.) Yamabushi will sometimes be seen flitting through downtown Kyoto begging and chanting sutras, or standing in inward-facing circles jangling their sistrum-staffs in rhythm at the train station while staging for a climb. They prefer the cheap, raw Golden Bat cigarettes. Yamabushi have a number of mountain centers, especially in the Dewa Sanzan region of Tohoku. Then there's Mt. Ontake, where many women climb, and shamanesses work in association with Yamabushi priests who help them call down gods and spirits of the dead. At one time the men and women practitioners of mountain religion in its semi-Buddhist form provided the major religious leadership for the rural communities, with hundreds of mountain centers.

The "Yamabushi" aspect of mountain religion apparently started at Omine, in eastern Wakayama Prefecture, the seat of En-no-Gyōja's lifelong practice. The whole forty-mile-long ridge with its forests and streams was En's original zendo. Two main routes lead the seven or eight miles up, with wayside shrines all along the route. Although the whole ascent can be done by trail, for those intent on practice the direct route is taken — cliffs scaled while chanting the Hannya Shingyo. Near the top there is an impressive face over which the novices are dangled upside down. There are two temples on the main summit in the shade of big conifers. When you step in it is cooler, and heady with that incense redolence that only really old temples have.

A jangling of shakujo staffs and the blowing of conches in the courtyard between buildings.
A fire-circle for the *goma* or fire ceremony — mudras hid under the sleeves — and the vajra-handled sword

brought forth. Oil lanterns and a hard-packed earthern floor, the *uguisu* echoing in the dark woods. A Fudō statue in the shadows,
focussed and steadfast on his rock,
   backed by carved flames,
        holding the vajra-sword and a noose.

He is a great Spell-holder and protector of the Yamabushi brotherhood. His name means "Immovable Wisdom-king." Fudō is also widely known and seen in the larger Buddhist world, especially around Tendai and Shingon temples. Some of the greatest treasures of Japanese Buddhist art are Fudō paintings and statues. His faintly humorous glaring look (and blind or cast eye) touches something in the psyche. There are also crude little Fudō images on mountains and beside waterfalls throughout central Japan. They were often placed there by early Yamabushi explorers.

A great part of the Shingon teaching is encoded onto two large mandala-paintings. One is the "Vajra-realm" (Kongō-kai) and the other the "Garbha-realm" (Taizō-kai). They are each marvelously detailed. In Sanskrit "Vajra" means diamond (as drill tip, or cutter), and "Garbha" means womb. These terms are descriptive of two complementary but not exactly dichotomous ways of seeing the world, and representative of such pairs as: mind / environment, evolutionary drama / ecological stage, mountains / waters, compassion / wisdom, The Buddha as enlightened being / the world as enlightened habitat, etc.

For the Yamabushi these meanings are projected onto the Omine landscape. The peak Sanjo-ga-dake at the north is the Vajra Realm center. The Kumano Hongu shrine at the south end is at the center of the Garbha Realm. There was a time when — after holding ceremonies in the Buddha-halls at the summit, the yamabushi ceremonists would then walk the many miles along the ridge — with symbolic and ritual stations the whole way — and down to the Kumano River for another service at the shrine. Pilgrims from all over Japan, by the tens of thousands, were led by Yamabushi teachers through this strict and elaborate symbolic journey culminating in a kind of rebirth. A large number of pilgrims now make a one-day hike up from the north end, a few do a one-day hike up at the south end, but it's rare to walk the whole Great Ridge.

In early June of 1968 three friends and I decided to see what we could find of the route. My companions were Yamao Sansei, artist and fellow worker from Suwa-no-se Island, Saka, also an island communard and spear fisherman, and Royall Tyler, who was a graduate student at that time. He is now an authority on Japanese religion.

Fudō Myō-ō
Gyokuren-in, Mt. Hiei

Early morning out of town. From Sanjo *eki* in Kyoto take the train to Uji. Then hitch-hike along thru Asuka, by a green mounded *kofun* ancient emperor's tomb shaped like a keyhole, as big as a high school. Standing by quiet two-lane paved roads though the lush fields, picked up by a red tradesman's van, a schoolteacher's sedan — reflecting on long-gone emperors of the days when they hunted pheasants in the reedy plains. All ricefields now.

As we get into the old Yamato area it's more lush — deeper green and more broad-leaf trees. Arrive in Yoshino about noon — meet up with Royall & Saka (we split up into two groups for quicker hitching — they beat us) at the Zaō Dō, an enormous temple roofed old-style with *sugi* bark. A ridge rises directly behind the village slanting up and back to the massive mountains, partly in light cloud. Yoshino village of sakura-blooming hills, cherries planted by En-no-Gyōja ("ascetic" but it would work to translate it "mountaineer") as offerings to Zaō the Mountain King. In a sense the whole of Yoshino town stands as a *butsudan* / altar. So the thousands of cherry trees make a perennial vase of flowers — (and the electric lights of the village the candle?) — offerings to the mountain looming above. Here in the Zaō Dō is the large dark image, the mountain spirit presented in a human form, Zaō Gongen — "King of the Womb Realm." ("Manifestation (*gongen*) of the King (ō) of the Womb (*za*)."

I think he was seen in a flash of lightning, in a burst of mountain thunder, glimpsed in an instant by En the Mountaineer as he walked or was sitting. Gleaming black, Zaō dances, one leg lifted, fierce-faced, hair on end. We four bow to this wild dancing energy, silently ask to be welcome, before entering the forest. Down at the end of the vast hall two new Yamabushi are being initiated in a lonely noon ceremony by the chief priest.

Zaō is not found in India or China, nor is he part of an older Shinto mythology. He is no place else because this mountain range is the place. This mountain deity is always here, a shapeshifter who could appear in any form. En the Mountaineer happened to see but one of his possible incarnations. Where Fudō is an archetype, a single form which can be found in many places, Zaō is always one place, holding thousands of shapes.

We adjust our packs and start up the road. Pass a small shrine and the Sakuramoto-bo — a hall to En the Mountaineer. Walk past another little hall to Kanki-ten, the seldom-seen deity of sexual pleasure. Climb onward past hillsides of cherry trees, now past bloom. (Saigyō, the monk-poet, by writing about them so much, gave these Yoshino cherry blossoms to the whole world.) The narrow road turns to trail, and we walk uphill til dusk. It steepens and follows a ridge-edge, fringe of conifers, to a run-down old *koya* — mountain hut — full of hiker trash. With our uptight Euro-American conservationist ethic we can't keep ourselves from cleaning it up and so we work an hour and then camp in the yard. No place else level enough to lay a bag down.

I think of the old farmers who followed the mountain path, and their sacraments of Shamanist / Buddhist / Shinto style — gods and Buddha-figures of the entrance-way, little god of the kitchen fire, of the outhouse, gods of the bath house, the woodshed, the well. A procession of stations, of work-dharma-life. A sacramental world of homes and farms, protected and nourished by the high, remote, rainy, transcendent symbolic mountains.

SECOND DAY

Early morning, as the water is bubbling on the mountain

En-no-Gyōja
Tenkawa-mura, Nara

stove, a robust Yamabushi in full gear appeared before the hut. He had been up since before dawn and already walked up from Yoshino, on his way to the temples at the top. He is the priest of Sakuramoto-bo, the little temple to En the Mountaineer. Says he's doing a 200 day climbing and descending practice. And he is grateful that we cleaned up the mess. The racket of a *kakesu*: Japanese Jay:

The Omine range as headwaters sets the ancient boundaries between the countries of Kii, Yamato, and Ise. These mountains get intense rainfall, in from the warm Pacific. It is a warm temperate rainforest, with streams and waterfalls cascading out of it. Its lower elevations once supported dense beech and oak forests, and the ridges are still thick with fir, pine, hemlock, and fields of wild azalea and camellia. The slopes are logged right up to the ridge edge here & there, even though this is in the supposed Yoshino-Kumano "National Park." (National Park does not mean protected land wholly owned by the public, as in the U.S. In Japan and many other countries the term is more like a zoning designation. Private or village-owned land may be all through the area, but it is subject to management plans and conservation restrictions.)

On the summit, center of the Diamond Realm, we visit the two temple halls, one to En the founder, and the other to Zaō. He makes me think of underground twists and dips of strata, the deep earth thrust brought to light and seen as a slightly crazed dance. And like Fudo, he is an incarnation of deep and playful forces. In Buddhist iconography, sexual ecstasy is seen as an almost ferocious energy, an ecstatic grimace that might be taken for pain.

We blow our conch, ring our shakujo, chant our sutras and dharanis, while standing at the edge of the five hundred-foot cliff over which I was once suspended by

three ascetics who then menacingly interrogated me on personal and Dharma points. In the old days, some stories say, they would just let a candidate drop if he lied or boasted. From the 7th century on no women have been allowed on this mountain. [Several college women who loved hiking changed that in 1969]. Elevation 5676 feet.

We descend from the summit plateau and are onto the branch trail that follows the ridge south. It is rocky, brushy, and narrow — no wide pilgrim paths now. We go clambering up the narrow winding trail, steps made by tree-roots, muddy in parts, past outcroppings and tiny stone shrines buried in *kumazasa*, the mountain "bear bamboo-grass" with its springy thriving erect bunches and sharp-edged leaves. We arrive at the Adirondack-type (open on one side) shelter called "Little *Sasa*" hut and make our second camp.

THIRD DAY

Rhododendron blossoms, mossy rocks, fine-thread grasses —
running ridges — wind and mist — it had rained in the night.
A full live blooming little tree of white bell flowers   its
limbs embracing a dead tree standing —
moss & a tuft of grass on the trunk.
The dead tree twisting — wood grain rising laid bare white —
sheen in the misty brightness. When a tree dies
its life goes on, the house of moss and countless bugs.
Birds echoing up from both steep slopes of the ridge.

And now we are in the old world, the old life. The Japan of gridlock cities, cheerful little bars, uniformed schoolkids standing in lines at castles, and rapid rattling trains, has retreated into dreamlike ephemerality. This is the perennial reality of vines and flowers, great trees, flitting birds. The mist and light rain blowing in gusts uphill into your wet face, the glimmer of mountains and clouds at play. Each step picked over mossy rock, wet slab, muddy pockets between vines. Long views into blue-sky openings, streaks of sunlight, arcs of hawks.

A place called Gyôja-gaeri — "Where the ascetics turn back". For a rice-ball-lunch stop. These trails so densely overgrown they're almost gone.

Now at Mi-san peak, the highest point along the Great Ridge, 6283 feet. Another place to stop and sit in zazen for a while, and to chant another round of sutras and dharanis. A little mountain hut a bit below the summit. White fir and spruce-mist blowing afternoon. Yellow-and-black eye of a snake. A fine polish and center line on each scale.

Here for the night. Tending the fire in the hut kitchen — open firepit on the dirt floor — weeping smoky eyes sometimes but blinking and cooking — sitting pretty warm, the wind outside is chilly. Lost somehow our can of *sencha*, good green tea. We have run onto our first hikers, the universal college student backpackers with white towels around their necks and Himalayan-style heavy boots. They had come up a lateral trail, and were shivering in the higher altitude cool. Hovering over the cook-fire stirring I mused on my family at home, and my two-month old baby son. Another sort of moment for mountain travellers.

Oyama renge — a very rare flowering tree "Magnolia Sieboldii" found here.

A *darshan*, the gift of a clear view of, a Japanese Shika Deer's white rump. Deep water   deep woods   wide. Green leaves — jagged and curved ones, a line-energy to play in. White-flowering low trees with red-rimmed glossy leaves.

We angle up an open flowery ridge and leafy forest to Shaka-dake, Shakyamuni Peak, and have lunch. Chant here the Sanskrit mantra of Shakyamuni learned in Nepal — "Muni muni mahamuni Shakyamuni ye svaha" — "Sage, sage, great sage, sage of the Shakyas, ye svaha." Shakya means "oak." Gautama's people were known as the "Oak Nation."

All this trip we have stayed over 5000 feet. Then stroll down a slope to the west into a high basin of massive broad-leafed trees, without a hint of any path, open and park-like. An old forest. A light wind rustling leaves, and a dappled golden light. Thick soft fine grass — Tibetan cat's-eye green — between patches of exposed rock. A rest, sitting on the leaves: sighing with the trees. Then a sudden chatter shocks us — a rhesus monkey utters little complaints and gives us the eye.

(Old men and women who live alone in the woods.
in a house with no trail or sign — characters of folktale or
drama —)

To hear the monkey or the deer
leave the path.

And I realize that this is the stillest place I had ever been — or would ever be — in Japan. This forgotten little corner of a range, headwaters of what drainage? Totsugawa River? Is it striking because it is seems so pristine and pure? Or that it is anciently wise, a storehouse of experience, hip? A place that is full, serene, needing nothing, accomplished, and — in the most creative sense — half rotten. Finished, so on the verge of giving and changing.

Maybe this is what the *Za* of Zaō's name suggests — za (or *zō* — Chinese *tsang*) means a storehouse, an abundance, a gathering, or in esoteric Buddhism, "womb." Sanskrit *alaya*, as in "storehouse of consciousness" *(alayavijñana)* or Storehouse of Snow: Himalaya. The three divisions of Buddhist literature are called zō. *Pitaka* in Sanskrit, "basket." Baskets full of the wealth of teachings. Could it be analogous to the idea of climax in natural systems? (Translating "Zaō" as "King of the Womb Realm" is the Imperial Chinese reading of his name. "Chief of Storage Baskets" would be the Neolithic translation. "Master of the Wilds" is the Paleolithic version.)

We walk back up to our packs. Down the east ridge, loggers are visible and audible high on the slope. Load up and push through sasa on down the trail. A view of a large hawk: some white by the head. Likely a *hayabusa* — falcon — to judge by its flight and dive.

(I find myself thinking we in America must do a Ghost Dance: for *all* the spirits, humans, animals, that were thrown aside.)

Zaō Gongen

— And come on a small Buddha-hall below Shaka-peak. We slip into it, for halls and temples are never locked. It is clean swept, decked out, completely equipped, for a simple *goma* service, with a central fire pit, an altar tray with vajra-tools, all fenced off with a five-colored cord, and a meditation seat before the fire spot. We know thus that there are villages below from which ascetics climb to meditate here. We are nearing the south end of the Great Ridge.

Another hour or so later, the trail that was following the top of the ridge has totally disappeared into the *kumazasa* and brush. It has started raining again. We stop, unload, study the maps, confer, and finally decide to leave the ridge at this point. We take the lateral trail east, swiftly steep and endlessly descending, stepping and sliding ever downward. Go past a seven-layer dragon-like waterfall in the steady rain. Sloshing on down the overgrown trail, find leeches, *hiru* on our ankles, deduced from the visible threads of blood. They come right off — no big deal. And still descending, until dark, we arrive at a place called Zenki, "Front Devil." (Zenki is one of Fudō's two boy imp helpers. Somewhere there's a place called "Back Devil.") We camp in another damp wooden hut along the trail. Someone has kindly left dry wood, so we cook by smoky firelight, and I reflect on the whole Omine route as we cook.

We are not far now from the Kitayama River, and the grade from here will be gentle. The Kitayama flows to the Kumano, and goes on out to the seacoast, ancient site of fishing villages and Paleolithic salmon runs. It would seem likely that from very early times, neolithic or before, anyone wishing to travel between the pleasant reed-plains of Yamato and this southern coast would have followed the Great Ridge. No other route so direct, for the surrounding hills are complex beyond measure, and the Great Ridge leads above it all, headwaters of everything, and sinuous though it be, clear to follow. The mountain religion is not a religion of recluses and hermits (as it would look to contemporary people, for whom the mountains are not the direct path) but a faith of those who move simultaneously between different human cultures, forest ecosystems, and various spiritual realms. The mountains are the way to go! And Yamabushi were preceded, by a mix of vision-questing mountain healers and sturdy folk who were trading dried fish for grains. In a world where everyone walks, the "roadless areas" are perfectly accessible.

The humans were preceded by wildlife, who doubtless made the first trails. The great ridge a shortcut for bears between seacoast fish and inland berries? All these centuries Omine has also been a wildlife corridor and a natural refuge, a core zone, protecting and sustaining beings. A Womb of Genetic Diversity.

FIFTH DAY

Next morning find the start of a dirt road going on down to the river. A pilgrims / hikers register on a post there, where we write "Sansei, Saka, Royall, Gary — followed the old Yamabushi route down the Omine ridge 5000 above the valleys walking 4 days from Yoshino and off the ridge at Zenki. June 11 to 16, 1968."

By bus and hitch-hiking we make it to the coast and camp a night by the Pacific. Hitching again, parting with Saka who must head back to Kyoto, we make our way to the Kumano "new shrine", Shingu. Dark red fancy shrine boat in the museum and an old painting of whaling. A coffeeshop has a little slogan on the wall, "chiisa no, heibon na shiawase de ii —" "A small, ordinary happiness is enough."

Travelling on, riding the back of a truck. Up the Kumano river valley running parallel to cascades of cool sheets of jade riverwater strained through the boulders. Houses on the far side tucked among wet sugi and hinoki, we are let off directly in front of Kumano Hongu at dusk. Found a nook to make a camp in, cook in, sleep the night. Riverbed smooth-washed granite stones now serve as the floor of the god's part of the shrine. Grown with moss, now that no floods wash over.

Then dreamed that night of a "Fudō Mountain" that was a new second peak to Mt Tamalpais in Northern California. A Buddhist Picnic was being held there. I walked between the two peaks — past the "Fudō Basketball Court" — and some *kami* shrines, (God's House is like the house the Ainu kept their Bear in?) and got over to the familiar parking-lot summit of Mt. Tamalpais. I was wondering how come the Americans on the regular peak of Tam didn't seem to know or care about Fudo Mountain, which was so close. Then I went into a room where a woman was seated crosslegged, told she was a "Vajra-woman" — *Vajrakanha* — a tanned Asian woman on a mat, smiling, who showed me her earrings — like the rings of a shakujo. Smiled & smiled.

6.30 AM the next morning we enter the center of the

Garbhadhātu at Kumano Hongu, "The Main Shrine at Bear-fields." On a wood post is carved:

"The most sacred spot in Japan, the main holy ground of the Womb Realm."

And it goes on to say that on April 15 every year a major fire ceremony is conducted here. Shinto, way of the spirits, outer; Buddha, way of the sentient beings, inner. It's always like this when you walk in to the shrine and up to the god's house. It is empty; or way back within, in the heart of the shrine, is a mirror: *you* are the outside world.

They say — Kannon is water — Fudō is uplift — Dainichi is energy.
Mountain and Water practice. Outer pilgrimages & inner meditations.
They are all interwoven: headwaters and drainages,

The whole range threatens & dances,
The subsiding
Mountain of the past
The high hill of the present
The rising peak that will come.

Bear   Field.

And poking around there, in back, we come on a carpentry shed, mats on the ground, and workers planing hinoki beams. With that great smell. We have run onto a *miya daiku*, a shrine builder, Yokota Shin'ichi. We chat at length on carpentry tools, and forestry, and the ancient routes of supply for perfect sugi and hinoki logs to be used in the repair of temples, and the making of sacred halls and their maintenance. I ask him how would one build a sacred hall in America? He says, "know your trees. Have the tools. Everyone should be pure when you start. Have a party when you end." And he says "go walking on the mountain." He gives us fresh fish, he was just given so much.

> deep in the
> older hills
> one side rice plains
>   Yamato
> one side black pebble
> whale-spearing beach.
> who built such shrine?

such god my face?
planing the beam
shaping the eave
blue sky
Keeps its shape.

Thinking,
"symbols" do not stand for things,
but for the states of mind that engage those things.
        / Tree / = tree intensity of mind.

We hitch-hike on up the Totsugawa gorge, cross the pass, and in some hours are out in the Nara prairies and ricefields. With *ayu* ("sweetfish") and *funa* (a silver carp, a gibel; lyrinus auratus) given us by Shin'ichi-san — tucked into a cookpot along with shredded ice to keep it cool, arrive in Kyoto by train and bus by 9 PM. We hello and hug and all cook up the fish — and brown rice for our meal. And I hold the baby, crosslegged on the tatami, back from the Great Ridge, linking the home hearth and the deep wilds.

That was 1968. It is doubtless drastically changed by now. The Yamabushi have much given way to hikers and tourists. Roads, logging, and commercial tourist enterprises spread throughout the Japanese countryside. Japan has extended its baleful forest-product extraction habits to the world. We in North America have nothing to be proud of, however. In the twenty some years since I returned to Turtle Island we have worked steadily to reform the US Forest Service and private logging practices. We are finally beginning to see a few changes. Nonetheless, in these years since 1968 Northern California, Oregon, Washington, British Columbia, and Southeast Alaska have been subjected to some of the heaviest logging and destruction of habitat in the twentieth century. As Nanao Sakaki ruefully suggests, "Perhaps we shall have to change Du Fu's line to read "The State remains, but the mountains and rivers are destroyed." ▲

L A U R E N   W.   D E U T S C H

SEARCHING FOR SANSHIN

An Interview with Hi-ah Park Manshin,
Lover of the Mountain Gods

Hi-ah Park Manshin *(a title of respect for a* mudang, *Korean shaman) specializes in ritual dance. Original artist, healer and teacher, she works at the level of the primordial state through ecstatic trance. Skilled in the healing arts, she communicates the needs of humans to the spirits, and oracles of the spirits to humans.*

I met Hi-ah Park during the 1990 Los Angeles Festival where she participated in a multi-cultural program about spirit and art, along with several Native Americans and a bevy of Buddhists. I had heard a report that the Native Americans earlier had tried to cancel

M U - A
E C S T A S Y

Carving by Kyu il Choi

their plan to do several sacred ceremonial rituals at this program if TV cameras or newspaper photographers were present. "What's ritual for," she remarked, "but to engage the spirits on behalf of people. Sharing the experience of rapture I have nothing to hide." She seemed a wise, old person, though she looked only 40. She told me she had "died many times."

The night of the presentation, she "performed" several dances of a traditionally longer kut, *ritual, going into a trance and deftly wielding a sword and a rainbow of flags before an altar resplendent with* dogk, *the many-layered rice cake, fruit, sticks of incense and other offerings placed in front of a gilded statue of Buddha.*

Out of a whirlwind of colorful costumes, loud drums (Native American and Korean), cymbals and gongs, and some 200 audience members dancing ecstatically, the "performance" finished in complete stillness. It was as if a weather front had moved in and blown the clouds away. We were at the trailhead, the ken, *keeping still, of the* I Ching, *that great mountaineer's bible. The buzz of mountain-top-seeking mind dissolved into silence, then plunged through formless ecstatic trance, leaving no footprints, taking the memories, too!*

At that point all I knew about Hi-ah Park was that she was born in Seoul and is considered the finest Korean traditional classical dancer of her generation. The first woman to be admitted to the Royal Music and Dance Academy and granted the esteemed rank of Court Musician, she gave an exquisite "performance" by any standard, but this was not just a dance recital on the second floor of a downtown Buddhist temple. She literally went a giant step further.

I have since come to realize that her life mirrors that of an intimate of Sanshin, Korea's Mountain God(s). As Canda a well-known author on Korean culture, explains in Korea Journal, *Sanshin is a "tangible, specific and personal entity," evident to human senses through vitality, power and mystery of the physical landmass as well as in dreams and visions. This, I was to learn, was Hi-ah Park's history. Canda's observation of Sanshin's having "awesome natural power in service of sacredness and wisdom," became her destiny.*

Shamanism is Korea's indigenous "religion," manshin — predominantly women — the ritual practitioners. For centuries manshin had been openly persecuted, their practices disrupted and shrines destroyed, their artistry desecrated to entertainment. The prevailing religious and social orders forced the practice of shamanism underground. It is still considered a curse to suggest that someone would grow up to be or to marry a mudang. That one of Korea's most acclaimed artists, an American citizen and university teacher became a manshin, has had an impact in Korea as well as globally.

After a number of years of quiet reflection following her initiation, Hi-ah Park decided to fulfill her destiny as manshin, to put her talents in service of the spirit and the people who seek her out. She currently works in Europe and the USA, teaching through performances, workshops and lectures, at many prestigious art centers, universities and mental health centers.

Whether clad in manshin's colorful robes performing a formal kut to the accompaniment of chang'go, *hourglass drums, and cymbals and gongs, or in a simple flowing white tunic dancing to the sounds of steel cello, bow chime, Chapman stick, Mongolian drum or a wall of gongs, Hi-ah Park shows us how the shaman warrior climbs the mountain, and dances with Sanshin atop the peak in* mu-a, *ecstasy.* ▶

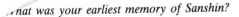

What was your earliest memory of Sanshin?

From very early childhood, I loved mountains. My memory of childhood is playing in the tiger cave near my neighborhood. Often there, I lost time and space while my family was looking for me. One day I climbed into the mountain deeper than usual, as if some invisible being was guiding me into the unknown world, and I found a big tree surrounded by a pile of stones. There unknowingly I bowed to the ground after respectfully gathering stones and placing them on top of the pile. That was my first encounter with Sanshin.

Did you encounter Sanshin on any other occasions prior to your initiation?

After teaching summer school in 1977 at UCLA, I retired to an avocado ranch located deep in the mountains. I left all worldly affairs behind, obsessed like a lover longing for the mountains. In the mountains I could feel the presence of something indescribably different, an exotic apparition, the spirit of which one can not find in a human; a beautiful, bewitching spirit embracing boundless joy. I journeyed to Yosemite, Mt. Rainier, Death Valley, and other places like the Grand Canyon. In Canyon de Chelly I was led by endless double rainbows to the White House cliff dwelling with its ancient *kiva*, subterranean ritual chambers. As I emerged from a ruined kiva a sudden thunderstorm came down upon me mercilessly. I fainted onto the sand, and in total surrender I offered myself to the spirits present. I awoke with the most incredible orgasm I have ever known, basking in the most luxurious ecstasy. The sky was replete with rainbows and the reflections of rainbows reaching every horizon. The mountain breeze passing through the canyon seemed to be coming and going in the rhythm of an inaudible chant. As I flowed into that chant my soul ascended as a flying unicorn, higher and higher into the sky. At last I was free and flying with such a feeling of exhilaration and joy that I wanted to cry, for I was experiencing the ecstasy for which I had been yearning so long.

Did you have any personal desire to be a shaman?

When I began studying shamanism in 1975, I had neither the wish nor the intention to become a shaman. I initially considered the whole process solely as an artistic endeavor, yet everything I encountered along the shamanic path seemed to create a thirst in me for spiritual fulfillment. I became a manshin after I was called to the profession through *sinbyong*, or initiatory illness.

What are the symptoms of shamanic initiatory illness?

I began to suffer from tedium and loneliness, without knowing any meaning to my life. My interest in mundane affairs and domestic chores waned completely, I suffered unbearable loneliness and longed for the mountains.

I spent many nights weeping endlessly or dreaming of impending death. In my dreams, I was imprisoned in the underworld and chased by wild animals. For about nine months, I endured sleepless and restless nights, until I had an incredible, lengthy dream of an ancient royal funeral procession.

My insomnia stopped right after this mysterious dream. I was happy without any specific reason. I felt elevated into the air, as if somebody was lifting me. After this funeral dream, my dream scenes started to change into lighter, celestial ones.

In one unforgettable dream journey, a white unicorn with wings took me through the Milky Way to an incredible, infinite space of deep, jet-dark indigo. In that place, I heard a deep and resonant voice ask me, "How are the people down there?" I still remember clearly the conversation with that invisible voice and the ecstatic feeling I had. Then the voice told me I had to go back to teach the people love. I felt boundless joy and, at the same time, sadness that I had to go back. Without any sense of waking up from a dream, I found myself in my room.

For a while, I was obsessed by this visionary dream and felt very connected with that other reality. Although I couldn't understand it, the other space was so clear that I now felt as if my waking state was the dream.

Why do shamans have to go through shamanic illness?

I believe that it happens because a person's spiritual body is starving from a lack of inspirational creativity. The initiatory sickness allows her to escape from the world and withdraw into the darkness, in order to experience her own rites of passage. In order to become a shaman, the person must go through years of introspection, personal torment, and progressive spiritual development. Without understanding the illness, one will never understand the spirit world.

How do you come out from sinbyong?

By reaching the point of *mu-a*, ecstasy, the death of ego. Ecstasy is a sensation which is encountered in our hearts. It is seeing and hearing with the heart, rather than just with eyes and ears. It is also a flame which springs up in the heart out of longing, to see and to become one with its truth (God). Atop this mountain there is such clarity that there is no duality.

What convinced you to become a manshin?

During my illness before my initiation, I had visions. In one, I saw Tangun, the heroic founder of the Korean nation who later became Mountain Spirit, sitting in a meditation posture within a yurt and wearing a red hat and robe. As I gazed intensely at that figure, we became one; then I saw myself sitting as Tangun. This clear vision of Tangun convinced me to visit my homeland after an absence of 15 years.

I didn't have any specific plan for my visit. However, from its start, everyone I met and everywhere I visited turned out to be connected somehow with shamanistic practices. Within a week, I was introduced to Kim Keum-Hwa, a well known Hwang-haedo manshin (from a western province of Korea). When I viewed a video of one of her shamanic rituals, I couldn't believe my eyes: I saw Kim Keum-Hwa wearing the same red robe and hat I had seen in my Tangun vision of a week before.

A week later I was introduced to her. When Kim came into the room in her house where I was waiting, we both shuddered. She told me she had the sensation that her spirits wanted to talk to me. She brought out a divination table and started to pronounce oracles: "Rainbows surround in all directions. The fruit is fully ripe and can't wait anymore!" She told me I was lucky to have surrendered to the spirits' orders and to have come to her. Otherwise, she said, I would have died, like an overripe fruit that

⨁ SITE-SPECIFIC SANSHIN ⸱⸱⸱⸱⸱⸱

Over 70% of Korea is mountainous and many of the "most famous" sacred peaks are in the northern part of the peninsula. Perhaps most notable is Mt. Taepaek (Myohyang-san in Yongbyon, north Pyongan Province), the spot chosen by heavenly god Hawan-in for his son Hwan-woong's earthly abode.

Tangun, founder of the ancient Chosun Empire and considered the first Korean, was born near a sandalwood tree to a patient, obedient bear-woman and Hwan-woong in 2333 BCE. He established his capital in Asadal (old name of Pyongyang) in Paegak-san where he eventually died, aged 1908 years, and became Sanshin of Mt. Kuwol. Other peaks sacred to Tangun are Mani-san (on an island in the mouth of the Han River) where it is said he established a rock altar, and Paektu-san (Mt. Whitehead).

Centuries ago you could find a cozy wooden hut, with thatched straw or tiled roof situated deep in the mountain. Today, anthropomorphic images of Sanshin appear everywhere fine arts and tourist mementos are found. Scrolls and screens depict Sanshin as a stately old man with a long beard leaning on a tiger, his messenger. The tiger, even the one playfully rendered as the mascot of the Seoul Olympiad, is also said to be Sanshin and Tangun.

Emille Museum

Sanshin icons were once prepared only for religious worship exclusively. To this end they were found only in the mountain spirit shrines in the samsinggak, three spirit hall, behind the golden hall in the Buddhist temple compounds, shamans' houses or at the ceremonial grounds of shamanic ritual. Korea's Emille Museum would be a good resource for further investigation on this topic.

On October 14th, 1993, the North Korean Academy of Social Sciences announced the discovery of the remains of Tangun (dating back to 3019 BCE) in a mausoleum located on Mt. Dae Pak just outside Pyongyang. The Korean Daily reported that North Korea fabricated the stories to stress that Pyongyang was Korea's original capital. Others speculated the announcement was tied to leader Kim Jong Il, heir to Kim Il Sung, whose title is expected to be taken from one of Tangun's names.

CAVEAT: If you're really looking for Sanshin in Korea, particularly Tangun, choose carefully whom you tell. The three "Cs" which have been dominating the political and social order north and south — Confucianism, Christianity and Communism — don't want anyone to find him, his being the national ancestor, with all that this powerful identity implies.

---

falls onto the ground and rots. Kim continued to explain that I had disobeyed two times previously and, consequntly, had had to go through unbearable pain and loneliness and near-death experiences. She warned that I should not resist anymore — the third time, there is no forgiveness. It was absolutely essential that I undergo the *naerim kut* without delay. On a more positive note, Kim told me she saw double rainbows stretched around my head, celestial gods surrounding me. She said that the warrior in me was so strong that I would want to stand on the *chaktu* (sharp blades). She predicted that in the near future I would be a famous shaman, and I'd travel all around the world. Then she set a date for the initiation — June 23, 1981. In less than two weeks, I was transformed into a new shaman.

What place did Sanshin have in your initiation ritual?

In preparation for the initiation ceremony, I had to climb up to the mountain to receive the Mountain Spirit by a purifying bath in a cold mountain stream early in the morning. My Godmother and I ascended a mountain north of Seoul. She asked me to climb up a steep, rocky cliff to get a branch from a pine tree. This task was the first test of the day. I did as she requested, performing the task necessary to receive Sanshin. We spoke as little as possible.

At the mountain altar I offered rice, rice cake, three different kinds of cooked vegatables, fruits, lighted candles and incense and *makghuli*, home-made rice wine.

As my Godmother chanted and beat a small gong, I held up the *Sanshin dari*, a long piece of white cotton cloth called *minyong*, white cotton bridge, through which the shaman receives the Mountain Spirit. My body started to quiver uncontrollably, a sign that the Spirit was entering me. I completely surrendered to the Spirit, turning off my internal dialogue, and entered into inner silence. I sensed light coming from every direction, and I started to feel drunk with the Spirit in me. It was at last a dramatic close encounter with the separated "Lover." I felt the ultimate completion of my primordial self before separa-

tion. I knew that the Spirit loved me and forgave my long resistance to accepting it. Bathed by the light of the Spirit, I felt clean and reborn. I practically flew down the mountain. I returned with my Godmother to the town in the valley below where her house would host the all-day ritual that was to come.

Could you describe some more details of the initiation?

The Korean term for initiation is *naerim kut*. I will explain the aspect of the ritual concerned with the descending spirits and identification and presentation of the deities which had already made their presence known through possession of my body.

At the initiation ceremony, the minyong was placed leading to the upstage portion of the house as a bridge between heaven and the earth. My Godmother and her assistant shaman, who serves as a messenger, sat where the minyong ended in heaven, to test my psychic ability and to determine if I could identify the deities who had descended on me.

A straw mat was placed downstage. Each question asked by the head shaman was repeated by her assistant. Instead of answering the questions directly, I began dancing. Then, kneeling down on the straw mat, I answered the questions orally. The dance seemed to heighten the trance state so that my answers came without thinking as if I had known everything already.

The first question was, "If you become a shaman, through which gate will you enter?"

I started singing in an occult way previously unknown to me. Again I danced until possessed and knelt down to wait for the next question.

"Which spirit is entering you?"

I answered, "Elwol Sung Shin and Okhwang Sangchae, spirits of the Sun, Moon and Stars and the Jade Emperor, are entering."

"Then reveal your true nature and find the symbolic paraphernalia of these deities," she ordered.

I stood, and walking upstage, grasped the *Il wrol dae*, sun and moon stick, a pine branch which I took from the

Photographs: page 78, Rob Sims; pages 81-82, 84-85, Kim Su Nam

cliff at the mountain, bundled together with a bronze mirror and covered with a white long-seeved gown, the costume of the deities.

After I danced, she asked me another question, "Which spirit did you receive this time?"

My reply was, "I received Sanshin, the spirits from the High Mountain and *Sa Hae Yong Wang Nim*, from the Four Direction Deep Ocean."

"Why did you receive it?" she asked.

"I obeyed the order from Tangun, the founder of Korea. He has told me to help infertile couples, to counsel parents and their children to love each other. Through him, I am guided to heal sickness and help those in poverty to find prosperity. Lastly, he advised me to engender love and respect among all people."

Acknowledging my remarks, the head shaman invited any other spirits that might be present to enter me. *Chil Sung*, the Deity of the Seven Stars or Big Dipper, *Taegam Nim*, the Spirit of High Nobility, *Chosang Nim*, Spirit of Ancestors, and *Obang Shinchang Nim*, Warrior of the Five Directions, came through.

As my Godmother had predicted, the kut climaxed with my dancing atop the chaktu.

How has the initiation influenced your dance?

Since my initiation, my understanding of dance changed completely. The inseparability of art and spirit became essential for healing myself, and eventually has helped others. My teaching and performing is at the level of the primordial state, mainly achieved through ecstatic trance. By integrating breath, sound, movement and theatre, I set the stage for the transformation of the audience and society.

You have been living outside Korea since the initiation. How does Sanshin Tangun fit in the global village?

Sanshin cannot afford any longer to wait on a lonely mountain top. I have been travelling a great deal since 1988, sharing Tangun's doctrine of *Hong Ik In Kan*, to be of benefit to all sentient beings, to engender love and respect among all people. Transformation is a fundamental concern of the shaman's ritual. One important function of ritual is that it makes you a member of the tribe, of society, and hopefully a member of the global community. Today it is especially important to return to tribal integration in a global sense.

What is Sanshin's message for us?

The nature and message of spirit is beyond mental condition; it is bliss of pure energy, pervading everything, *mu-a* / ecstasy. The Spirit, which is formless, speaks through me in ecstatic dance. Spirit is shy, but sword is sharp. It teaches us a powerful but direct process of purification. Through ecstatic dance, sound and breath meditation, it cuts through fear, conflict and confusion. Fear is transformed into plentiful, universal love, and suddenly, we understand that our lives are about much more than suffering; they are also about experiencing rapture. This only works for those who are willing to confront their dark side and surrender to the primal spirit.

KEEPING STILL

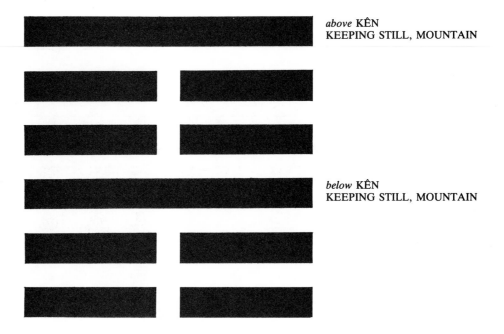

above **KÊN**
KEEPING STILL, MOUNTAIN

below **KÊN**
KEEPING STILL, MOUNTAIN

THE IMAGE of this hexagram is the mountain, the youngest son of heaven and earth. The male principle at the top, because it strives upward by nature; the female principle is below, since the direction of its movement is downward. Thus there is rest because the movement has come to its normal end.

In its application to man, the hexagram turns upon the problem of achieving a quiet heart. It is very difficult to bring quiet to the heart. While Buddhism strives for rest through an ebbing away of all movement in nirvana, the Book of Changes holds that rest is merely a state of polarity that always posits movement as its complement. Possibly the words of the text embody directions for the practice of yoga. ▶

艮。〔艮〕其背、不獲其身。行其庭、不見其人。无咎。

象曰、艮、止也。時止則止、時行則行。

動靜不失其時、其道光明。

艮其（止）〔背〕、止其所也。

上下敵应、不相与也。

是以不獲其身、行其庭、

不見其人、无咎也。

象曰、兼山、艮。

君子以思不出其位。

初六　艮其趾。无咎。利永貞。

六二　艮其腓。不拯其随、其心不快。

九三　艮其限、列其夤、厲薰心。

六四　艮其身。无咎。

六五　艮其輔言有序。悔亡。

上九　敦艮。吉。

THE JUDGMENT

KEEPING STILL. Keeping his back still
So that he no longer feels his body.
He goes into his courtyard
And does not see his people.
No blame.

True quiet means keeping still when the time has come to keep still, and going forward when the time has come to go forward. In this way rest and movement are in agreement with the demands of the time, and thus there is light in life.

The hexagram signifies the end and the beginning of all movement. The back is named because in the back are located all the nerve fibers that mediate movement. If the movement of these spinal nerves is brought to a standstill, the ego, with its restlessness, disappears as it were. When a man has thus become calm, he may turn to the outside world. He no longer sees in it the struggle and tumult of individual beings, and therefore he has that true peace of mind which is needed for understanding the great laws of the universe and for acting in harmony with them. Whoever acts from these deep levels makes no mistakes.

THE IMAGE

Mountains standing close together:
The image of KEEPING STILL.
Thus the superior man
Does not permit his thoughts
To go beyond his situation.

The heart thinks constantly. This cannot be changed, but the movements of the heart — that is, a man's thoughts — should restrict themselves to the immediate situation. All thinking that goes beyond this only makes the heart sore.

THE LINES

Six at the beginning means:
Keeping his toes still.
No blame.
Continued perseverance furthers.

Keeping the toes still means halting before one has even begun to move. The beginning is the time of few mistakes. At that time one is still in harmony with primal innocence. Not yet influenced by obscuring interests and desires, one sees things intuitively as they really are. A man who halts at the beginning, so long as he has not yet abandoned truth, finds the right way. But persisting firmness is needed to keep one from drifting irresolutely.

Six in the second place means:
Keeping his calves still.
He cannot rescue him whom he follows.
His heart is not glad.

The leg cannot move independently; it depends on the movement of the body. If a leg is suddenly stopped while the whole body is in vigorous motion, the continuing body movement will make one fall.
The same is true of a man who serves a master stronger than himself. He is swept along, and even though he may himself halt on the path of wrongdoing, he can no longer check the other in his powerful movement. Where the master presses forward, the servant, no matter how good his intentions, cannot save him.

Nine in the third place means:
Keeping his hips still.
Making his sacrum stiff.
Dangerous. The heart suffocates.

This refers to enforced quiet. The restless heart is to be subdued by forcible means. But fire when it is smothered changes into acrid smoke that suffocates as it spreads.
Therefore, in exercises in meditation and concentration, one ought not to try to force results. Rather, calmness must develop naturally out of a state of inner composure. If one tries to induce calmness by means of artificial rigidity, meditation will lead to very unwholesome results.

Six in the fourth place means:
Keeping his trunk still.
No blame.

As has been pointed out above in the comment on the Judgment, keeping the back at rest means forgetting the ego. This is the highest stage of rest. Here this stage has not yet been reached: the individual in this instance, though able to keep the ego, with its thoughts and impulses, in a state of rest, is not yet quite liberated from its dominance. Nonetheless, keeping the heart at rest is an important function, leading in the end to the complete elimination of egotistic drives. Even though at this point one does not yet remain free from all the dangers of doubt and unrest, this frame of mind is not a mistake, as it leads ultimately to that other, higher level.

Six in the fifth place means:
Keeping his jaws still.
The words have order.
Remorse disappears.

A man in a dangerous situation, especially when he is not adequate to it, is inclined to be very free with talk and presumptuous jokes. But injudicious speech easily leads to situations that subsequently give much cause for regret. However, if a man is reserved in speech, his words take ever more definite form, and every occasion for regret vanishes.

Nine at the top means:
Noblehearted keeping still.
Good fortune.

This marks the consummation of the effort to attain tranquility. One is at rest, not merely in a small, circumscribed way in regard to matters of detail, but one has also a general resignation in regard to life as a whole, and this confers peace and good fortune in relation to every individual matter.

COMMENTARY ON THE DECISION

KEEPING STILL means stopping.
When it is time to stop, then stop.
When it is time to advance, then
    advance.
Thus movement and rest do not miss
    the right time,
And their course becomes bright and
    clear.

Mountains & Mythology

Sketch by Dee Molenaar, *American Alpine Journal*, 1964

In mountainous countries mythology comprises the identification of one or many holy mountains. The symbolic values of a mountain are primarily:

1. *The movement upwards.* The eye moves upwards as an expression of elevation, increase of any positive kind.

2. *Ascension.* A person moving upwards is symbol of a person increasing in every positive way.

3. *Highness.* The elevation reached and the difference in altitude in comparison to the environment, symbolizes excellence, nobility, majesty, steadiness, coolness, superiority.

4. *Transcendence.* Every "ascension" is a passage to the beyond, a rupture of the level, a passage from the region of the trivial or profane to that of sur-passing, over-whelming importance. In short: to reach the mountain top is to transcend the human condition, reaching the unreachable.

5. *A mountain is the nearest to heaven.* Or: mountains "touch" the heavens, and are therefore considered to be "the center" in the sense of the meeting-place between the heavenly and the earthly.

6. *The struggle towards the summit,* towards the highest quality. The way up, the difficulty, the fatigue, of this struggle. Ritual ascension is a "difficult ascension."

7. *The unreachable.* The passage to the beyond, "transcendence," may be possible or not possible for humans. The highly valued unclimbableness of mountains symbolizes the unreachableness of the absolute — absolute virtue, power or also immortality.

The condition of man is in a long and varied cultural tradition conceived as an unstable and dynamic condition. In the vertical dimension man is always in a condition of elevation or fall. He neither can reach a summit nor fall to the absolute bottom. He cannot rest without falling, nor can he attain any height definitely: he cannot dwell or occupy the height. He is always on the way, up or down. He is longing for the paradise, but is unfit to stay there.

All the major "ideals" which man struggles towards are more or less unattainable. Only hypocrisy and untruthfulness can give him the passing sense of having reached the ideal.

This holds good of truth also in the sense of scientific truth. Research is search for truth, science or knowledge in the sense of "truth arrived at" is an ideal, not anything accomplished.

Some of the symbolic values of mountains are such that for humans to reach *the summit involves transgression or violation of a cultural belief or attitude.* In a Chinese cultural tradition it is a plus for a human being to climb its sacred mountains. In Hindu and Tibetan cultural traditions, it is not. The people below the sacred mountain Gauri Shankar (Tseringma, "The Mother of the Long Good Life") voted unanimously for forbidding expeditions to try to scale it. But the government of Nepal did not even react to their formal request not to open access to the mighty walls of the great peak — for economic reasons.

The ideal, the unreachable is not reached! The terrifying condition of being always on the way, of being unable to reject the ideals, is transcended. The unconquerable cannot be conquered.

Thus the ascension of the great summits is a profanation, a negation of the difference between God and man, the death of the urge to mount any further.

But the climbers find that they cannot rest, so they climb more summits, and perfect their equipment until it no longer is any supreme achievement to reach the summits. These abdicate as symbols of the unreachable.

UNREACHABLENESS AND JOY

Against this trend there is a trend to accept the terrifying condition of being essentially on the way. On the one hand, unreachableness of all we long for, of all ideas that can command our respect, is acknowledged. On the other hand, the meaningfulness and joyfulness of the struggle "upwards" is also acknowledged.

In recognition of this, the few unclimbed, old, majestic mountains, which for thousands of years in many cultures have been supreme symbols of the unreachable, should be left unclimbed. ▲

KYOTO: SPIRITUAL WONDERLAND

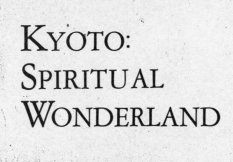

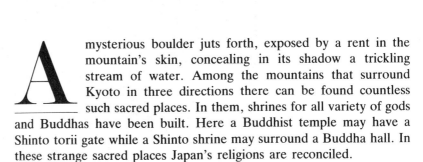

A mysterious boulder juts forth, exposed by a rent in the mountain's skin, concealing in its shadow a trickling stream of water. Among the mountains that surround Kyoto in three directions there can be found countless such sacred places. In them, shrines for all variety of gods and Buddhas have been built. Here a Buddhist temple may have a Shinto torii gate while a Shinto shrine may surround a Buddha hall. In these strange sacred places Japan's religions are reconciled.

Originally, the whole of Kyoto was a sacred place. This fact becomes clear as soon as one looks at the city geomantically, but this spiritual power has been lost in the heart of the modern city. Yet in its surrounds, scattered throughout the encircling mountains, there are many locales that maintain their psychic power. Many of these still serve as the focus of active popular religious practices.

From among Kyoto's many remaining sacred places, I would like to introduce one: the Raccoon-dog Valley of Acala[1] (Tanukidani Fudōson). Raccoon-dog Valley is set in the gorge of Kasho Mountain which is aligned on the city's northeasterly compass point. This places it just at the front of the city's *kimon* or demon gate. The temple complex is arranged on the climax of a hill with a wide view of the city below.

One bright sunny spring afternoon I lazily strolled up the hill from the Ichijo Temple bus stop, taking pleasure in the quiet of the Shisendo

2. *Benzaiten (Saravati) is the goddess of music and eloquence, and as one of the Seven Gods of Happiness also brings wealth, wisdom and happiness. Usually she holds a biwa or lute. Originally the deification of a river in India, she is popularly regarded as the wife of the Indian god Bhrama (Bonten).*

1. *Acala (Fudōson) or Acalanatha (Fudōmyō-ō) is a fearsome deity borrowed from the Hindu pantheon. Originally depicted as a deformed slave, his role in Buddhism is to deal harshly with evil thoughts and desires when gentler methods have failed. The grim faced and flaming Acala cuts evil from the worshipper with his ever drawn sword, and should that fail, he throws out his rope to yank the lost sole from wrongdoing and bind fast the afflicting evil. Acala is a lesser manifestation of the Celestial Buddha Virochana (Dainichi), who is central to the esoteric Buddhist pantheon, and although rarely seen in other Buddhist countries, Acala has long been a prominent deity in Japan.*

district. My usual course would have taken me north from the gates of Shisendo past the Shrine of the Heron Forest and on to the Monastery of Mañjuśrī. But on this day I decided not to join the crowds of tourists herding into Shisendo and instead walked straight east up the Shisendo road. For some reason I had always thought that Shisendo was at the tail of a dead end street, but beyond it I discovered the Hachidai Shrine, and past this it led still farther up the slope of Mount Kasho. After an incline of five- or six-hundred meters, the roadway opened into a wide overlook. There I noticed a signboard that announced: "Raccoon-dog Valley of Acala and Places of Prayer."

A strange sense of anticipation hung about this place and with the expansion of my view at the overlook my spirits brightened. To have simply headed back down the hill at this point would have already amounted to an utterly satisfying walk, but the path that led up into the depths of the mountain invited me onward.

As I walked on I was soon met by a long, seemingly endless stone stairway. At every turn along this climb there was arranged a religious device and at each was placed a cordially written signboard detailing the correct method of worship for that particular deity or place. I performed the required rite for each as I came to it.

First, there was a Water Pavilion where I ritually purified myself with the water of a cascading fall. Next, after walking through a great

3. *The Seven Gods of Happiness are 1) Ebisu, an indigenous Japanese deity originally worshipped by fishermen, but popularized as an all purpose god of happiness. He is thought to be the son of Izanagi and Izanami, sun and moon gods in the Japanese creation myths, and he is usually depicted as a fat man with large earlobes. He often rides or is accompanied by a giant carp. 2) Taikokuten (Mahakala), the god of the kitchen, is of Indian origin and was brought to Japan and popularized by the Tendai sect of esoteric Buddhism. He usually carries a large bag over his left shoulder and a mallet in his right hand, and he often stands on a large sack of rice. 3) Bishamonten (Vaisravana), also of Indian origin, is the foremost of the four great Buddhist guardian deities. As defender of the north, he is guardian of the Buddhist Law and giver of virtue and happiness. Popularly he is regarded as the husband (sometimes father) of Kichijoten (Sri-mahadevi) (see 6 below). Bishamon usually stands on one or more girmacing dwarfs and is dressed in full body armor with a staff in his right hand and the jewel pagoda of happiness held high in his left. 4) Benzaiten. See note 2 above. 5) Fuku-roku-ju, is a deification of the attributes of happiness, wealth and longevity. He resembles a Chinese Daoist immortal with a long white beard and an elongated forehead. He holds a staff from which dangles a sutra scroll and he is usually accompanied by a crane. 6) Jurojin, is of similar Chinese origins and is so close in appearance to Fuku-roku-ju that he is commonly replaced with Kichijoten (Sri-mahadevi), a beautiful Buddhist deity of Indian origin. She is always dressed in lavish, flowing drapery, and she holds up the jewel of happiness just as her husband Bishamonten holds up the jewel pagoda. 7) Hotei, is the deification of Budai Heshan, a sixth-century Chinese Zen monk. He is jovial, fat and always carries with him a huge cloth sack filled with useless trifies.*

stone torii, I came to an eerie Benzai[2] of the White Dragon (Hakuryubenzaiten) set into a grotto. Here, in accordance with the instructions, I chanted the mantra *"On-sora-sobateiei-sowaka"* five times while ringing a bell. Then after pausing in front of each of the Seven Gods of Happiness[3] I suddenly came upon a life-size standing bronze statue of the Great Teacher Kobo.[4] He seemed to beckon me on toward the hall of the Great Teacher and the Light. Once there I was given the opportunity to choose from a plentiful menu of spiritual activities including a thirteen-Buddha pilgrimage, an 88-holy-sites walk, and a version of the Shinto 100 supplications. By the time I had ascended the 250 Stone Steps for the Expulsion of Evil, and come face to face with the Three Shinto Gods of Great Miracles[5] both my mind and body were in a state of elation.

I was lost in this strange space, utterly divorced from that of the modern cafe-bar on Shirakawa Street where only a few minutes before I had eaten lunch. The spiritual distance I had traversed during this short walk made my head spin.

Above me, built onto an overhanging precipice, I could now see the Central Hall of the great evil slayer Acalanatha. On the way up to it I had to pass through an additional series of sacred spots. At each I stopped and performed the prayers and incantations as advised. First there was a waterfall of Miyamoto Musashi's[6] Ascetic Practice. Then there

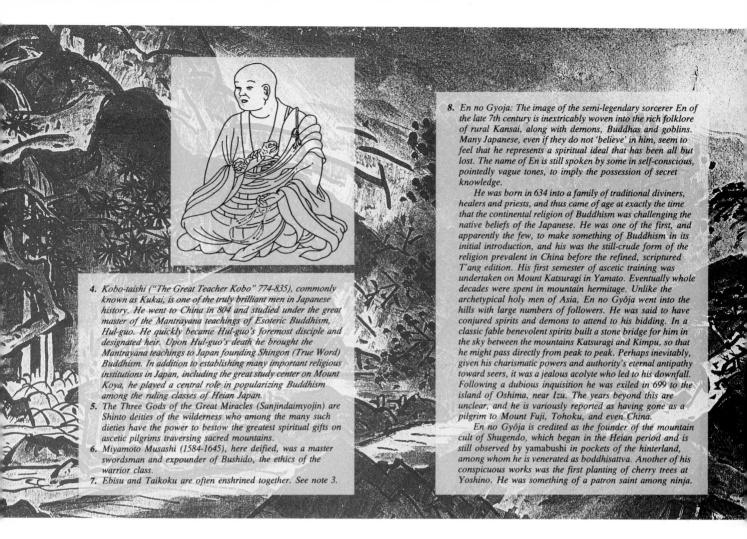

8. *En no Gyoja:* The image of the semi-legendary sorcerer En of the late 7th century is inextricably woven into the rich folklore of rural Kansai, along with demons, Buddhas and goblins. Many Japanese, even if they do not 'believe' in him, seem to feel that he represents a spiritual ideal that has been all but lost. The name of En is still spoken by some in self-conscious, pointedly vague tones, to imply the possession of secret knowledge.

En no Gyōja was born in 634 into a family of traditional diviners, healers and priests, and thus came of age at exactly the time that the continental religion of Buddhism was challenging the native beliefs of the Japanese. He was one of the first, and apparently the few, to make something of Buddhism in its initial introduction, and his was the still-crude form of the religion prevalent in China before the refined, scriptured T'ang edition. His first semester of ascetic training was undertaken on Mount Katsuragi in Yamato. Eventually whole decades were spent in mountain hermitage. Unlike the archetypical holy men of Asia, En no Gyōja went into the hills with large numbers of followers. He was said to have conjured spirits and demons to attend to his bidding. In a classic fable benevolent spirits built a stone bridge for him in the sky between the mountains Katsuragi and Kimpu, so that he might pass directly from peak to peak. Perhaps inevitably, given his charismatic powers and authority's eternal antipathy toward seers, it was a jealous acolyte who led to his downfall. Following a dubious inquisition he was exiled in 699 to the island of Oshima, near Izu. The years beyond this are unclear, and he is variously reported as having gone as a pilgrim to Mount Fuji, Tohoku, and even China.

En no Gyōja is credited as the founder of the mountain cult of Shugendo, which began in the Heian period and is still observed by yamabushi in pockets of the hinterland, among whom he is venerated as boddhisattva. Another of his conspicuous works was the first planting of cherry trees at Yoshino. He was something of a patron saint among ninja.

4. *Kobo-taishi* ("The Great Teacher Kobo" 774-835), commonly known as Kukai, is one of the truly brilliant men in Japanese history. He went to China in 804 and studied under the great master of the Mantrayana teachings of Esoteric Buddhism, Hul-guo. He quickly became Hul-guo's foremost disciple and designated heir. Upon Hul-guo's death he brought the Mantrayana teachings to Japan founding Shingon (True Word) Buddhism. In addition to establishing many important religious institutions in Japan, including the great study center on Mount Koya, he played a central role in popularizing Buddhism among the ruling classes of Heian Japan.

5. *The Three Gods of the Great Miracles (Sanjindaimyojin)* are Shinto deities of the wilderness who among the many such dieties have the power to bestow the greatest spiritual gifts on ascetic pilgrims traversing sacred mountains.

6. *Miyamoto Musashi* (1584-1645), here deified, was a master swordsman and expounder of Bushido, the ethics of the warrior class.

7. *Ebisu and Taikoku* are often enshrined together. See note 3.

was an Acala of the Water, a Shrine for Ebisu and Daikoku[7], and another to the Great Bodhisattva of Godly Transformation.[8] Finally there stood Ksitigarbha (Jizo) as the Water Child.[9]

With the grand and expansive view from the Hall of Acalantha I was absorbed into a yet higher plateau of my ongoing natural high. I sat down on a bench provided in the rest area and as beads of sweat formed on my forehead, drank a can of Mitsuya Cider from the vending machine. (For some reason this was the only drink the machine had.) It was like holy nectar.

Beyond the Main Hall there awaited a Pilgrimage to the Temple at the Heart of the Mountain, yet another spiritual pathway. When I had finished walking up this wondering path past the thirty-six statues of Acala's Pages (doji)[10] each with accompanying mantra, and reached the Hall for the Avatar of the Dragon of Good Fortune at the top of the mountain, I felt as if I had surely arrived at the doorstep of absorption into enlightenment.

Purification by waterfall, mountain pilgrimages, mantra chanting, the 100 supplications, prayers and evil expulsion... If we apply contemporary language to these practices the terms that emerge are those of spiritual healing and sports. With these one can obtain benefits for both mind and body.

If one discovers the technique to enjoy such things then Kyoto reveals

9. *Ksitigarbha as the Water Child (Mizuko Jizo) is a Jizo for the protection of the souls of dead children.*
10. *Acala is known to have 36 child-like assistants (Doji).*
11. *The Fushimi Inari Shrine extends up a mountainside along a range southeast of Kyoto. It is famous for its thousands of bright red torii and the many guardian fox statues that populate the shrine. The fox is the guardian beast of all Inari (Rice God) shrines.*
12. *Kurama Temple, dedicated to Bishamonten, and Kibune Shrine, the site of an important water purification festival, are both hidden in the mountains directly north of the city.*

itself as a kind of wonderland. This should make apparent the foolishness of paying exorbitant fees to be given the privilage of standing in line at a few famous temples in some packaged tour. The true "Kyoto Mountain Tour" should include a walk to the mountain top through the ten-thousand vermilion torii at Fushimi Inari,[11] or an excursion from the Deep Mountain Hall of the King of Hell at Kurama Temple to the Kibune Shrine of Pure Water.[12] Such masterpiece walks can rival any Disneyland adventure, and of such Kyoto has many.

In the dramatically materialistic civilization of our current age the level of interest in the spiritual world is still surprisingly high. The entire city of Kyoto can be thought of as a spiritual apparatus, a kind of spiritual amusement park if you will, and for this it should be given more attention. Kyoto is still a mysterious and eternal spiritual wonderland.

▲

Translation and notes by James Heaton
Drawings by Tanaka Makiko

THE SACRED AND THE PROFANE

Gunung Batukau

Tanah Lot

Emerging breathless from the dank river canyon which runs behind my Ubud *losman*, I climb the slippery path to the plateau, hurrying out of the shadows, spooky even in the morning light. New rice shoots emerge in the neat fields to the east of the narrow walkway, while to the west, harvest is well under way. The morning mist rises to greet the dawn, perhaps to carry the spirits of the ancestors who so many centuries ago shaped these terraces. Holy Gunung Agung, the "Mother Mountain" of Bali, is swathed in a gossamer *sarong* as the sun rises behind her, casting haze yet across the row of mountains to the west. Although I rose early, I am still too late to catch the duck-masters, leading their flocks into the paddy behind their little white flags; the fields are already aquack with hundreds of fluffy ducklings, earnest in their neat double function of keeping both weeds and pests down, while fattening up for the next temple ceremony (or tourist dinner).

A diamond in the center of the archipelago now ruled by Indonesia, Bali is the last stronghold of ancient Hindu culture in a Muslim sea. Yet even before the Hindi princes arrived in the 9th century CE, the rice terrace culture was well established. I try to imagine this landscape untold millennia ago; before the mountain slopes and plains were shaped by human hands, before the water was coaxed into the irrigation canals which now flow like a network of arteries throughout the island, bringing the precious resource first to this community, then to another, first to this field, then to another, in a constant

interaction between mankind and his economic needs, and the gods and their demands; and all within the ebb and flow of nature and its complexities. The Rice Goddess, Devi Seri, determines how and when the rice should be planted, and her earthly intercessors keep their schedules in line with the help of calendar experts who somehow manage to keep Bali's three interlocking calendars in synch.

The island of Bali — a mere 5620 square kilometers — is one of the world's most remarkable examples of a high density population making a living on a limited area of land. It is almost impossible to imagine, from the minutely tended fields stretching before me, a time when people didn't manipulate the land. The volcanic soil, when cultivated through wet rice agriculture, has a remarkable fecundity; nitrogen is fixed by microscopic plants in a cycle which, when left unimpeded by so-called improved agricultural techniques, renews itself endlessly.

Every inch is known: either cultivated, or in small patches, many of which are on the banks of the deep river gorges, allowed to remain wild — in such treacherous places lurk the myriad subterranean spirits, who also need a home. Better, as the Balinese see it, they should be left a place alone to their own devices. And a regular bit of propitiation does no harm, in one aspect of the ways in which what secular observers might consider to be a superstitious and profitless series of rites, a perfectly viable, proven ecosystemic approach to a self-contained economy is maintained.

I reluctantly make my way back to my brick losman, falling in step with a group of people making their way into the fields. "Salamat pagi!" "Salamat PAGI!" — the morning greeting rises and falls with the cadence of a dance drama. The women carry phenomenal burdens upon their heads, negotiating the slippery trail between fields with the grace of gazelles and a singsong greeting to the odd foreigner out so early this morning.

The poise of the people reflects the care with which they maintain balance within their world: the parameters of culture, nature and spirituality all interacting in an intricate harmonious dance for centuries, to form a weaving so tight as to seem virtually impervious to outside influences. The flowers of this complex culture — the dance, visual arts and music — have so charmed outsiders, that they perhaps safeguard it from the destructive momentum of industrialization. Tourism is Indonesia's second highest earner of foreign income, and to kill the golden goose would seem foolish even in modern acculturating, "democratic" politics.

At home, Niwayan makes the morning offering as I sink into my veranda chair. She smiles shyly, intent on her task. She proffers a small square of banana leaf — in the center of which are a few grains of rice and a flower blossom, topped by a neatly balanced smoldering stick of incense — to the various gods which protect the household. She will soon take up the day's work, carrying loads of bricks, balanced on her head as gracefully as she now carries the offering basket. Up and down the stairs, countless times, she delivers the materials for another tourist bungalow being put up on their compound. I ask, "Did you carry the bricks for this building?" "Oh, yes," she smiles. And I look at the structure which keeps the daily rains from my head with renewed respect.

But on this day, I can't linger over my *kopi* Bali and pancake; it's time to go to the mountain. A ceremony at the oldest — and one of the most sacred — of Bali's countless temples will reach its climax today, and I have been invited to join the pilgrims who have, over the past five weeks, made the journey to the area's mother temple. Somewhat self-consciously, I am dressed in appropriate temple garb — sarong and lace blouse and an immense golden sash: a lovely effect which after the first few minutes does nothing but fall apart! However disheveled I feel, my escort, a young Balinese called Pung, is the picture of cool elegance in his white tunic and golden sarong. We hop into the jeep and away we go — off to the mountain that is his home.

Our journey is mutually beneficial. He needs to get back to his home village, Dadia, to discuss arrangements for his upcoming 22nd birthday, as well as bring his little sister, Ketut, down from the village to Ubud, where she will start junior high school. I want to escape the tourists in Ubud; we're both happy. I rent the jeep — he fantasizes he's Mario Andretti.

While Gunung Agung is unquestionably the "holiest of holies" to the Balinese, it is but one of a system of moun-

PHOTOGRAPHS BY BETH LISCHERON

tains that form a kind of geo-spiritual gridwork across the island. The nine major peaks are each assigned a direction (the eight cardinal points plus the center), colors, gods and goddesses, tools, weapons, and characteristics. The spiritual and ritual interweavings of aboriginal animism and the arrival sometime around the 9th century CE of Hindu god-kings, have over the centuries, achieved a bewildering involution, as some anthropologists have dubbed it, of belief and ceremony, virtually impossible and pointless to either untangle or analyse. And even the pseudo-scientific New Age Ley Hunters have involved themselves; as the writings of Jose Argulles attest, Gunung Agung is considered one of the major points of intersection for the many energy ley lines believed to encircle the planet.

It is towards the western chain of mountains that we are headed. Pohon, Lesong, Batukau and Sagauang run on an east-west axis, and flank the central plain which supports the vast majority of Bali's population of some 2.3 million. Remote Pura Lahur temple is perched high on the steep forested slope of the 2275-meter Gunung Batukau; it is one of the nine directional temples, and guards the west. After the most important mountains of Gunung Agung and Gunung Batur, (which are thought to be the twin halves of the sacred Hindu Mahameru, split when the mountain "landed" on Bali), Batukau ranks high on the scale of these Olympian games of sanctity.

Pung maneuvers the jeep through well-ordered prosperous villages, dodging dogs, chickens and children: the Balinese leg of the "white-knuckle Grand Prix" which I've experienced with other young South East Asian friends. The narrow roads are lined by temple standards and altar platforms every twenty meters or so; the excitement mounts as we approach as, beginning this very afternoon, some 2,000 pilgrims will carry the numerous visiting gods, "in town for the month," as it were, down to the sea at Tanah Lot temple for a ritual purification bath, and then back to their home temples.

We fall in line behind a scooter, roaring along at some 70 kliks an hour with a young woman perched elegantly side-saddle on the back, hanging onto the lidded square basket which contains her temple offering. We're getting close. Pung slows the jeep and edges into a parking lot already overflowing. Deserted food stalls line the street; for now, people make their way straight to the temple up the hill. The senses reel; the vivid contrasting colors of the women's clothing, the pungency of incense, floral oils and frangipani blossoms intermingle with the cool montane forest air. Already we can hear the *gamelan*, and soon we can see the temple complex itself: a collection of austere black-thatched buildings, mounting the slope. We pause to sluice cool water on our hands and feet before entering the first precinct of the complex.

A priest urges us to join the latest group of penitents, and we kneel and accept a basket of blossoms from which Pung passes me a few brilliant fragments, to raise between my joined fingers while the prayer is offered, and then to tuck into my hair. The priest intones through a loudspeaker while another walks among the throng, sprinkling holy water which we catch in our upturned hands. This is repeated three or four times, and we are ready to enter the main compound; already a crowd is at our backs, waiting patiently to take their turn for the ritual ablution.

I do feel strangely welcome; any glances the local people cast in my direction are of mild curiosity. I notice the only other foreigners here — a huddle of camera-heavy German tourists, who look even more awkward than I do, bulky in their borrowed sarongs and Birkenstocks. I feel a touch more "inside" — if only by contrast! But there's no time to indulge the serpent of smugness, as the gong has rung, and once again, Pung and I take our place with the crowd, kneeling on the concrete. The same procedure is repeated — flowers, prayers, holy water, and this time, a few grains of rice to press to our foreheads, to protect us against any malevolent spirits who might be lurking outside the sanctified grounds. Away we go. While it may seem perfunctory, it's clear from people's faces that they are deeply moved to be here. Many greet friends and family, and the spiritual and social functions of the occasion are seamlessly woven together.

Moving out through the grounds, we join the thousands of people who line the street, as the procession falls into place. Perambulatory gamelan instruments swing on bamboo poles, tall standards, prayer flags flutter

in the wind, to form a vanguard around the small statues, carried aloft as the temporary dwelling places of the visiting gods. The shrill high notes of the occasional flute pierce the hum of the waiting throng. Suddenly, they begin to move. Within moments, the parade that will take some four days to reach the ocean, cascades down the slope like a waterfall of rainbows. Young men walk hand in hand; mothers and daughters glide along arm in arm, their heads for once free of the ubiquitous offering baskets, for all has been left at the temple.

The ritual purification at the sea has its roots in the ubiquitous ceremonial use of holy water. In Bali, the mountains are the most sacred; within this spiritual geography, it follows that the sea is the most profane. However, as Fred Eiseman points out in his classic work on Balinese religion, *Sekala and Niskala*, the sea was the progenitor of the water of immortality, brought forth by a monumental collaborative effort of the gods and demons. When the gods won, the demons sank into the sea and under the earth; and perhaps for this reason the sea is, spiritually speaking, a perilous place. The fact that the ocean currents surrounding Bali create some of the most hazardous waters in the world surely reinforces the taboo. However, when approached with proper ceremony, the sea's waters also have purifying virtues, and are indispensible to the balance which must constantly be maintained. The gods will be cleansed and refreshed with holy water carried from different temples, as well as sanctified sea water, before returning to their resting places.

When asked, Balinese people will only say they get a good feeling when they think about Gunung Agung, although it is not a forgiving master (for this mountain is thought to be male). The two dragons which make their home in its caldera are infamous for their dramatic fits of pique when the appropriate propitiations fall a tad behind schedule, as was the case in 1963. The centennial ceremonies had been put off by a couple of years, and when the volcano registered its disapproval by massively erupting just days before the ritual was to occur, thousands of people lost their lives, homes and rice fields. However, "sudden poor, sudden rich": today the lava flow that destroyed so many rice terraces in its search for the sea, is being mined to provide asphalt for the ever-expanding network of roads that inexorably cover the island.

Scooting ahead of the procession by several days, a roaring afternoon's drive from Pura Luhur brings us to the sea at Tanah Lot; dismayed by the jarring raucousness after the natural sounds in the highlands, I am embarrased by the coarseness of the tourist trade, of which I am inevitably a part, simply by being here — as post-modern physics recognizes, you effect what you observe, simply by observing it. Tanah Lot is so picturesque as to be cloying; and the incongruity of the thought that, in another few days some 2,000 pilgrims will arrive here to ritually purify the gods, makes my mind reel. Sacred mountains, profane sea: the cultural prostitution to which Tanah Lot has been subjected shadows this unseen reality.

We pay our few shekels (donation for temple upkeep) and are immediately drowned in hordes of pushy tourists (at this time of year, mainly ethnic Chinese and German) and the pre-adolescent postcard and shell-necklace vendors of the daily dusk feeding frenzy. The temple itself is mercifully roped off to the tramp of heretic feet, but the sunset is mauled by a thousand shutters a day. We find a seat on the crest of the hill overlooking the tiny island fortress, and order warm Bintang and orange squash. Little sister Ketut (who hasn't said a word all day) seems overwhelmed by the noise and foreigners; Pung says she is sad at leaving Papa.

I am reminded of the scene in Mervyn Peake's underground classic *Gormenghast Trilogy* where an enterprising lunatic charges an entrance fee to other lunatics to sit on benches for daily cliff-side sunset viewing parties. Pung appreciates the irony, and I break off my story as a middle-aged German woman virtually steps on little Ketut to videotape the sunset for the relatives back home. She is surprised when I suggest (in German) that she's standing on someone, and although she makes a huffy apology, it's clear she thinks this tiny Balinese girl is merely in the way of the view.   ▲

BOROBUDUR

An Architectural Mandala of the Pilgrim's Path

TEXT BY HEINRICH ZIMMER
PHOTOGRAPHS BY OHKI AKIRA

BOROBUDUR

An Architectural Mandala of the Pilgrim's Path

THE CENTERPIECE of a Tibetan mandala — where Buddhas are grouped in a circle around one central Buddha — recalls, in a miniature form, the stepped terraces of Borobudur in Java. To which genre this impressive structure belongs is a question still unsettled. But however one may ultimately explain the figurative detail of this monumental edifice, one thing is clear: Borobudur must be regarded as the most impressive mandala the art of Buddhism has ever created in the visible world as a symbol of its truth.

The cryptic message of the wealth of forms confined within its symmetrical plan will never be deciphered if its grand design is understood merely as a self-contained construction — and that is how it does appear to an untutored eye. Borobudur is a place of pilgrimage. Both its elaborately figurative ornamentation and the architecture of its galleries and passageways that ascend one over the other must be understood in the light of their functional purpose; the intent is that the pilgrim make his way through the structure in spiraling ascent until he surmounts its topmost height. The purpose of Borobudur is to release a spiritual process in the pilgrim during his ascent through sculpture-embellished terraces to the unadorned summit, to bring about a complete transformation of his sense of being, a transformation by nature related to the activity of meditation as practiced by the adept of the Tibetan mandala described above. The austere geometric plan of its construction, in which peripheral rectangles serve as both the underpinning and enclosure for inner circles, seems designed to provide space for the parallel development, in some purposeful sequence, of an inner spiritual process and of the impressive concept of Being experienced during that process. In the same way, the figurative ornamentation seems

designed in its entirety to set off in its own fashion the rigorous geometry of the architectural complex, which is experienced inwardly and outwardly by the pilgrim as he is drawn into the series of terraces in his spiraling ascent. Between the structure's basic horizontal and vertical plan and its wealth of figural ornamentation, there exists the same absolute ideational relationship that obtains between the painted mandala's linear design and its world of figurative symbols.

The architectural design of Borobudur invites the pilgrim at his approach to undertake the physical effort of a circling climb that has a spiritual purpose. This function links Borobudur with older, related structures such as the Thūpārāma and Ambaśthala *dagobas* in Ceylon and the most ancient representatives of this type on the Indian mainland in Sānchi and Bharhut. But the physical activity they require and the spiritual activity they seek to engender are less complex than the activities initiated by the structure of Borobudur. Consequently, their architectural form and ornamentation are simpler. It is not surprising that the form and purpose of these ancient relic mounds undergo, in this late masterpiece of their historical development, a transformation into a mandala of monumental proportions. Here it is simply a matter of finding reflected in architecture what we discovered earlier in the technique of *samādhi*. In ancient Buddhist times, the use of the mandala as a means to Nirvāna was alien even to that technique. Within the Buddhist store of forms it appears as one more part of the inexorable absorbtion of Hindu ideas and symbols into Buddhism, an influx marking one of the major developments in the history of that religion. The magnificent structure of Borobudur, so often described, deserves special mention within the context of this present study because the initiate's visual and physical experience during the ascent constitutes a transposition of the Buddhist path of yoga, which utilizes the mandala technique, into three-dimensional tangibility — a concrete representation of the Buddhist path to Nirvāna.

Even the simple, unterraced plan of the domed structure in Bharhut is designed, with its relief-embelished enclosure, to engender a spiritual experience in the pilgrim treading his pious path in a clockwise direction; while his eyes are scanning the extensive series of reliefs with their scenes of the Buddha Śākyamuni's millennia-long journey to the Enlightenment which is Nirvāna, the pilgrim, even though far from his ultimate goal, as he traces the path of the "Shower of the Way," anticipates that path inwardly in contemplative meditation all the way to Nirvāna, here made tangible by the central domed structure. A pilgrimage to Bharhut presented the believer with the opportunity to experience palpably that legendary Buddhist tale recounted in the story of the Master's evolution, which from the remotest of ancient times has served the faithful as an exemplary model. Entering the sacred precincts of the stone enclosure, he would undertake to pace off, in the fullness of his knowledge, an exhaustive symbolic *imitatio* of the Buddha and, in following the Master through successive reincarnations from *samsāra* to Enlightenment, he would be supremely aware of the similarity to his own path and goal.

But at Borobudur the pilgrim's feet and spirit complete symbolically a different journey as they follow the spiral path to the very top, over terraces adorned with images and cupolas; from the phenomenal world of the senses, replete with forms, from the soul-flattening division of consciousness into the Self and the Other (that is, World), the pilgrim makes his way homeward to the Pure Void.

Four rectangular terraces with shivered outline, set one over the other, encompass a circular center section where three stepped circles descend, so to speak, toward them from the surmounting cupola at the peak. Their rectangular passageways are a world full of forms. From one end to the other embellished with pictorial friezes that are divided by pilasters in bas-relief and interrupted by four sets of stairs, they tell, on the lower two levels, the tale of the infinite number of Śākyamuni's lives: his path of preparation, his maturation to Buddhahood, his Enlightenment and proclamation of Truth. Their story corresponds to the motifs in the relief on the stone parapets of Bharhut. In them, the Pure Void presents itself as *nirmānakāya*. Happy though the content of the scenes along the passageway may be, its elevated sides create for the pilgrim a sense of confinement. For the outer balustrades of the lower galleries rise up like walls, and are adorned with images, as are the inner walls forming the base of the next terrace above. In pursuing his course, the observer finds himself inescapably hemmed in on every side by shapes and figures laden with meaning. Only high overhead does he perceive the blue presence of pure Emptiness.

Not until the pilgrim has reached the last of the multi-cornered terraces does the flood of imagery subside. The outer wall gives way here to a lower, cupola-crowned parapet without images, allowing the form-free vault of the heavens to emerge on the pilgrim's left. Beginning with the upper rectangular galleries, the pilgrim leaves the form-filled world of the senses behind, and enters the plane of form-filled inner vision: their decorative reliefs are devoted to the *dhyānibodhisattva* Samantabhadra, and to the coming of the Buddha Maitreya, whose glory has never been beheld by mortal eye, but only inwardly envisioned.

Samantabhadra, the "Kindly in Every Respect," is a favorite luminary in the Buddhist pantheon. As a *dhyānibodhisattva*, he belongs to the spheres of unfolding, which may be attained only through meditation (*dhyāna*). His name identifies him as the symbolic embodiment of Total Compassion, which is the only possible quality fit for him who possesses the highest Knowledge of the undifferentiated Emptiness of all names and forms. The *Śrīcakrasambhāra Tantra* tells of him in an ordinance for a devotional exercise dedicated to the "Bearer of the Diamond Weapon," Vajradhara. In Buddhist Tantrism he is one of the most exalted symbols representing the state of perfection, pure Emptiness. He is pictured as being

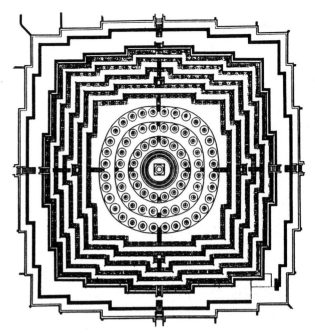

Top View of Borobudur

two-armed and in ecstatic union with his Śakti. Like Mahāsukha, he is a variant of a type of Śaivite image, a symbol of the not-yet-unfolded divine essence which, with its *śakti*, is both two and one.* The *Śrīcakrasambhāra Tantra* gives instructions concerning the path that lifts the Buddhist practitioner into Vajradhara's state: practice in the twofold pattern of meditation — in the paths of unfolding and subsequent enfolding of the unfolded — leads to two stages of *samādhi*; this is where the distinction between the seer and his vision vanishes, along with the division between the Self and the Other, the division of consciousness. In essence, these two levels of *samādhi* are the same, but they manifest themselves in different ways. The lower level is brought about by the will, using yoga techniques; the higher level breaks upon the adept spontaneously, but only after long training. In the latter case, Nirvāna has become the adept's second nature. Continuous cultivation of this highest of all states favors him with the ultimate wisdom (*prajnā*) that lies beyond all worldly knowledge. But part of this regimen is the perfect imitation of the exemplary path of the *dhyāni-bodhisattva* Samantabhadra, the "Kindly in Every Respect." If the goal is to achieve Nirvāna, then it is a matter of first adopting the bodhisattva's essential quality — the practicing of that love which extinguishes the unreal difference between the I and the Not-I — and then making that quality one's own second nature through practicing it.

---

* During the successful invasion of Hindu symbols into the Buddhist world of forms, Vajradhara assimilated the five highest *dhyānibuddhas*. His being embraces the more ancient Buddhas belonging to the four corners of the earth — Vajrasattva, Ratnasambhava, Amitābha, and Amoghasiddhi — who can combine themselves into a mandala around Vairocana, the "Sun"-Buddha, who forms the fifth one in the center.

After this, the way leads along the bodhisattva's twelve-step path to perfection — to Buddhahood. Total Compassion, the great virtue of Those Who Know, confers miraculous powers. These are the signs that signal one's entry into the diamond state of Vajradhara, whose hands bear the diamond Thunderbolt of Truth and the Bell of Compassion. As the very embodiment of Total Compassion, Samantabhadra is the adept's noblest escort on the path to the Enlightenment that is Nirvāna.

Continuing upward past this elaborately figurative, relief-studded part of Borobudur, the pilgrim arrives at the upper circular terraces. Here, seventy-two smaller cupolas made of fretted stone are clustered around one large, raised, centrally located cupola whose surface is completely unperforated. In this area, the extravagant number of sculptural and ornamental forms has vanished: all those images which drew their subjects — humans, animals, and flowers — from both the external, sensual world and its reflection in inner vision. Here a whole range of Nirvāna symbols juts up, row upon row, into the pure void of the celestial dome that arches above in a vivid, uniform blue, extending from the zenith down to the surrounding horizon of mountains and jungle. But the rows of latticed cupolas, ranged above one another on the three ascending circular terraces, were still not symbols of the Supreme State, since each one contains a Buddha figure that the stone fretwork does not quite hide from view. The cupolas are emblems of the higher worlds of form-free contemplation that constitute the stage just prior to Nirvāna. Above them all towers the crown of the whole edifice, a massive central dome. This architectural feature also contains a Buddha, but the figure is completely concealed from view behind an all-enclosing, unperforated, arched exterior. The form of the surrounding latticed cupolas represents an intermediate stage between the massive central dome and the cupolas of the lower balustrades that are cut in half, as it were, to form niches exposing their *dhyanibuddhas* fully to view. The latticed cupolas form a connecting link between those lower symbolic forms, perceived in inner vision, and the symbol of blissful Being situated at the very top. Placed halfway between these two types of symbols, the cupolas guide the pilgrim, by means of architectural forms and the ideas underlying them, from the precincts of form-filled inner vision right up to eternal Nirvāna, to that one single cupola in the center of all the others; they are images of the form-free, transitional stage between the spheres of inner visions, which do have names and forms, and that nameless and formless state which conceals itself from itself.

In the devotional ascent demanded of the pilgrim by Borobudur's upward-spiraling passageways, he is presented with more than the opportunity simply to imitate Śakyamuni in body and mind. Here, Pure Emptiness, which human consciousness divides into the Self and the world of forms, returns to Its true state; It ascends symbolically through the figure-filled world of visions and the senses, then passes through the realm of form-free contemplation up to Its Nirvāna that has no beginning; Emptiness casts aside, one after the other, the fetters of Ignorance that conceal the true nature of Emptiness from Itself; the fetters are left lying behind, as are the lower terraces during the ascent; Emptiness becomes the extinguished Buddha, without name or form; It becomes the Emptiness that is the essence of all phenomena. The whole of Borobudur acts as a *yantra* for the external, tangible surroundings, in which the pilgrim finds his homeward path leading from the mandala's outer reaches — which are various forms of consciousness, the world, and the Self — toward its heart: to the pilgrim's own true, ineffable essence.

The meaning of Borobudur is basically found in the way the symbol of the Buddha image is presented: it is placed in a sequence of stages progressing upward from the structure's lowest levels to its summit. In the reliefs on the narrative and descriptive friezes, the symbol of the Buddha is shown interacting with human beings and the world of nature. On the next higher level, in the cupolas opened to form niches, the Buddha symbol, in disengaged solitude, is visible to the pilgrim who gazes up to it in contemplation. It is totally visible. In the latticed cupolas on the topmost, circular terraces, the Buddha is at the point of disappearing from view, just as a Buddhist yogi's mind, in form-free contemplation, is at the thin line dividing conscious from unconscious. The domed structure at the peak conceals the symbol entirely. On each of these four levels, the initiate comprehends the identical nature of the Buddha symbol. And he understands that it signifies nothing less than his own essential, innermost being, which is Nirvāna and Enlightenment, even though these are still shrouded in Ignorance. He develops the lower sphere of sensual perception by walking through Borobudur's galleries and allowing its world of symbolic images to unfold before his eyes. He then lifts himself up above that realm of *nirmānakāya*, transcending and melting it away by progressing to the intermediate level and entering the levels of the symbols of inner vision. But this realm of *sambhogakāya* is also left behind and transcended when he arrives, by way of the circular terraces of form-free vision, at the topmost symbol of Nirvāna. Confronted with this ultimate symbol, he experiences his very self as *vajrakāya*, and knows: "*Om:* my essence is diamond. I am the pure diamond of all pure adamantine Essence." ▲

From Artistic Form and Yoga in the Sacred Images of India *by Heinrich Zimmer, © 1984 by Princeton University Press. Excerpt reprinted with permission of Princeton University Press.*

BUILDING THE SACRED MOUNTAIN

Tsukuriyama in Shinto Tradition

造り山

1　Groundbreaking ceremony for the Indian pavilion at Osaka Expo. (*Mainichi Daily News*, June 27, 1969)

PRIME MINISTER Indira Gandhi came to Osaka in 1969 to quiet the earth. Through the ritual act of cutting grass with a sickle, she commenced construction of the Indian pavilion for Expo '70. This Indian ceremony was particularly appropriate for the occasion because it is similar (though not directly related) to *karizome no gi*, the first part of the common Japanese groundbreaking rite. The Japanese audience certainly felt the allusion to the whole of the Shinto ceremony, which continues with the breaking and plowing of a mound of sand.

The *jichinsai* or earth-quieting rite is performed by a Shinto priest before the construction of virtually every building in Japan. What it signifies can be interpreted in various ways. Many students of religion would view it as a symbolic reenactment of the divine creation of the world. I believe it is a reiteration of the human act of clearing and occupying land, which was profoundly important in many agricultural societies and left deep cultural imprints. (For example, the German word *raum* (space) and the English room come from the verb *roden* which means "to make a clearing in the forest.") Specifically, the artificial mound in this ubiquitous Japanese ceremony seems to derive from the Shinto *shimeyama* (signifying-mountain) which is fabricated as a place for a deity to descend to, and which in turn originated as a mark of human occupation.

The sacred mountains and pseudo-mountains which play such a large role in indigenous Japanese rituals are usually *tsukuriyama* (造り山), (mountains built by the human hand as sacred objects). The artificial mountain, as we shall see below, is the original genre of the sacred mountain. Let us examine how the belief developed that a deity would take up residence in a tsukuriyama.

MOUNTAIN DEITIES

In the beginning, the gods created the mountains and the mountains were gods. So say the oldest records of Japanese mythology in the high tradition, the histories compiled for the imperial court in the early 8th century. Both of them, *Kojiki* and *Nihonshoki*, contain two relevant legends from "the age of the gods."

1. The first divine couple, Izanagi-no-mikoto and Izanami- no-mikoto, circumambulate the central pillar of heaven and give birth first to the islands of Japan, then to the sea, the trees, the wind, the plains, etc. These were produced in the form of deities which embody and protect the phenomena. After the deity of the trees and before the deity of the plains, Ōyamatsuna-kami (Great Mountain-Ruler Deity) is born.

2. Izanami dies from burns sustained during the birth of her final child, the fire deity. Out of anger, Izanagi kills the fire deity, and eight mountain deities (or mountains) spring forth from its body.

The first legend is of course an element of a cosmogony, an account of the creation of a universe called Yamato. The second probably refers to volcanic eruptions, which in prehistoric times gave rise to new mountains on land and in the sea.

2 The three steps of the earth-quieting rite (*jichinsai* or *tokoshizume*): cutting *sakaki* evergreen sprigs with a sickle (*karizome* or *ugachizome*); opening a conical sand mound with a hoe (*kuwaire*); and plowing the sand with a spade (*sukiire*). The symbolic mountain of sand (*morizuna* or *imisuna*) is placed off-center in the sacred rectangle marked by bamboo poles and a shimenawa straw rope. The central point is reserved for a *himorogi*, a temporary altar to a Shinto deity. (From *Kenchiku no gishiki to saiten*, Kashima Kenkyujō Shuppankai, 1975)

MORE FERTILE than those brief official accounts is what might be called the lower tradition, the body of beliefs which make up Shinto folk religion. In this sphere, the Shinto *yamanokami* or mountain deity[1] plays multiple and pervasive roles.

In many parts of Japan it is believed to have a dual existence, as a mountain deity in winter and a field deity (*tanokami*) in summer. It is ritually brought down in the spring to dwell in the fields and watch over the crops until autumn, when it is ritually brought back to the mountains. (There are variations: In parts of Kyushu and Okinawa it is an ocean deity in the winter. On the Noto Peninsula it hibernates in the farmhouse within the final bit of the rice harvest.)[2] The annual transformations may originate from an ancient belief in a grain spirit which died at harvest time and was reborn in the spring, and was associated with the birth and death cycle of humans, which in turn came to be intimately connected to the growth of rice.[3]

In ancient times the word *yama* (mountain) signified the place beyond the village, the abode of animals and the source of wood and edible plants. Its basic aspect was not the landform or summit, but the forest. In fact, "forest" survives today as one meaning of the word yama and its written character, and there are many old documents in which the usual character for forest is written for "yama." Studies by Yanagita Kunio and associated folklorists indicate that a deity known as yamanokami is in no sense felt to be the mountain as such. Indeed, in agricultural rituals the deity is brought down in a tree (this is its temporary abode or *yorishiro*).

The yamanokami of modern times has been described as a syncretic deity with four identifiable aspects which date from various eras:[4]

1. The guardian deity of hunters, foresters and wood-

3　Painting from 1234 of a mountain in completely natural state, marked only by a torii, which is regarded as a deity-body. (From Kageyama Haruki, *Shintaizan*, Gakuseisha, 1973)

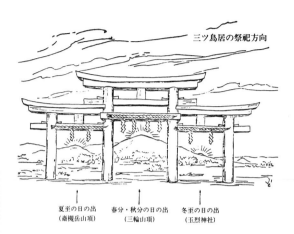

4　Three-bay torii at the foot of sacred Mt. Miwa, in relation to the extreme annual positions of the rising sun. The modern scholar who discovered these correspondences regards it as a seasonal clock.

workers, the patron of animals and the lord of the forest. Offerings are made to her in connection with the taking of game or timber, and to request protection in the forest. She communicates with people through the medium of a boar, monkey, hare, fox, etc. Female gender is usually ascribed, and women are not welcome in the realm of this jealous deity. This aspect seems to have originated with the Jōmon culture of hunting and gathering (to 200 BCE).

2. As the deity of agriculture, the yamanokami enters the fields, which in their earliest form were patches of forest cleared for temporary use. With the spread of arable land and the decrease of forests, rituals developed to carry the deity, in the vessel of a tree or branch, to the fields. In that vicinity it becomes visible in such forms as leaves or flowers placed where water enters the fields; a scarecrow-type guardian (*kagashi* = mountain-guide child); a sheaf of rice ears (*hokake*) hung at the village shrine or family altar; or a sack of seed-rice kept at home through the winter. This aspect probably dates from the Yayoi period (200 BCE – 250 CE) when metallurgy and wet rice cultivation began.

3. Through an association of the blessings of family and village ancestral spirits with the blessings of the field deity, the yamanokami took on the aspect of collective ancestral deity. The ancestral sprits were likewise believed to make periodic visits to the villages, generally at the new year and thee midsummer Bon festival. The mountains took on an aura of awe as the belief developed that they were the abode of the sprits of the dead. However, there is by no means a complete identity of the collective ancestral spirit and the yamanokami.

4. It is also to some extent the yamanokami which is carried to the home at the new year, via the pine branch

which is placed for two weeks outside the gate or doorway (*kadomatsu* = gate-pine). One name by which it is known is *toshigami*, which now means new-year-deity but in ancient times meant the deity of the harvest, by which the years were counted.

The bringing of this combined mountain/field/ancestral deity into the village for veneration once each year, usually at harvest time, led to a division of the village sanctuary into three: a mountain shrine, a field shrine and a village shrine. The early phases of Shinto (Nature Shinto and Storehouse Shinto) emphasized three elements which especially reflect the agricultural aspect of the mountain deity: the mountain with its water sources, the rice paddies fed by that water, and the human settlement which depends on both of them for survival.

In nature-oriented folk Shinto, then, there is no sacred mountain in the sense of a physical manifestation of a deity. The mountain territory is simply the temporary dwelling place of a non-stationary deity or deities. The mountains may be entered and their fruits enjoyed, as long as the ritual conventions are followed. The yamanokami are in essence a set of faces for the mysterious regenerative powers of nature. The rituals which express hope or gratitude for their blessings function also as brakes on exploitation, pointing to an awareness of the need to sustain the resources of nature for future generations.

SACRED NATURAL MOUNTAINS

A new strain of Shinto, characterized by a substantial shrine building to house a *goshintai* (August Deity Body), developed from about the 7th century. The first such deity halls resembled older raised-floor rice storehouses,

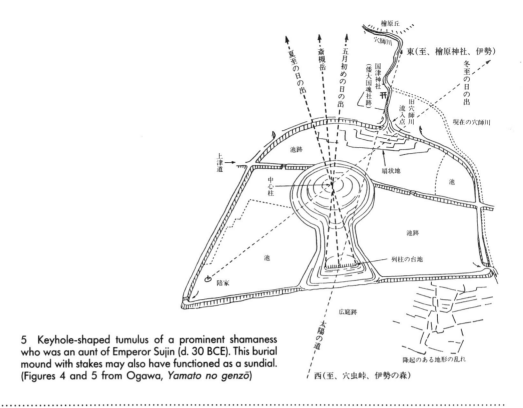

夏至の日の出　斎槻岳　五月初めの日の出　東(至、檜原神社、伊勢)

檜原丘
穴師川
国津神社
(倭大国魂神社跡)
旧穴師川流入点
現在の穴師川
冬至の日の出

上津道
中心柱
池跡
扇状地
池

陪冢
池
池跡
列柱の台地
太陽の道
広庭跡
隆起のある地形の乱れ

西(至、穴虫峠、伊勢の森)

5 Keyhole-shaped tumulus of a prominent shamaness who was an aunt of Emperor Sujin (d. 30 BCE). This burial mound with stakes may also have functioned as a sundial. (Figures 4 and 5 from Ogawa, *Yamato no genzō*)

which hark back to the agricultural developments of the Yayoi period, and also imitated the architecture of Buddhist temples, which were built in Japan from the 6th century.

Naturally the physical and ritual structures of Deity-Hall Shinto were also strongly influenced by the already-ancient cult of the composite, dynamic mountain deity. While the celebrated early shrines of Ise, Izumo, Sumiyoshi and Kamigamo (Kyoto) each have distinctively designed deity halls, they have in common the vital ritual connection to the mountain from which the deity is believed originally to have descended. Even today, the deities are periodically brought down anew for the duration of the main festivals. Another type of early shrine, notably those at Suwa, has no deity hall but is centered on an *ombashira* (August Pillar), a log from the sacred mountain related to the shrine.[5]

Eventually the concept of the fixed, sacred space was applied to the mountain itself, in shrines where the goshintai is considered to be present without a deity hall. This is the *shintaizan* (mountain as deity body), and here the whole natural mountain is indeed held sacred, with entry forbidden unless one completes special purifications. The best known of the many *shintaizan* in Japan is Mt. Miwa, at the southeast corner of the Yamato basin, which is marked by an unusual triple torii.

Sacred and ordinary mountains are experientially different to the believer, but phenomenologically identical to the non-believer. What converts a mountain into a *shintaizan* is a particular system of religious programming and signage. I suspect that the mountain-as-deity-body was a relatively late fixation of the originally dynamic mountain/field/ancestor deity. It parallels the way in which many other Shinto deities are regarded as fixed to such features as waterfalls, wells, rocks and even islands.

There is some evidence that the identity of the deity and the mountain was a late or lateral trend. One scholar has concluded that the deity-body mountains at the center of the Kasuga, Hachiman, Sannō and Kumano cults originated from fusions of Shinto and Buddhist practices no earlier than the 7th century, and were superimposed upon agricultural or ancestral shrines of much older origin.[6] Also, over time various Shinto mountain shrines were built within precincts which were first demarcated as Buddhist temple grounds, as part of the extensive trend within both religions to seek the protection of each other's deities, and in some cases to pair or merge them.

In sum, neither the official creation myths, nor the common belief in mountain deities, nor the mountain-as-deity-body point to an indigenous Japanese veneration of natural mountain as deities.

SACRED ARTIFICIAL MOUNTAINS

The sacredness of human artifacts may be more informative than the sacredness of nature, for they present a definite physical trail of the human mind at work. Mountain-type artifacts which are traditionally sacred in Japan include graves and certain Shinto ritual objects.

On the popular level there is a vague linkage between mountains in general and the sanctity of departed spirits. Yama (mountain/forest) has been a synonym for "grave" since ancient times. This may be connected to the small mound which is made when burying a corpse. Probably it was also linked to the widespread former custom of dual graves, a burial grave (*umebaka*) for the physical remains, and a visiting grave (*mairibaka*) for memorial worship. In the oldest known practice, the burial grave was never vis-

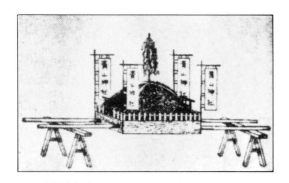

6, 7 Mountain *yorishiro* used today as temporary abodes for deities during festivals. Aoyama-san ("honorable blue mountain"), a portable shrine made of cedar needles, is carried on the shoulders of children during the annual Aoyama Festival at Matsumoto (from Hafuri, *Yama no utsurikawari*). The model of Mt. Fuji is a portable shrine carried in the August 26 fire festival at Yoshida, Yamanashi. The torii with a sanctifying *shimenawa* rope and the ritual offerings indicate that it is regarded as a sacred mountain.

8 These *shimeyama* (man-made mountains that mark the descent of a deity), constructed for imperial enthronement ceremonies during the Heian era, are among the oldest on record. They were about 10 meters high, and built around a central pine tree. Representatives of each of the two localities which prepared the Daijōsai rice offering fabricated a mountains in the Shinsenen garden and carried it into the Imperial Palace grounds. (From Mishina Akihide, *Shinwa no sekai (Nihon no rekishi, dainihen)*, Shūeisha, Tokyo, 1974)

ited after the official period of mourning.[7] Burial graves tended to be at rather inaccessible mountain/forest sites, which may have given rise to the common belief that mountains are the land of the dead.

From the dawn of history through the 7th century, every ruler of Japan was buried in an artificial mountain precinct called *misasagi* (August Tumulus) or *sanryo* (Imperial Mountain). The size and shape varied considerably. From about 215 BCE to 580 CE, the imperial tumulus was a large hill with two to four terraces, surrounded by a wide moat. The largest known example, 500 meters in length, is the mausoleum of Emperor Nintoku (d. 399) near present-day Osaka. Typical of its time, it is keyhole-shaped ("square in front, round behind," as the Japanese describe it) with a torii at the front, and from ground level it resembles an ordinary Shinto sanctuary centering on a sacred mountain. Tumulus construction ceased when the imperial household switched to Buddhist funeral rites, beginning with the cremation of Empress Jitō in 703. It was not until the passing of Emperor Meiji in 1912, during the ascendance of State Shinto, that the practice was renewed in accord with ancient procedures.

The origin of the gigantic imperial burial mounds is not clear, nor is the significance of the unique keyhole shape. There may well be some linkage to Korean and ultimately Chinese models. A leading specialist in the design of Yamato sacred sites believes they were shaped and oriented to function as seasonal clocks for farming, perhaps in connection with a solar cult imported by Korean artisans and shamans, and the moats served in part as reservoirs for irrigating rice paddies.[8] We may learn more if and when the government allows serious investigation of the tumuli. But from everything that is known so far, it seems reasonable to regard them primarily as graves. Spectacular though they may be, they are sacred in the way that all burial sites are considered sacrosanct in many cultures. In the end they are graves rather than sacred mountains.

AN ARTIFICIAL MOUNTAIN is used in certain Shinto rituals as the *yorishiro*, the temporary abode to which a deity is believed to descend when it is invoked for a festival ceremony. Japanese folklore and Shintoism scholars generally believe that the mountain yorishiro originated as a fabricated model of a natural sacred mountain. The theology behind this idea is that a deity residing in the "high plain of heaven" can be called down by people to the summit of a "divinely selected fire mountain," and then guided down (usually in a tree) to the festival site. This gives rise to the theory that the vessel prepared as its abode during the festival is an iconic mountain. This type of yorishiro has been called a *shimeyama* or signifying mountain (標山 , also pronounced *shirushiyama*), that is, a mountain which marks the temporary presence of a deity.[9]

Two portable shrines which are used today in local festivals are frequently cited as evidence for the theory that such tsukuriyama or built mountains originated as models of natural sacred mountains. These and other examples are shown in Figures 6 – 9.

Over time, "yama" has become a very flexible term indeed in its application to Shinto sacred artifacts. Objects known as yama include not only natural and artificial sacred mountains, but also movable and immovable artificial mountains, and there are even artificial yorishiro

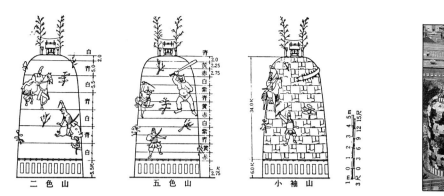

二色山　　　　　　五色山　　　　　　　小袖山

9　The *okiyama* (placed mountains) at the Idate Hyōzu Shrine in Himeji are related to three sacred mountains in the vicinity. Standing 16 meters high and 9 meters across at the base, they are reconstructed every 21 years during the Mitsuyama Daisai (Great Festival of the Three Mountains), held most recently in April 1993.

. . . .

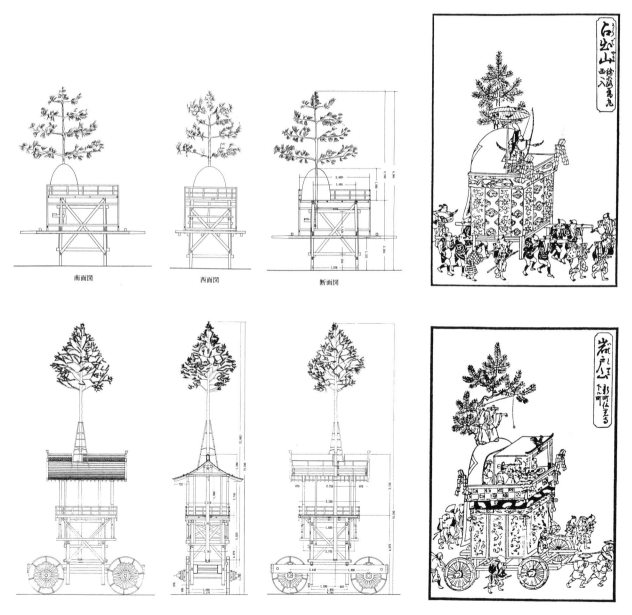

南面図　　　　　　西面図　　　　　　　断面図

10, 11　Floats used in the 1100-year-old Gion Festival of Kyoto are known collectively as yama, and also broken into the two categories of yama (technically *kakiyama* or *katsugiyama* = carried mountain), and *hoko* (halberds, named for the pointed wooden pillar at the top, and related by origin to the shimeyama in Figure 8). An ongoing shift in the usage of the word "*yama*" is illustrated by the Iwatoyama float at the right, one of three which resemble the pulled, wheeled hoko floats but are classed as yama along with the simpler, smaller and older, portable floats, which are topped by miniature mountains. The only hint of a mountain on the pulled floats is the pine or cedar branches at the top, harking back to the tree-type yorishiro. (Woodcuts from 1844 and structural drawings from the 1960s, from *Gion Matsuri*, Kyoto Bunka Kanko-kyoku, 1968)

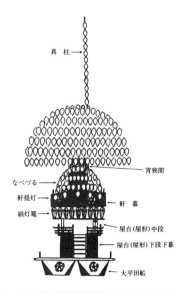

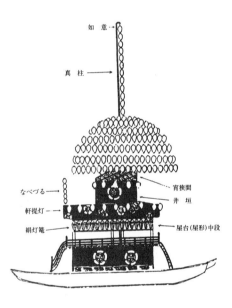

12 During the Tsushima Festival of the Tsu Islands, villagers celebrate the reinvocation of the deity with a *danjiri* (pleasure vehicle) made of lights and floated on a river at night. This mountain of light consists of 336 paper lanterns around a central pillar of 12 lanterns, mimicking the oldest known form of the artificial sacred mountain.

GÜNTER NITSCHKE

which do not resemble a natural mountain but are, or once were called yama. The devolution of the yama form is caught in action in the classification of the floats of the Gion Festival, as explained at Figure 10. Various wheeled floats (*dashi*) and covered performance stages (*yatai*) are among other types of objects used in local festivals which are known to have derived from the mountain yorishiro. Generally speaking, the mountain as yorishiro tends to disappear under a growing exuberance of decorations. Although the original meaning of the mountain as archetypal sacred artifact is often long forgotten, it still serves as a powerful visual image in such unexpected forms as a mountain of light.

FROM ARTIFICIAL TO NATURAL SACRED MOUNTAIN

Returning to the accepted genealogy which claims that the artificial sacred mountain is descended from the natural sacred mountain, I believe that it is seriously flawed, and that it has the whole story backwards. To begin with, there are some simple facts which it cannot explain. Moreover, it is associated with a conceptual framework which deserves to be questioned.

The facts: First, there are many yorishiro fabricated for Shinto rituals which have neither any visual resemblance, nor any historical or etymological linkage to a physical mountain. Actually, there are far more yorishiro made in the likeness of a pillar than of a mountain. Second, what delineates a Shinto artifact as sacred, whether or not it looks like a mountain, is not the shape but the straw rope (*shimenawa*) which is ritually placed around it or over its entrance. The so-called yama which do not look like mountains are visually recognizable as yorishiro only by these sacred ropes. Third, there are yorishiro with a shape clearly imitative of a natural mountain (e.g. Figures 10 and 12), which have no relation to an existing sacred mountain or a mountain deity. These data suggest that sacredness may flow from human artifacts to natural mountains.

Conceptually, the primacy of the natural sacred mountain accords with a theory of religion which has become an established paradigm of human evolution. Seminally articulated by Mircea Eliade, this theory holds that religious/metaphysical awareness precedes and inspires the building and making of objects. "The work of the gods, the universe, is repeated and imitated by men on their own scale." By this interpretation, a constructed dwelling, sanctuary, grave, city or even a country constitutes an *imago mundi*, an analogy of the builder's conception of cosmogony. "The creation of the world becomes the archetype of every human gesture, whatever its plane of reference may be."[10]

Research by myself and others into the origin of human building and the relation between building and religion indicates that the Eliadian picture is only part of the panorama of history, and not the earliest part. My thesis is that archaic people slowly explored and mentally contructed (that is, named) the wider world and ultimately the universe in analogy to what they had first learned when occupying and building their immediate surroundings. This approach, known as architectural anthropology or the anthropology of building, begins by looking at the actions of an a-religious (not anti-religious) culture which preceded those of the religious culture with which Eliade

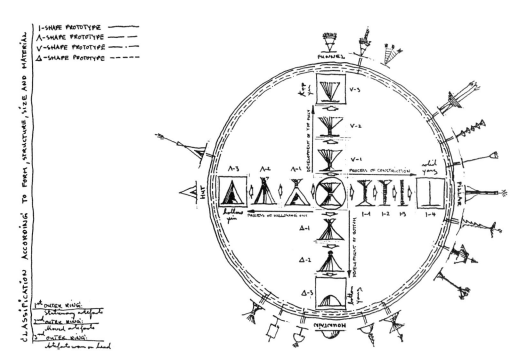

13 Formal typology of present-day sacred Shinto artifacts, illustrating the theory that they derive from an archetypal bundle (*shime*) of grass. The prototypes are the pillar (constricted bundle), the hut (hollowed bundle), the mountain (bottom-flared bundle), and the funnel (top-flared bundle). (From Nitschke, "Shime...")

is chiefly concerned. Those actions of *homo faber* have a great influence on the actions and beliefs of *homo religiosus*.[11]

In the study of Shinto rituals, several Japanese ethonologists have noted that mountains, pillars, simple huts, and other objects can hold identical roles despite differences of shape. On the hypothesis that all of these deity vessels may have a common source, I made an exhaustive survey of the forms, names and ritual manipulations of Shinto sacred artifacts, and suggested a general theory of their origin.[12] The main points are:

• Shinto yorishiro derive from what were originally markers constructed to signify occupation of land or ownership of property. Over the course of time, these marks of human territory were sacralized or deified.[13]

• The etymology of one of the oldest indigenous Japanese words, *shime* (which in verb form means "binding," "occupying," and "signifying"), points to a knot or bundle of grass or other plants as the simplest and likely the oldest form of the occupation marker.

• The archetypal shime or bundle can be theoretically construed to be the origin of four formal prototypes of the artifacts common in Shinto ritual: the pillar, the hut, the mountain, and the funnel. Nowadays most sacred artifacts have a composite character combining two or more of those forms.

In terms of the sacred mountain, these are the consequences of my theory: The sacred mountain which is *built* as the temporary abode of a deity seems to precede the concept of the natural sacred mountain, and the *secular* built mountain (as either an occupation marker or a simple dwelling) seems to precede the sacred built mountain. But this model of the evolution of Shinto sacred

artifacts does much more than simply remove the built mountain from the shadow of the natural mountain. It proposes that the people of Japan originally constructed their own deities and continue to do so, retaining control over where and when they visit certain artifacts.

IN THE BEGINNING, then, humans created their space, and later they created their gods. Such is the thrust of architectural anthropology, and such also is the approach of Jean Gebser, an anthropologist whose works offer a paradigm of human cultural development which is more expansive than the religion-centered paradigm of Eliade. Gebser posits five stages of the evolution of human consciousness: 1) the archaic stage, characterized by a sense of undifferentiated unity between self and nature, and hence completely without deities; 2) the magical stage, with the emergence of a self differentiated from nature, and the appearance of idols and rituals; 3) the mythical stage, where polytheism and mysteries take central cultural roles; 4) the mental stage, with the full-fledged ego in opposition to the body and to nature, where monotheism and ceremonies appear; and 5) the state of transparent consciousness where a new unity is reached, as in the original practice of Buddhism.[14]

At the primal stage of consciousness, a crucial part of human life is the creation of space — making territory, clearing space, building a home. No doubt one of the earliest constructive skills was binding, and this seems particularly apt in assessing the earliest period of Japanese culture, c. 8,000 to 200 BCE, which is called the "rope pattern" (Jōmon) period, after the knot and braid designs which were commonly impressed on artifacts with straw ropes.

In the development of language, the precedence of

14 Hypothetical reconstruction of a Jōmon dwelling. (Musashino Museum)

15 Shrine of a *yashikigami* (ancestral deity of house and grounds) at Hōki village in Nagasaki. In an annual rite of renewal, the mountains receive a fresh layer of reed grass and a new shimenawa rope. This is a pure example of the mountain prototype in Figure 13.

GÜNTER NITSCHKE

human action over contemplation has been asserted by the etymologist Jost Trier. He concludes that in the Indo-European language family generally, "analogies are drawn from things made to things natural." Concerning building in particular, he wrote, "The human dwelling is the greatest source of analogies made by ancient man. It metaphorically supplies a part of the language which is later used for the understanding of the world, the cosmos as a whole..."[15]

No such critical investigation has been made into Japanese etymology, but along the same lines it is tempting to suggest that the word for mountain (*yama*) could have derived from the word for house (*ya*). Hypothetical reconstructions of Jōmon dwellings do look like tiny mountains, consisting entirely of a roof (*yane* = house-root). The word for a Shinto shrine, *yashiro*, originally meant house-substitute or house-enclosure. The oldest surviving examples of yashikigami shrines made from reeds or straw have the same sort of mountain-of-grass form as the hypothetical Jōmon dwelling. Could the mountains have taken their very name from built dwellings and shrines? Likewise, the earliest form of the Chinese ideograph for "tree" resembles a bundle more than a natural tree, and it is quite conceivable that it originally depicted a human artifact.[16]

Shintoism as practiced in Japan today belongs mainly to the magical and mythical stages of the evolution of consciousness, with roots running deeply into the earlier, archaic stage. The farmer worships a mountain deity in a rite of spring, the priest breaks ground by cutting into branches and an artifical mountain, the emperor venerates a tree cut from a sacred mountain and buried beneath a shrine as a symbol of a sun deity. In this day and age, can one really believe in those rituals? It is fitting, in a way, that they are generally thought to be founded on a mystical, mythico-magical sacredness of "nature." Yet the realities of nature and society today cry out for a recognition of the fundamental role of human actions in naming and manipulating the world. Knowing that we have fabricated our deities may help us to quiet the Earth. ▲

NOTES

1. The Shinto term *kami*, often translated as "god" or "gods," does not denote an omniscient, omnipotent personal God, but rather a series of invisible, superhuman powers and energies residing in various natural phenomena such as the sun, a waterfall, a tree or a rock. "Deity" seems best to translate this elusive concept, which belongs partly to the magical and partly the mythical levels of human consciousness. See D.C. Holtom, "The Meaning of Kami" in *Monumenta Nipponica*, Vol. III and IV, Tokyo, 1940-41.
2. On mountain/field deity rituals, see Gunter Nitschke, "Daijosai and Shikinensengu," Parts I and II in *Kyoto Journal*, No. 12 (Fall 1989) *and* 13 (Winter 1990): II, p. 18-19. For more in English on rituals and deities of rice production, see Hirayama Toshihiro, "Seasonal Rituals connected with Rice Culture" and Naoe Hiroji, "A Study of Yashiki-gami, the Deity of House and Grounds," both in Richard M. Dorson, ed., *Studies in Japanese Folklore*, Kennikat Press, Port Washington NY, 1973.
3. Hori Ichirō, "Mysterious Visitors from the Harvest to the New Year" in Dorson, 1973.
4. Nelly Nauman, "Yama no Kami, Die japanische Berggottheit" in *Asian Folklore Studies*, Vol. XXII, Tokyo, 1963.
5. On deity-hall designs and rituals, see Nitschke, 1990, p. 20-21; 1989, p. 11.
6. Kageyama Haruki, *The Arts of Shinto*, Weatherhill/Shibundo, Tokyo, 1973.
7. Mogami Takayoshi, "The Double Grave System" in Dorson, 1973.
8. Ogawa Kōzo, *Yamato no genzō* [The Original Image of Yamato], Yamato Shoʾō, Tokyo, 1973.
9. Hafuri Miyashizu, *Yama no utsurikawari* [Transformations of the Mountain], *Kōza Nihon fuzokushi, daijūhen*, Tokyo, 1959. His summary of the accepted theory of mountain yorishiro is the source for the terms *shimeyama/shirushiyama* and *tsukiyama*.
10. Mircea Eliade, *The Sacred and the Profane*, Harper & Row, 1961, pp. 35, 45.
11. Early works in English in the area of architectural anthropology include Joseph Rykwert, *The Idea of a Town: Anthropology of Urban From in Rome, Italy and the Ancient World* (1976), Kevin Lynch, *What Time is This Place* (1972), Nadar Ardalan, *The Sense of Unity: The Sufi Tradition in Persian Architecture* (1971), Jeffrey Meyer, *Peking as Sacred City* (1976), and Nitschke, "Shime..." (see below). In Japanese, there are books from the early 1970s by Izumi Seeichi, Yoshizaka Takamasa, Ishige Naomichi and Ueda Atsushi. Recent books include Nold Egenter, *Architectural Anthropology — Research Series,* Structura Mundi, Lausanne, 1993 (8 volumes, trilingual English/German/French); and Gunter Nitschke, *From Shinto to Ando: Studies in an Architectural Anthropology in Japan,* Academy Group Ltd., London, 1993
12. Gunter Nitschke, "Shime — Binding/Unbinding: An Investigation into the Origins of, and the Relationships between, Human Building, Human Sign-Systems and Religious Beliefs in East Asia," *Architectural Design*, Vol. XLIV 12, London, 1974.
13. See Kurata Ichirō, "Sen'yūhyo no hattatsu" [The Development of Occupation Marks] in *Keizai to minkan denshū*, Tōkai Shobō, 1948.
14. Jean Gebser, *Ursprung und Gegenwart* [Origin and Present, Volume 2 of the Collected Works], Novalis Verlag, Schaffhausen, 1986 (my translation).
15. Jost Trier, *Lehm — Etymologien zum Fachwerk* [Clay — Etymologies concerning Half-timber Construction], Simons Verlag, 1951, p. 21; and *Holz* [Wood], 1952, p. 54 (my translations).
16. Nitshke, "Shime...," p. 757.

The author is indebted to Stephen Suloway, for editorial collaboration.

DRAGON-CAVES & WATER-FLAMES

In Praise of Chinese Pagodas

The Great Pagoda (Da ta), 11th century, near Ning Cheng, Inner Mongolia. Photograph by Marilyn Gridley

RED-MOUNTAIN County government officials commandeered forty jeeps for the academicians' pilgrimage over non-existent roads to the famous and newly restored White Pagoda in eastern Inner Mongolia. This sacred symbol of Sumeru, the Buddhist World Mountain, with sparkling "water-flame" (*shui-yan*) at its pinnacle, is one of many pagodas that have survived in various states of preservation since the precursors to the Mongols built them in the tenth and eleventh centuries A.D. This pre-Mongol tribe, Khitan (source for the word Cathay), worshipped the sun before embracing Buddhism which, in promising victory in any endeavor undertaken with its blessing, held much appeal for Khitan rulers, as it did for the Tang Chinese, the Toba Turks, and in fact, most of the rulers who embraced Buddhism, hoping to secure and expand their earthly kingdoms. Climbable Buddhist pagodas, like the White Pagoda, served two purposes: they were strategically useful watchtowers in military maneuvers, and they were important symbols equating the stability and power of the state to the stability and power of the "World Mountain."

Like these original patrons, the Chinese archaeologists who, with the blessing of the Bureau of Cultural Relics, have been restoring the White Pagoda and many others, have two purposes: to pay homage to China's architectural heritage and to capture tourist monies. The latter task is not easy, because many of these sacred structures are in difficult-to-reach mountainous terrain where natural and man-made mountains enhance each other. To add to the lure, therefore, China is building museums to house the treasures they have unearthed from the sacred cavities of these pagodas — their "dragon-caves" below ground and their "heavenly-palaces" near their top. On walls above display cases, photographs of precious relics and elevation drawings of the pagodas show the very spots where the treasures lay protected for centuries. Panels of text describe the pagodas and their relics in great detail, their size to the centimeter, their shape, what they are made of, how they were made. The key question, how the builders made them sacred, often goes unanswered. The reports of pagoda excavations and restorations also rarely tackle questions of sacred meaning. This reluctance does not reflect a lack of interest so much as a pragmatic wariness in the wake of

the Cultural Revolution. That time of heightened persecution of religion in general included the deliberate destruction and desecration of sacred man-made symbols of Mt. Sumeru. Many climbable pagodas, for instance, became multi-storied latrines. The government actively suppressed scholarship of the religion and its temples until the late 70s. Now, slowly, older scholars and a few young ones are venturing gingerly back into the field of religious symbolism and meaning. Monastic communities are once again tending temples; aged monks are again teaching acolytes the meanings of sacred mountains.

Inscriptions often name the patron rulers, but it is the skill and ingenuity of the anonymous builders that inspire awe — awe at the engineering feats required to raise the tallest ancient masonry and wooden structures in the world; awe at the equally wondrous ways in which the builders have made these mountains sacred symbols of power and stability, of cosmic creation, of cosmic force of life in death. A structure that issues from the marriage of the Indian stupa and the Chinese watchtower, the pagoda can be, like the stupa, a sacred symbol of the *paranirvana* of Shakyamuni (the historical Buddha), that is, his death and entry into nirvana. At the same time the pagoda is a symbol of life, the creative forces of the universe embodied in the cosmic Buddha, Vairocana. The Buddha images sculptured in relief on the outside or sculptured in the round on altars within, emanate from Vairocana to encompass in their ken all directions, including up, down and center. The images make the pagoda a three-dimensional mandala, a diagram of the Buddhist cosmos, a way to visually conceptualize the inconveivable immensity of the sacred realms.

The sacred symbols of the creative forces of the universe are explicit: the lotus petals encircling the pagoda at the base and body, the pillar/mast rising through the pagoda, the water-flame shining from the pinnacle. In China and in Chinese scholarship, I have never heard of, nor read, any reference to, the procreative symbolism of pagodas other than in the most abstract terms of cosmic creation. Perhaps the sexual symbolism is not so embarrassing as it is embarrassingly obvious. But the Chinese consistently show a propensity to cover up the voluptuous quality of Indian art when they adapt it, and Buddhism came to them, of

The White Pagoda, 1049, at Quingzhou, Inner Mongolia

course, in the form of Indian art as well as Sanskrit sutras. To understand the sexual symbols incorporated into the sacred man-made mountain, scholars must turn to Indian and Western studies of the Indian origins of pagoda symbolism in the stupa and Hindu temple.

The pagoda mast, which pierces the dome and umbrellas of the pagoda, is the *vajra*, the diamond thunderbolt, spike or pin with which Indra fixed the world mountain and cleaved the head of the serpent Vrtra whose "role was to obstruct or lock up the waters of fertility within the [Primordial] Mound."[1] The mast is the top of the pillar that penetrates the pagoda at least to the heavenly palace, and often to the dragon-cave or underground "palace."

In an otherwise splendid book about ancient pagodas in China, Luo Zhewen notes that "people said" these underground cavities were "sea-holes," that "pagodas were built to repress [sea waters], if a pagoda crumbled, sea water would rush out and the area would be submerged under flood." He goes on to write that "after the founding of the People's Republic, scientists made a lot of investigations about the basements of many ancient pagodas, [and] this mystery was at last solved." He explains that the people relating this "imaginary tale" simply did not understand the fact that the real function of the underground cavity is to contain the sacred relics, and when "underground water seeped into many of the pagoda cellars forming deep wells, . . . mystified observers mistook them to be sea-holes."[2]

By defining the water in the dragon-cave simply as evidence of a leaky basement, scientists have literally thrown the baby, lots of babies, out with the bathwater. The people's "imaginary tale," their "superstition," had preserved at least some of the rich symbolism of the water in the relic chamber. The water certainly can symbolize in part the waters of fertility unlocked by Indra's diamond thunderbolt. The scientists are correct that the function of the cavity is to contain the sacred relics, but the water is also important in that function: according to legend, Buddha prophesied that "his relics would one day be taken to the serpent world mythically located in the waters."[3]

The symbolism of the lotus pedestals that ring and "support" the pagodas also depends on water imagery. The lotus symbolizes Buddhism as a gloriously resplendent flower that grows out of the muddy waters of this earth. Adrian Snodgrass writes eloquently of the lotus as the "support of the world. It is identified with the waters that uphold the total cosmos, . . . or with the grounds (*prthivi*) of existence, the Earth, extended on the back of the Waters." Further, the lotus "is identified with the Earth Mother, Laksmi, Padma ("Lotus") who gives birth to, nourishes and supports all life."[4]

Hindu temples also can inform us about these symbols in the stupa/pagoda structure. In the temples, "the foundation deposit, buried in a pit that often descends to the water table and is filled with water, pertains to the Waters of Substance (*prakrti*); the deposit at the summit pertains to the vivifying presence of Essence (*purusa*); the *linga* or image that is located between

them on the vertical axis is the result of their union."[5] Some of the earliest extant Buddhist monuments, the Asokan pillars, Susan Huntington tells us, "reached below the earth to the water table." She interprets this not as a structural deficiency but a "probable allusion to their conceptual source in the cosmic ocean."[6]

The meaning of the water-flame, the shui-yan — often the most beautiful single ornament on many pagodas — likely derives from what Adrian Snodgrass, quoting from a Brahmanic text and A.K. Coomaraswamy, calls the "Brahmanic concept of the Golden Egg: 'Agri at one time cast his eyes upon the waters. "May I pair with them," he thought. He united with them, and what was emitted as his seed, that became gold. Therefore the latter shines like fire, being Agni's seed, hence it is found in water, for he poured it onto the Waters.' Agni, cognate with Fire and with Breath, descends into the Waters to awaken the potentialities of form contained therein, and produces the Golden Embryo of the Universe."[7]

The pagoda builders a millennium ago surely believed that "to build a stupa is to repeat mimetically the Buddha's primordial action of setting the Wheel of the Dharma in motion; "it is to recreate the Buddha's cosmogonic and ordering action, whereby chaos is structured and the Way revealed."[8] Let us hope that China, in its commendable efforts to preserve these structures, does not lose sight of the ways of preserving as well the rich symbolism of these sacred man-made mountains. ▲

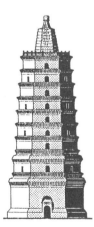

NOTES . . . .

1. John Irwin, "The Axial Symbolism of the Early Stupa: An Exegesis," in *The Stupa: Its Religious, Historical and Architectural Significance*, ed. by Ann Libera Dallapiccola (Wiesbaden, Franze Steiner Verlag, 1980), p. 22. 2. Luo Zhewen, *Ancient Pagodas of China*, (Beijing: Huayi chubanshe, 1990), p. 29. 3. Irwin, p. 26. 4. Adrian Snodgrass, *The Symbolism of the Stupa*, Cornell University, Ithaca, New York, 1985, p. 98 with reference to the *Maitri Upanisad* VI. 2 in R. E. Hume, *The Thirteen Principal Upanisads*. London, 1931, and Heinrich Zimmer, *Myths and Symbols in Indian Art and Civilization*. New York, 1946, pp. 90ff. 5. Snodgrass, p. 267. 6. Susan J. Huntington, *The Art of Ancient India*, New York: Weatherhill, 1985, p. 45. 7. Snodgrass, p. 160. 8. Snodgrass, p. 88.

JAMES ROBSON

POLYMORPHOUS SPACE

The Contested Space of Mt. Nanyue

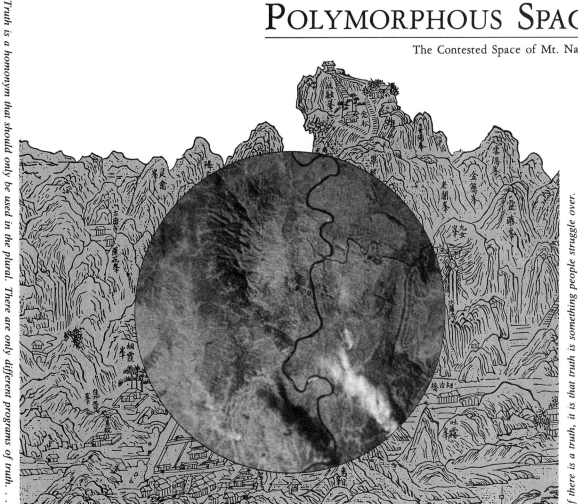

Truth is a homonym that should only be used in the plural. There are only different programs of truth. . . .

— Paul Veyne, Did the Greeks Believe in Their Myths?

If there is a truth, it is that truth is something people struggle over.

— Pierre Bourdieu, "A Lecture on the Lecture."

A GEO-HISTORICAL VIEW OF SACRED SPACE GROUNDING SACRED MOUNTAINS

An early Greek myth relates a story about Thales (c. 624-546 BCE) who, while contemplating the stars high above, fell into a well. A Thracian slave woman laughed at the soaked Thales, and reprimanded him for having his head in the sky and not observing what was directly under his own feet. To the ancient Greeks this story exhibited the dilemma of a theorist who had lost his ground. In Greek history, incidentally, Thales is credited with abandoning a metaphysical thesis for understanding the earth (as was common in his day), and forwarding a down-to-earth (chemical/material) thesis, attributing everything to water.

Since the time of Thales, technological advancements have provided us with the capacity to view the earth from the stars. For modern thinkers such as Hegel (whose name Georges Bataille and Jacques Derrida have enjoyed pointing out sounds like eagle) and Descartes, a bird's-eye view was considered a philosophical ideal which provided a privileged all-encompassing vision.

The privileged perspective of a high-altitude gaze became, however, the target of fierce criticism among French thinkers.[1] Maurice Merleau-Ponty, for example, "was deeply suspicious of what he called *pensée au survol*, the high-altitude thinking which maintained the Cartesian split between a distant, spectatorial subject and the object of his sight."[2] "High places attract those who wish to look over the world with an eagle-eye view. Vision,"

Merleau-Ponty suggests, "ceases to be solipsist only up close."[3]

Although Merleau-Ponty was primarily concerned with the effects of a distant gaze on the human being as an object of analysis, one might also apply his critique to traditional views regarding sacred geography, and sacred mountains as objects of analysis. Traditionally, sacred mountains have been perceived as if from a high-altitude universalizing perspective (philosophical), with little regard for what happens on the ground, namely their cultural, social, political, or economic dimensions. This approach has lead scholars to treat sacred mountains as ahistorical phenomena and sublimate their differences in favour of an imperialistic view, following Mircea Eliade, that mountains share an inherent numinous power that is revealed to humans through hierophanies and epiphanies. Although sacred mountains have traditionally been considered to "have an extraordinary power to evoke the sacred,"[4] should we accept uncritically that viewpoint without first providing detailed analyses of specific mountains, including the complex geo-historical contexts for their perceived sacredness?

To avoid falling into a well of ungrounded metaphysical speculation about sacred mountains, my premise is that sacred space cannot be understood from a sectarian/univocal perspective, that it is produced and maintained by historical agents, that it is often the locus of competing claims to the legitimate representation of the sacredness of that space, and is, in the end, territory to be gained or lost. In other words, sacred space is here considered a culturally constituted phenomena that cannot be sepa-

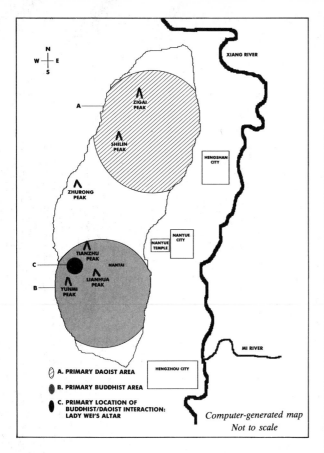

A. PRIMARY DAOIST AREA
B. PRIMARY BUDDHIST AREA
C. PRIMARY LOCATION OF
   BUDDHIST/DAOIST INTERACTION:
   LADY WEI'S ALTAR

Computer-generated map
Not to scale

rated from the conditions of its construction and its maintenance, nor can it be analyzed separately from its historical, economic, political and social contexts.

The object of this analysis will be Mt. Nanyue (also known as Mt. Heng) a sacred mountain located in south/central China (modern day Hunan province). Mountains in China offer a plethora of material for studying Chinese religious traditions, and the interactions between those traditions, since throughout Chinese history they have been the sites of religious retreats, pilgrimages, and large monastic centers. Yet, most writings about China's sacred mountains do not take into consideration the complex interaction between the religious institutions that occupied those sites, nor do they consider that those sites may have been the focus of competing claims by different religious traditions. Therefore, it will be asked here: What happens, when two religious traditions attempt to claim a sacred mountain as their own?

In the case of China, it seems, there were no univocal Buddhist or Daoist sacred mountains, there were no purely sectarian spaces. Space in China was polymorphous and the locus of competing claims by different religious traditions and institutions to define and control it, a processes that often lead to violent interactions. For interpreting the polymorphous character of sacred space in China we might want to consider the advice of the spatial theorist Henri Lefebvre: "Just as white light, though uniform in appearance, may be broken down into a spectrum, space likewise decomposes when subjected to analysis; in the case of space however, the knowledge to be derived from analysis extends to the recognition of conflicts internal to what on the surface appears homogeneous and coherent and presents itself and behaves as it were."[5]

MT. NANYUE: A BRIEF GENEALOGICAL HISTORY

According to an eighteenth century gazetteer of Mt. Nanyue, the Nanyue Temple at the foot of the mountain was divided into two halves, with Buddhist Temples on the right side and Daoist

Abbeys on the left side. Even today the precincts of the Nanyue Temple are shared by Daoist and Buddhist monks who go about their daily activities in peaceful coexistence. This apparent harmony between two religions that have been traditionally perceived as 'peaceful/serene Buddhists,' and 'go-with-the-flow Daoists,' however, has nor always characterized the nature of the relationship between the Daoists and Buddhists on Mt. Nanyue. The history of Nanyue's development as a sacred mountain provides a useful background for understanding the conflict that ensued between these two religious traditions between the sixth and the eighth centuries.

Mt. Nanyue is a range of mountains that runs parallel with the Xiang River 湘 河 . Although it is often referred to as a single mountain, its sacred purlieu is actually made up of seventy two peaks. This geological arrangement is mirrored in the architecture of the Nanyue Temple (Nanyue Miao 南 嶽 廟) at the base of the mountain, which has 72 columns, each purported to be 72 feet high. The Nanyue range lies on an almost direct North-South trajectory, and its highest peak, *Zhurong Feng 祝 融 峯* , is 1290 meters above sea level. Among Nanyue's seventy-two peaks, five were designated as the major peaks, *Zhurong Feng, Sigai Feng 紫 蓋 峯 , Yunmi Feng 雲 密 峯 , Shilin Feng 石 廩 峯 ,* and *Tianzhu Feng 天 柱 峯 .* On these five peaks and among the sixty seven other peaks various religious institutions settled and shaped the mountain with their hands as well as their minds.

Mt. Nanyue's pre-imperial history remains relatively unknown, though there is some evidence which suggests that prior to its imperial role it had been the site of an influential local fire cult for several hundred years.

In the Han dynasty (206 BCE-220 CE) Mt. Nanyue was integrated into a dominant mountain cultic system developed by the Chinese imperium, known as the Five Marchmount system (Ch. *wuyue*). Within this system of five mountains, Mt. Nanyue was instituted as the southern sacred mountain, became the locus of imperial rituals, and was overlaid with myths associating the mountain with well known imperial sovereigns of the distant past, namely the Blazing Emperor Yandi. In other words, the imperial cult used fabricated myths to claim legitimacy to the mountain by virtue of having been associated with Mt. Nanyue from the time of the early (mythical) sage emperors. Therefore, Mt. Nanyue was not exempt from imperial processes of territoriality and governmentality, in fact its consitution as a sacred mountain was used to legitimate those processes.

Beginning in about the fourth century Mt. Nanyue came to be inhabited by Daoist recluses who came to the mountain in search of numinous mushrooms and ingredients for their alchemical endeavors. At about the same time Mt. Nanyue was included in the expanding network of Daoist sacred sites in China. According to Daoist conceptions of sacred space, China was criss-crossed with sacred sites that were believed to be the terrestrial paradises of the immortals. These sacred sites were systematized into Daoist categories of ten greater and thirty-six lesser "grotto-heavens" and seventy-two "blissful realms." Mt. Nanyue was considered to be the home of one "grotto-heaven" and four "blissful realms."

By the Tang dynasty (618-906) Mt. Nanyue was home to large Daoist institutions, was filled with Daoist toponyms (to name was to claim), and was associated with a vast array of mythical Daoist immortals. Most of the Daoist temples and abbeys at Mt. Nanyue were built in the northwestern part of the range, except for one significant site, the stone altar of the Daoist priestess Wei Huacun (or Lady Wei), which was located in the southern section of the mountain. This site became an important site mentioned in narratives describing conflicts between Buddhists and Daoists on Mt. Nanyue.

Lady Wei had been a libationer in her earthly existence, but when she shed her mortal remains she became the celestial couterpart of the deity of the Southern Marchmount and was described as an astral divinity whose crystaline body was illuminated by her luminescent vital organs, which shined like precious gems. In her tenure as Lady Wei of the Southern Marchmount she revealed a series of Daoist scriptures to eminent Daoist monks. These texts, which now consitute a substantial section of the Daoist Canon, had been transmitted to her by 'realized ones' from the heaven of highest clarity. During the Tang dynasty, Lady Wei became the object of a large cult offered by Daoist priestesses on Mt. Nanyue. This cult to Lady Wei was centered around her stone altar in the southern part of the mountain at the base of Heavenly Pillar Peak.

Mt. Nanyue's transformation into a Daoist sacred mountain was the result of the Daoist usurpation of the prior imperial perogative to the control of the marchmount's perceived powers, and underlines the importance of avoiding static interpretations of sacred space. Conceptions of Mt. Nanyue's sacredness were defined and re-defined throughout its history.

During the fifth century, Buddhist practioners began to arrive at Mt. Nanyue and proceeded to establish themselves in the southeastern part of the mountain. Eventually, that part of the mountain became filled with Buddhist toponyms (to name, once again, was to claim), and the site of numerous large temples and monasteries. Therefore, by the seventh century it is possible to detect two distinct geo-specific areas of Buddhist and Daoist influence. The Daoists were well entrenched in the northwestern part of the Nanyue range and the Buddhists in the southeastern section.

One of the first influential Buddhist monks to arrive at Mt. Nanyue was Huisi (515-576).[6] Huisi built a large Buddhist monastic institution, the Fuyan Monastery, in the vicinity of the already established Daoist site at the base of Heavenly Pillar Peak.

The story of Huisi's arrival at Mt. Nanyue, as it is preserved in the Buddhist Canon, is particularly revealing for what it has to say about the Buddhist attempt to constitute Mt. Nanyue as a sacred Buddhist mountain.

"One day after his arrival at Nanyue, Huisi ascended to the top of Zhurong Peak (Zhurong was the old god of fire). The spirit of the mountain was then engaged in a game of chess.[7] The spirit then greeted the master and asked: "Master, why have you come here?" Huisi answered: "To implore my benefactor for a plot of useful land." Mountain spirit: "It is agreed." Huisi then threw his khakkhara (a Buddhist priest's staff), thus determining his place. [Commentary: Today this is the site of the Temple of Glorious Happiness (Fuyan si 福嚴寺).] The spirit added: "Master, henceforth you occupy a blessed terrain. As for me, the disciple, where am I to live?" Huisi then rolled an oblong stone that came to rest on a flat area of land, which he bequeathed to the spirit. The spirit of the mountain then begged to be given the Buddhist precepts. Huisi consented and gave to him the essentials of the Law."[8]

Huisi's interaction with the spirit of Mt. Nanyue served as a foundation myth for the institution of Buddhism on Mt. Nanyue. It is significant to note that when Huisi approached the mountain spirit he was engaged in a game of chess, which in Chinese Daoist lore is an essential characteristic used to signify a place as an abode of the immortals. Therefore, it seems that when Huisi arrived at Mt. Nanyue the mountain spirit was perceived as a Daoist, and in need of redefinition. Another significant feature of Huisi's interaction with the mountain spirit was the fact that he obtained land. This land became the site where he built Mt. Nanyue's first major Buddhist monastic center, the Fuyan Monastery. From an economic perspective it is important to emphasize this Buddhist territorial acquisition, since Buddhist monastic estates grew into some of the largest landholding institutions in the Chinese empire, and that territorial claim also included control over one of Mt. Nanyue's main water sources that provided irrigation for the cultivation of rice, a large cash crop of this region. Finally, this story informs us that Huisi conferred Buddhist precepts on the (Daoist?) mountain spirit, thus confirming the Buddhist attempt to transform Mt. Nanyue from a Daoist sacred mountain into a Buddhist sacred mountain. As we will see, though, this transformation did not go uncontested.

THE BUDDHIST PERSPECTIVE

Although the above story of Huisi's arrival at Mt. Nanyue is a polemical treatise written by Buddhists to legitimate their claim to Mt. Nanyue, it does preserve some useful historical information. We know from other Buddhist sources that Huisi's fame and popularity seems to have grown rapidly at Mt. Nanyue, and perhaps due to that fame he aroused jealousy among Mt. Nanyue's Daoists, who perceived him as a threat to their hegemony on the mountain.

In the first year of the Taijian reign period (568), a Daoist of the Jiuxian temple [Jiuxian guan 九 仙 觀], Ouyang Zhengze observed that the mountain possessed a superior breath (qi 氣), conspired with the others and said: "This breath has as its master a prince of the Buddhist Law (dharma) who wears coarse garments.[9] If he flourishes then our Law will decline." He has pierced the heart of the mountain, gathered stones for divination, and interred arms in the mountain.

This passage informs us that, following their recognition of Huisi's presence at Mt. Nanyue, the Daoists decided to do something about the serious threat he posed to their insitutions, reported him to the emperor, and accused him of storing arms at Mt. Nanyue in order to mount a rebellion. The story, as it is preserved in the *Further Biographies of Eminent Monks* (compiled by Daoxuan in 645), says:

Because those of the heterodox teachings (i.e. the Daoists) harbored jealous hatred to Huisi, they secretly reported him to the Lord of Chen. They falsely accused the northern monk Huisi of receiving subsidies from the state of Qi [a rival state of Chen], and of digging into and destroying Mt. Nanyue. Subsequently an imperial envoy arrived at the mountain, where he saw two tigers roaring angrily, and he became terrified and fled. After several days the envoy was allowed to enter the mountain, at which time small bees came and stung Huisi's forehead. Subsequently, large bees came and ate the small ones, they gathered in front of Huisi then scattered and left. The Lord of Chen prepared an investigation without paying heed to this ominous sign. Not long after... one of those who had plotted against Huisi died a sudden death, and the second was eaten by an enraged dog. The symbol of the bees was thus affirmed by this miraculous corroboration. The emperor acknowledged Huisi's virtue and welcomed him to the Xixuan Temple in the capital.

This text relates how later Buddhists attempted to counter the Daoist accusations against Huisi, and in fact reversed the roles of accuser and accused. Here, Huisi is aided by the natural forces of Mt. Nanyue (tigers and bees), thus confirming his innocence and the mountains support for him, and therefore of the Buddhists not the Daoists.

Other sources, emphasizing Huisi's thaumaturgical powers, say that he agreed to go see the emperor but told the envoy he would go on his own accord, he then threw his almsbowl into the air and rode in it to the capital, a feat that is memorialized in the toponomy of Nanyue Shan as the Throwing Almsbowl Peak (Zhibo Feng 擲 鉢 峯).[10] Once in the capital he proved his innocence to the court. When it became clear that the accusations against Huisi were false, the emperor visited him, "had enjoyable conversations and loaded him down with gifts."[11] Shortly thereafter Huisi returned to Mt. Nanyue and continued his teaching as he had been doing before. The Daoists at Mt. Nanyue offered Huisi a gift of several hundred *mou* of land, the revenue of which permitted the purchase of incense for the cult and essentials for a monastery. Once again it is significant to notice the forfeiture of land, which came to be referred to by the local people as the 'Retribution of the Daoists Farm.'[12] Huisi accepted the land and in order to record the facts of this case for posterity he inscribed them on a stone which he hid.

Hindus attack the Ayodya Mosque, a site they claim is Hindu sacred ground, in December 1992.

THE DAOIST PERSPECTIVE

Daoist textual sources also confirm the presence of Buddhists on Mt. Nanyue, however, instead of depicting them as pacifistic monks out to spread the *dharma*, they are presented from the opposite perspective as hoodlums intent on destroying and desacralizing a Daoist sacred site. The site in question, Lady Wei's stone altar, was as we have seen, the locus of an important Daoist cult on Mt. Nanyue. It is understandable that her altar became the site of discord between these two religious traditions since it was the only major Daoist site that was located in the southeastern part of the Nanyue range, which was the region of the mountain that saw the largest influx of Buddhists between the sixth and eighth centuries. Significantly, Lady Wei's altar was located at the base of Heavenly Pillar Peak, precisely where Huisi's Fuyan Monastery was built. The following story about Lady Wei's altar might therefore be read as a Daoist attempt to legitimize their control over a sacred site on Mt. Nanyue, which was in threat of a Buddhist takeover.

THE CONTESTED SPACE OF LADY WEI'S ALTAR

Nanyue Wei furen xiantan yan 南嶽魏夫人仙壇驗
*[An Examination of the Immortal Altar of Lady Wei
of the Southern Marchmount]*

The altar of Lady Wei is located in front of the Central Peak (Heavenly Pillar Peak) at the Southern Marchmount. On the top of a great rock there is a large rock exceeding ten feet square. It has a stable appearance, with a round base and a level top. [However] it is perched tenuously and it seems that if it were pushed by one person it could be toppled. Yet, when many people [push on it] it remains firm and stable. It is said that because strange and divine things happen there, spirits, immortals and anchorites frequently come to reside there. Strange and wonderful clouds, as well as numinous qi [氣] often obscure its top.

*Suddenly, ten or more Buddhist monks (*naseng 衲僧 *lit.*

patch robed monks) carrying torches and staffs arrived at the altar during the night. These monks wanting to inflict injury waited for the immortal Gu to return to her residence. But, the immortal Gu was at that time inside her residence on her bed and the monks did not see her and left. Reaching the Lady Wei's altar they pushed it over and ruined it. Then there was a loud, angry sounding rumble. Hearing this they raised their torches to try and illuminate it. The first could not move in the face of this strange and supernatural intervention. Eventually they were able to flee and made it to a distant village. Then of the ten monks nine were devoured by tigers. One of the monks, who hadn't agreed with the others' evil actions at the time they attacked the altar, was spared the wrath of the tigers. When he returned to his village and told his story, people from near and far were astonished.[13]

This passage presents the Buddhist monks on Mt. Nanyue as aggressive, violent, and intentionally out to harm the Daoist caretaker of Lady Wei's sacred stone altar. It is significant to note that the Daoist priestess was protected by tigers who subsequently devoured the Buddhists with pious devotion. Tigers, as we saw in the story of Huisi above, were traditionally presented in Buddhist hagiography as protectors of Buddhist monks and defenders of the *dharma*. In this story, however, the Daoist legitimacy was grounded in a (super?) natural act, whereby the natural forces at Mt. Nanyue were now on their side. It is also pertinent to note that the one monk who had not been party to the attack on the altar was not killed by the tigers. It seems the Daoist author of this story was inclined to acknowledge the Buddhist concept of karmic retribution.

The movement of this essay from high-altitude ungrounded speculations about sacred mountains, down to the consideration of a specific site and what acually took place (literally) there in the constitution of its perceived sacredness, has led us to rethink the traditional categories used to discuss sacred mountains in China. By treating sacred space as a culturally constituted phenomena which cannot be analyzed separately from the historical, sociopolitical and economic contexts of its creation and maintainence, we have been able to go beyond a static/univocal interpretation of sacred space. Sacred space in China was in a constant state of definition and redefinition throughout history. Underneath a thin layer of apparent homogeneity, characterized as sectarian sacred space, we found their was a terrain of highly complex poymorphous space, within which competing religious traditions (in this case Buddhists and Daoists) attempted to legitimize claims to the land as well as the 'true' representation of the sacred character of that space.

By realizing that sacred places are not static unchanging entities devoid of complex cultural interests, we may move to a better understanding of the transformations affecting other "sacred places" around the world (Native American sacred mountains, the Holy Lands of Israel, Tibet, and Ayodya Mosque in India come to mind.) In the end, the history of the interaction between different religious traditions at Mt. Nanyue seems to affirm Pierre Bourdieu's classic dictum, "if there is a truth, it is that truth is something people struggle over."[14]   ▲

NOTES ···

1. See Martin Jay, "In the Empire of the Gaze: Foucault and the Denigration of Vision in Twentieth-century French Thought," in David Couzens Hoy, ed., *Force Fields: Between Intellectual History and Cultural Critique*. New York: Routledge, 1993, especially the chapter titled "The Rise of Hermeneutics and the Crisis of Ocularcontrism." 2. Jay 1989: 178 3. Maurice Merleau Ponty, *The Visible and the Invisible*. Evanston: Northwestern Univ. Press, 1968: 4. Edwin Bernbaum, *Sacred Mountains of the World*. San Francisco: Sierra Club Books, 1990: xiii. 5. Henri Lefebvre, *The Production of Space*. Cambridge: Basil Blackwell, 1991: 352. 6. Huisi is well known as the founder of the Tiantai school of Buddhism and was the teacher of the

influential Chinese monk Zhiyi. 7. An illusion to the geographical configuration of the multiple peaks of Nanyue which, from far away, appear as a two players engaged in a chess party. 8. *Fozu tongji*, T. 49,2035, p.179c. 20-26, Paul Magnin, *La Vie Et L'Œuvre de Huisi*. Paris: École Française D'Extrême-Orient, 1979: 56-57. 9. An illusion to a Buddhist monks robe. 10. *Nanyue Zongsheng ji* 1062b. 9ff. 11. Magnin 1979: 62-63. 12. Magnin 1979: 63-64. 13. Du Guangting, *Daojiao Lingyan ji*, TT 590, fascicle 325-326. 14. Pierre Bourdieu, "The Lecture on the Lecture," in *In Other Words: Essays Towards a Reflexive Sociology*. Stanford: Stanford University Press, 1990: 185.

B R U C E   R .   C A R O N

Magic Kingdoms

Towards a Post-modern Ethnography of Sacred Places

MODERNITY, POSTMODERNITY, AND THE SACRED

In what might, to some, seem a facile, iconoclastic maneuver, this essay will posit certain similarities between self-professed sacred places and other places that make quite different claims. These similarities — specifically the need to establish, remake, defend, and promote their claims about *place* — ties sacred geographies with other, urban geographies (Las Vegas, for example), national parks (the Grand Canyon), restaurant chains (MacDonalds), and "Magic Kingdoms" (Tokyo Disneyland). By this I am not lumping together the individual claims of these various places, but, instead, I will look at the similarities in the strategies used by institutions to support their claims about place, and also the similar effects these strategies have on the subject/consumer of the institution/place.

A couple things I cannot do in this piece: such as discuss the reverse side of this topic, of what differentiates "the sacred" place from Las Vegas (except to say that the sacred is a synthetic notion, not to be taken whole before breakfast); and, I will not try to describe or expand the semiological discussion about Disneyland, to which many others, including Umberto Eco and Jean Baudrillard, have contributed. The notion that Disneyland resembles a "sacred" place is not my own. Others, most recently Masako Notoji's 1990 study of Disney parks, *Dizuniirando to iu seichi* (The Sacred Land called "Disneyland"), have made this (metaphorical) suggestion. I wish to add some additional social geographical weight to this idea.

My intention is to introduce a few theoretical problematics of current interest in the social sciences to the notion of — and the study of — "sacred" geographies in late modernity. "Modernity" is also a synthetic term used to describe historically embedded but increasingly globalized institutions and practices. I am fairly comfortable with Anthony Giddens's outline of modernity's main features (he links this to the institutions and effects of global industries and capitalism, and to an increase in the means of surveillance and communication) and also those of "post-modernity" as a reflexive moment in late modernity instead of something essentially different.[1] (Note: "The Modern," like "The Sacred" goes down better in the plural, particularly when dealing with other people's modernities and sacralities.) A variety of institutions make claims about individual sacred places. Each institution makes its own claims, based on the history of its own institutional discourse. But all sacred places are equally subject to the mechanisms of modernities that pre-empt their claims. The conflict between modernities and sacralities shows up in the differences between the maps used for the domains of each.

LOST IN SPACE

Places in general, and sacred places with some central emphasis, share the necessarily opaque qualities of "place-ness," as opposed to what Lefebvre termed the "illusory transparency"[2] of the uniform, univocal, modern social space, a space devoid of life — including anything resembling the sacred — and which does not allow opacity of any sort. This is the panoptic space of the prison yard or the modern city mall. As Anthony Giddens also noted,[3] the disembedding mechanisms of modernity evacuate historical idiosyncratic localities (what I call "places") in favor of re-embedded globally-organized spaces. In terms of knowledge, too, this modernist notion of a vacuous undifferentiated universe where physical and metaphysical laws apply uniformly — the space of experimental reason that defies local aberration; the space of scientific *truth* — leaves no room for other truths. Just so, the reality claims of the unitary global space impinge upon the reality claims of other, necessarily smaller, localities, leaving no space for other places.

A univocal purview of global geographical science has succeeded in "re-placing" the plurality of sacred geographies around the globe — and even beyond. The orbiting Hubble Telescope (despite its manufacturing flaws) stretches our vision to the edges of the universe, while tunneling electron microscopes reveal the contours of individual atoms, leaving little space left for heavens or even hells. Back on Earth, the continual surveillance of the entire surface of the planet is now accomplished via satellite. This promotes a uniform conceptualization of global geography. The planetary-scale perspective is also reified by global geographical data bases, Space-Shuttle photography, and coordinate systems that elide local social (including sacred) boundaries in favor of, say, topographic, ecological, or navigational information. All of this satisfies the underlying notion that space is only an empty container, made insignificant by its simple ubiquity. The result is a space completely liable to being charted by its internal contours and external boundaries — the transparent, visible, *mappable* space of modernity. Today there are maps of modern states and cities which show not only mountains, rivers, streets and buildings, but also distributions of populations by a wide range of social variables. In general, "mappability" is a good measure of the amount of modernity in any location.

MAPPING THE SACRED

Those places called "sacred" are usually, by contrast, unmappable in the modern mode. At least the maps which would tell about their absolute location on some planetary grid, or about their elevation, climate, and geology, do not, and cannot, speak about what makes these "sacred." Maps of sacred geographies are a different genre entirely from those we would recognize and accept as even being "maps." Their sacred contours are unavailable for satellite verification, and the computation of their area and topography do not translate into a useful measurement of distance for any practical purpose. These spaces are traversed in quite different fashion.

What type of maps do I mean here? There are two primary types of maps of sacred places. The first are generated directly by practices within the place, inscribed on the memories of the practitioners and never actually written down. The performance of the practice is itself the map. For example, the travels of an *omikoshi* during a Shinto festival demarcate the boundaries of the festival community. The second type of "sacred map" is also derived from practices, but acquires a textual/textural form. Such texts/maps attempt to reassemble the spatial logic of the practice of the place. These are composed of various genres and forms: poems, songs, epic narratives, sculptures, mandalas, drawings or paintings. However, they are never (for reasons we will soon discover) *maps*, in the modernist sense.

There is also a transitional form of map between what we would generally describes as a "map" and this other genre of maps (which are no less maps, even though we may be discomforted by their description as such). This is the pilgrim's map, which charts the course from the outside to the place of sacred practices. The pilgrim's map to Tokyo Disneyland does, indeed, resemble and rely on those charting technologies which usually describe the built environment of Japan: mass transit maps. However, once the boundary of the "Magic Kingdom" is at hand, a map of a different sort is in order. In the map of Tokyo Disneyland, like all maps of sacred places, what is not

described is at least as interesting as what is described.

Sacred geographies include invisibilities that can never be made visible: entrances into other worlds; rocks, statues, buildings, mountains that house deities; pathways that lead the initiated to esoteric visions. Maps of these places are, by definition, incomplete. They invite, they intrigue, but there comes a point where they will not inform. Maps of sacred places can never show their entirety, as this would reveal the arbitrary ground of the enterprise. To reveal this is to allow what Barbara Meyerhoff described as "that fatal perspective of recognizing culture as our construct, arbitrary, conventional, invented by mortals."[4]

The brochure to Tokyo Disneyland does not describe what happens behind the numerous doors for "Staff Only." In fact, those few who are able to join one of the behind-the-scenes tours of a Disney park are not allowed to take photographs. As Susan Willis noted, back-stage photography breaks the visual barrier between what the public is allowed to experience and what the staff must do *outside the purview of the consumer* to create the desired consumer experience. "The unbroken seamlessness of Disney World, its totality as a consumable artifact, cannot tolerate the revelation of the real work that produces the commodity."[5]

In Disney parks, the authority to move (or the prohibition to pass) into those back-stage spaces marks the *disparity* between the two levels of knowledge required by the production and the consumption of the experience of the place. Yet a similar spatialized knowledge/power distinction operates in all "sacred" places, and is tied closely to the "magic," the "mystique," the place acquires by its becoming known as sacred, and by the need to control and reproduce this mystique over a period of years. Detailed modern maps exist for all the spaces and machinery above and below ground at all the Disney parks. These are reserved only for the eyes of those who engineer the Disney magic.

MYSTIQUES OF THE SACRED

The mystique of any place (sacred, magical, or simply romantic) is managed by practices intended to exert control over its "reality claims." In his book *Frame Analysis*, Erving Goffman directs us to a useful starting point in the discussion of such practices. Goffman follows a line of reasoning that was articulated back in the 60s (the 1860s that is) by William James:

> *"Instead of asking what reality is, he [James] gave matters a subversive phenomenological twist, italicizing the following question* Under what circumstances do we think things are real? *The important thing about reality, he implied, is our sense of its realness in contrast to our feeling that some things lack this quality. One can then ask under what conditions such a feeling is generated, and this question speaks to a small, manageable problem having to do with the camera and not what it is the camera takes pictures of."*[6]

"The camera," here, represents the institutionalized practice of framing reality. The practice (and its institution) thus becomes the object of study, replacing any notion of un-framed "reality" in this role.

In Tokyo Disneyland, physical reality is framed by the clever use of façades, plantings, and semiotic devices that create the motifs for the various "lands." The close physical proximity that "Fantasyland," "Adventureland," and "Westernland" have to each other (which is revealed in the guidemap) is obscured by the labrynthine pathways that connect them and the thin visual obstructions that separate them. The outside world is also not a part of the Disney experience (no borrowed landscape here). The simulation of wide vistas and broad plazas and gardens was made possible by constructing several of the major rides underground. Subterranean rides also allow the use of darkness to obscure and magnify the scale of the simulated environments. Meter-tall Caribbean pirates are designed to be perceived as giants in their meticulously scaled-down mise-en-scène. Above ground, the pathways within the "Kingdom" have a centripetal,

The procession of the omikoshi during a Shinto festival marks the territory of the shrine and spatially defines its community of worshippers. Here is a detail from an early Edo-period (17th century), six-fold screen depicting the procession of the Hie Sannō Festival in Sakamoto on Lake Biwa. Los Angeles County Museum of Art: gift of Jerry Louise and Robert Johnson.

mobius effect, always bringing the visitor back from the edge to the center: to the World Bazaar (to Main Street). The entire park feels much larger than it "really" is (no scale is provided on the map). One reason why Tokyo Disneyland "feels" bigger than its Anaheim cousin is that there is no Matterhorn, no mountain. Rather, the Cinderella Castle was moved to the very center of the park and enlarged — it serves as a human-made mountain, a vertical *axis mundi* at the Magic Kingdom.

"Disney-ality" is also crafted by hiding the mechanical, electrical, and labor-intensive production of the entertainments, rides, and restaurants. The daily grand parade seems to come from nowhere, fill the central plaza with dancing and music, and then simply disappear. The parade's apparently effortless, "magical" appearance and disappearance is central to its overall effect. Such ritualized spontaneity happens continually throughout the park.

At any Disney park, the *ritual* mystique of its place is maintained, in large part, by the practice of simulating spontaneous emotion. On the Jungle Cruise, for example, the boat driver (who doesn't actually drive the boat) must feign surprise at the "unexpected" attack of a crocodile and get off a lucky shot with his pistol. The timing and the tone of this charade is not convincing to any skeptical adult, but adults, and children too, are expected to leave their skepticism (and, in L.A., their own pistols) at the gates of the Magic Kingdom. And so, the moment of surprise is maintained.

Each day at Tokyo Disneyland recreates its opening day. Every day is presented as special. There is a parade today, the visitor learns. Actually there is a parade every day. (As Mircea Eliade noted, managing time perspectives is generally implied in practices that support the mystique of all sacred places.) This, the *temporal* mystique of Tokyo Disneyland, is also maintained by the simple fact that for a good number of the crowd, today is their first day at Disneyland, and for many of the rest, there is a desire to reproduce the experience of their first day. So too, every employee — particularly those wearing the complete body-costumes of Disney cartoon characters — is required to exhibit a spontaneous enthusiasm made even more remarkable on a sweltering Kanto August day, but remarkable enough any time considering it must be repeated again, and again, and yes, once again. The staging of displays of "spontaneous" emotion is a strategy designed to help the visitor forget that today is just like every other day in a Disney park.

STRATEGIES OF THE SACRED

It is much easier when discussing Tokyo Disneyland — instead of places with reputed antiquity and sacrality — to consider what Goffman suggests and talk not about the ultimate reality of, say, the "Jungle Cruise," but rather of the instrumentality that creates the illusion of its reality, and the desire that makes us want to experience the Jungle Cruise *as though it were real*. What is important, however, is that this same methodological "move" is available — and thus, at some point, unavoidable — for the discussion of any sacred place. This move brings into focus not the *a priori* quality of any "sacred" place, but rather the *strategies* used to create and maintain such places.

The strategies of the sacred are, again, not so very different from those of the "profane" world. For example, take practices of concealment that promote a differential knowledge of a situation. In a game of cards, all players are expected to have similar knowledge about the deck and about the actual lay of dealt cards around the table. Everyone knows their own cards and can only guess at those of the other players. Any attempt by one or more participants to expand their own visual range, while limiting those of others, (by means of marked decks, hidden mirrors, etc.) describes what would normally be considered "cheating." More generally, as Goffman notes, "the social front that an individual presents to his various associates during his daily round allows them to make some assumptions about his social worth and moral standards, the latter including, importantly, the practice of candor and openness."[7] Everyday interactions depend upon rather rigid assumptions of candor and openness between individuals. These assumptions are liable to doubt and suspicion if there is any reason to suggest that candor and openness are, in fact, a strategic front.

One more notion needs some description before we can shed some light on the strategies of the sacred. This is the notion of an individual's *ken*. The term "ken" is used here in both its physical, visual/audial sense of *perceptabilities*, and its knowledge/power sense of awareness and *complicity*. The former responds more to the physical setting of a place, and the latter to its social practices. Concealment strategies serve to limit the ken of the subject. They put a narrower frame on the subject's awareness/perceptions than is available to the author of the strategy.

This type of strategy can only work if the subject is also unaware that his ken has been so manipulated. For this reason, additional strategies are needed to conceal the first one. A strategy that limits the ken of a subject — while extending one's own for strategic purposes — requires additional practices to suppress the subject's suspicions of the "innocent" underpinnings of the situation at hand. Very simply, it is not enough to conceal *what* one does not want the other to discover, it is also imperative to also *hide the very possibility that one is concealing anything at all.*

The visual sequestering of the working areas of the Magic Kingdom is not sufficient in itself to produce the desired effect. A second level of hiding is accomplished by eliding the fact that anything is actually hidden. For this reason, the doors for "Staff Only," are themselves hidden from view, placed around blind corners, behind fake rocks or plants, or simply unmarked and camouflaged as parts of walls. As previously discussed, the real workings of a Disney park go unnoticed. Even the removal of trash is accomplished continuously by an underground conveyor system so that garbage trucks do not interfere with the fantasyland ambiance. The act of hiding is itself hidden from view. This is essential for institutional "mystique" management.

MODERN DOUBT, POSTMODERN SUSPICIONS

Goffman's careful separation of practices that suppress *doubt* from those that suppress *suspicion* provides an extremely valuable insight into the history of the study of sacred places and institutions. We can see the modernist approach as one directed at the level of *doubt*, a critique of the content of the actual knowledge/place claims of the sacred. The modernist (scientific) reading of the sacred works mainly on this level — it adds an external source of doubt to any claim about the sacred. In physical and geographical terms it illuminates and elides any hidden qualities within the physical universe, a territory for which it makes its own claims. And so while there are many places that claim sacrality, we continue to see modern spaces re-placing sacred places in numerous locations around the globe.

The sacred place is maintained through a few necessary deceptions, accomplished not only through the use of myths, but also through the confidence provided by ritual practices (which mask their own arbitrariness). Again, two moments of concealment are needed. In terms of knowledge (rather than geography), the first moment of concealment is the hiding of certain aspects of knowledge (thereby suppressing doubt in the subject), and the second, the hiding of the fact that there is actually a broader frame to the knowledge (thereby suppressing suspicion). The former is simply a discursive aspect of any knowledge, but the latter involves the ideological use of the same knowledge.

In terms of geography (rather than discursive knowledge) the first moment is the physical (visual/audial) sequestration of zones (peaks, caves, forest groves, etc.). The second is the further concealment of the earlier fact of this geographical sequestration. Commonly, the latter concealment is done by using "the Sacred" as the putative source of the geographical sequestration practices. The sacred is credited with creating itself in a rule-governed place that cannot subsequently be violated — which is simply to say "the sacred was here before we got here and we can do nothing but obey its rules." This is a type of deceit; and, even though it may well be an ancient one, it is performed in the present for an institutional advantage. (Here, my own suspicions are showing.) In examining the construction and maintenance of sacred places (and knowledges), the question of "How is suspicion suppressed?" comes to the fore. This question is directed not at places, but rather at *institutions* of the sacred. Let us pursue this a bit further.

INSTITUTIONS OF THE SACRED

Modern doubt has managed to divide geography from the sacred without denying institutions of the sacred the strategies they use to control access to "sacred knowledge." Institutions of the sacred have not had the same scrutiny as sacred places. More specifically, the scientific critique of claims about sacred places has had little effect on those parctices that suppress *suspicion*. This

may, in part, account for the curious fact that some institutions of the sacred are faring much better than sacred places in general. But why is this so?

It must be noted that some religious institutions have joined the "other side" in the modern critique of sacred places. While most East and South Asian religious institutions continue to be centered around immobile places of practice (mountains, caves, rivers, rocks, trees), many institutions that claim control over sacred knowledge in Europe and North America have, over the last six hundred years, relinquished an interest in the control of such sacred places. Beginning with the early English Lollards in the late fourteenth century, Protestant Christian critiques of religious practice have also been critiques about the need for and legitimacy of any sacred place. "Replacing" these is the human body itself, as a metaphorical "temple," and scripture (the Bible read in the vernacular) as a moveable site of practice. These practices created a break between geographically disembedded (Protestant) knowledge claims and those of other, historically/geographically fixed "religions." What does this mean?

In part, it suggests that some religious institutions have a history of abetting the "modern" critique of sacred places. This critique can no longer be described as merely a secularizing critique, but rather one that also takes an active part in institutional conflicts (such as those between Protestant Christianity and Buddhism in various Asian nations). And, by using the same arguments as their secular academic critics, these "institutions of the sacred" suppressed suspicion of their own institutional strategies.

I am not suggesting here that the Protestant Reformation was actually planned as a strategy to suppress suspicion, but rather that this outcome is an unintended, and mostly unquestioned, consequence of the long history shared between liberal Protestant religious institutions (and also their evangelical desires) and Euro/American academe. In what I am calling a postmodern moment, the reflexive critique of institutions, including those of "modern science," is beginning to break through the silence that surrounded the institutional management of knowledge/power. The desires of modern science, which were hidden beneath its façade of objective neutrality, are now coming into critical focus. Recent contributions to the history of science (Popper, Kuhn, Gould, and Lyotard come to mind) have exposed many of the strategies the scientific community uses to suppress suspicion. Similar critiques of religious institutions, such as Allan Grapard's just-published study of the early Japanese Kasuga cult, have also revealed strategies centered around the control of sites of religious practice. Social science is now moving away from its earlier role as an (unreflexive) agent in the spread of modern scientific *doubt* to a new role: that of a reflexive critic of institutions and their practices.

EMOTIONAL CONTROL & DE-CONTROL

"Doubt management" is vital to the promotion of places. The "mystique" or reputation of any place, from a Pure Land Temple to a ramen restaurant, is liable to doubts. For this reason, the minor suppression of doubt[8] is more or less implicated in the maintenance of places generally, as an entrance requirement for the activity that sustains the place. "Forgetting" one's doubt is simply a cover-charge one pays to experience the place-as-place. The desire to forget (which is different than the desire to believe) underlies all of the practices that provide such an experience. A Disney park provides an excellent example of forgetting as a requirement of the experience of place.

A Disney park's seamless semiological and physical place saturates the consumer's ken for the duration of the visit, prompting the *forgetting*, which is, as Willis also noted, precisely what the consumer pays for. The Disneyland mystique requires the consumer to forget that all the spontaneity has been pre-programmed, and that none of the proffered risks are in any way risky. The complicity of the consumer is generally required for this forgetting. The consumer agrees to accept the circumstances *as they are presented.* Disney customers open themselves up to

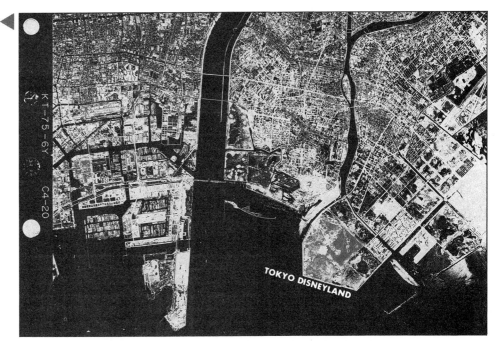

Aerial photograph of Tokyo Bay and the site of Tokyo Disneyland. Aerial (and satellite) photography opens up a modernist, panoptic perspective of places.

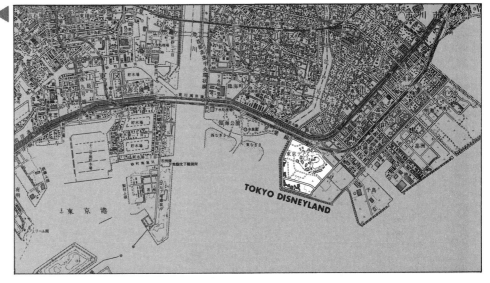

Land-use map of the environs of Tokyo Disneyland. Notice how the "sacred geography" of the Magic Kingdom becomes flattened and normalized in this modern map.

The Disney guide to Tokyo Disneyland. A semiotic buffet that serves up the main attractions (while it hides the working areas) of the Magic Kingdom. Notice the use of the Cinderella Castle as a central monumental structure, a human-made mountain, in the absence of the Matterhorn.

129

the Magic Kingdom's heavy dollop of nostalgia and vertiginous bodily thrills. This forgetting is pre-programmed by the institution but it is also managed by the consumer for his/her own advantage, in order to generate the desired (and paid for) experience of the place. We must not presume that consumers abjectly surrender to the Disney experience, but rather explore how consumers manage their own forgetting.

The desire to forget — the "urge to merge" — leads to the practice of what Featherstone calls the "de-controlled control of the emotions."[9] This practice of emotional self-management allows the consumer to experience the mystique of various places in a single day as though each were real, without acquiring a durative belief in their sometimes conflicting reality claims. A higher level of emotional control — and an expanded ken — is maintained in this effort, under which a greater degree of emotional relaxation is possible. The shriek of the consumer at the "surprise attack" of the mechanical crocodile on the Jungle Cruise (a display of de-controlled emotion) marks the forgetting; but the laughter that immediately follows marks the higher level of emotional control the consumer still maintains. Doubts are not actually abandoned in this process, but rather they are temporarily ignored, forgotten but not gone. Virtuoso consumers now "dive into" a place (a Jungle Cruise ride, say, or a Cuban restaurant), emotionally "submerge" themselves, and reemerge later unaltered (emotionally "dry"), ready for the next dive. This ability to control the de-control of emotions is a fundamental consumer skill in cities where each doorway on the market street offers up a highly aestheticized ambiance in competition with its neighbor — and in a world where a plurality of religious institutions offer up conflicting knowledge claims and sacred geographies.

THE ETHNOGRAPHY OF SACRED PLACES

Let's review a bit here. That *places* can be described separately from the spaces they "occupy" is an essential notion for social geography. This transformation of its space is the first requirement in the creation and maintenance of any place, sacred or not. So too, there are processes in modernity that "de-place" places, illuminating their spaces with maps that show no trace of their placeness, which was there a minute ago but now cannot be found. Global geographical science (in the service of the nation state) opens up all spaces to an illusory transparency which denies places anywhere to hide. The differences between spaces and places can be read from the maps that apply to each.

We have also seen how hiding places and hiding practices are integral to the fabrication of sacred places. Sacred *practices* share an essential structural feature with confidence games and practical jokes: they hide some aspect of their intentions or meanings and so fabricate an experience for the person subjected to (thus the subject of) the joke, or the con, or, indeed, the sacred. Sacred *places* — and Magic Kingdoms — also share an essential structural feature with hospitals and restaurants: they hide from view those places where the real action happens (operating theaters, kitchens, and inner sancta) and so fabricate a façade for the subject of the surgery, the salmon mousse, or, again, the sacred.

Where does this leave us, and better, where does it all lead? The main outcome — also the desired effect — of a postmodern ethnography of sacred places, and of places in general, would be

to free up the internal debate about their individual reality claims. This is done at the cost of institutional priorities rather than at the expense of sacred places themselves. Denying institutions the strategies that control suspicion makes them vulnerable to further examination of their intentions and practices. This opens up the sacred place and its knowledge to *those doubts that are implicit to its own reality claims.* The underlying moral/political notion here is that suspicions (likewise imaginations and desires) belong to the consumer and should not be managed beyond the consumer's ken by any institution. The democratization of knowledge about sacred places is central to the postmodern ethnography of these. Notions of "belief" and "believer" are transformed in this process: belief becomes a plural, reflexive, fluid *commodity*, and the believer its savvy consumer.

The commodification of belief within what Giddens calls a "reflexive project of the self" allows the consumer to choose and to "play with" their belief. Discursivized and subject to continual negotiation, such a belief is acquired and discarded with little effort. This belief marks the relationship the *consumer wishes to have* with the sacred place. "Postmodern" belief would not be dependent upon institutional strategies that constrain the ken of the consumer of the sacred, but linked to each individual's desires and personal, reflexive project of the self. Of course, such a belief is antithetical to institutionally regulated belief and belief systems. These believers make lousy followers when it comes to acquiescing to authoritative institutional demands; their commitment to an institution is much less reliable than is convenient for an institution. But this does not mean that their commitment to places of sacred practice or to practices in sacred places is any less durable. These believers are simply street-wise, self-aware consumers of the sacred.

A postmodern ethnography of a sacred place is something like a combination of the following: a "consumer's guide" to the sacred place; a self-help book with instructions on the reflexive belief in and appreciation of this place; and a critical history of the institutional practices that now claim control over this. Although the requirements of the proffered experience of each sacred place are different, all such experiences are open to a consumer-generated "de-controlled control of emotions." The goal is to free consumers of the sacred to make personal choices about their belief in (and doubts about) a particular sacred place.

Places that claim to hold the sacred within their boundaries can tell us much, including much about what it takes to make a "place" on this planet where globalized, uniformly modern space continues to elide what used to be local, and special, and full of history and knowledge. But even as the sacred place is vulnerable to practices of modernity, it is also liable to institutional strategies that obscure its knowledge for institutional purposes.

The future of sacred places depends upon critical knowledge of the practices of both modern scientific institutions and those institutions that claim control over sacred places. ▲

NOTES

1. Anthony Giddens, *The Consequences of Modernity*, Stanford: Stanford University Press, 1990. 2. Henri Lefebvre, *The Production of Space*. trans. by Donald Nicholson-Smith. Oxford: Blackwell, 1991. p.27. [Originally published as *La production de l'espace*. Paris: Editions Anthropos. 1974.] 3. For a discussion of Giddens's use of time-space relations see: Derek Gregory, "Presences and absences: time-space relations and structuration theory," in David Held and John B. Thompson (eds.), *Social Theory of Modern Societies: Anthony Giddens and His Critics* Cambridge, Cambridge University Press, 1989, Pp. 185-214. 4. Barbara G. Meyerhoff, "A Death in Due Time: Construction of Self and Culture in Ritual Drama." in John J. MacAloon(ed.), *Rite, Drama, Festival, Spectacle*, Philadelphia, Institute for the Study of Human Issues, 1984, p. 152. 5. Susan Willis, "Disney World: Public Use/Private Space," *South Atlantic Quarterly* 92:1 Winter 1993, Pp. 119-137, p. 135. 6. Erving Goffman, *Frame Analysis*, Boston, Northeastern University Press, 1984, p. 2. 7. Erving Goffman, *Frame Analysis*, p. 110. 8. The more general suppression of *both* doubt and suspicion may very well be unnecessary for the maintenance of places as such, but is pursued for other, institutional purposes. There are aspects of Disney parks that are hidden for reasons that have nothing to do with the maintenance of the "Magic," and everything to do with profit motives and corporate security. The ethnography of sacred places would open up the institutional strategies that would separate the consumer from her suspicions, her cash, her time, and her own life-project skills and desires. 9. Mike Featherstone, *Consumer Culture and Postmodernism*, London: Sage, 1991, p. 126.

MUSICAL CHAIRS FOR MOUNTAIN GODS

STEPHAN KÖHLER

The wind played with the loose end of the straw rope, entwined with a zigzag of white paper. At each gust, the rope struck the weathered post of the Shinto gate at a different angle. Atop this hill, only a few dried-up shrubs and weeds remained. The landscape was a man-made desert. A couple of stones were draped in white cotton cloth. In this setting, their inscriptions took on new meaning. On this peak they were sovereign. A narrow cast-iron gate opened upon an area surrounded by a fence of hand-carved stone. Ends of candles, burnt matches, and dried-up *sakaki* twigs were the evidence of people coming up here to pray.

Two months later, this hill had lost 30m of height, and the silhouette of an earth mover had replaced the soothing shadow of the wooden gate to a once holy area. The old god had been displaced by one of man's favorite tool-toys, a bulldozer.

"I would not let anybody touch that mountain and shrine; when the negotiations on the Gifu Mino Golf Course began six years ago, I opposed as much as I could. I had to give up. The temptation of a big chunk of money to the families owning the land was stronger than my spiritual considerations," explained Fukeji Furuta, caretaker and leader of the group of Ontake Mountain god believers. "Every year in May, about 15 people would come up with offerings; dressed in a white gown, I would then hold the ceremony. This year we had to move the god to a new location east of here, a mountain much lower. In a way it makes it easier for elderly persons to come up and pray."

"Were the holy stones wrapped in white cotton cloth so that the god inside them would not see the bulldozers coming?" I asked naively.

"No, when the holy stones are wrapped in cotton, the spirit inside them returns temporarily to its origin, the peak of the holy Ontake Mountain in Nagano Prefecture. Only in that empty state, can these stones be touched and moved."

"Do you think the god is happy in the new location?"

"I hope so..." His voice sounded tired and broken.

▲▲

My workshop is located near this scene in Oyada, part of Mino City, Gifu Prefecture. It's worth a visit. Maybe we have the highest sand dunes in Japan now, bigger than the ones in Tottori Prefecture. The ripples are not engraved by the wind, but by endless steel treads. To the west, the golf course eats its way through the mountains. Toward the south, Mino City Hall is making a group of mountains disappear to make a place for a "Tecno Park," though more slowly than expected, since the scraping seems to be more expensive than anticipated, or recession has narrowed the number of potential tenant companies. To the east, the Mino Country Golf Course has applied for permission to build nine more holes.

Two years ago, on the peak of the highest mountain of "Tecno Park" was a little Inari shrine, weathered and shaky. The trees had all been shaved away around it; I found there an abandoned pheasant's nest, with three cold eggs inside. Half of the mountain had been cut away and the shrine looked as if it were going to fall off the cliff soon.

"What is going to happen to the shrine?" I asked people in Oyada.

"They will take it away, the god has been moved a while ago."

"The god has been moved..." This line fascinated me the first time I heard it. Gods seem to be movable, just like any commodity. "Nature as such is god. A big rock, an old tree, a stream, a river, and of course mountains, can be gods." Most Japanese give me this statement, when we talk about Shinto concepts. However, few individuals refer to these principles and dare to stand up and speak out against the commercial rape of nature. Annual construction budgets must be spent, and people prefer clubbing white balls along artificial lawns to taking a hike on a mountain trail. I'd expected persons who hold priestly positions and carry out functions in Shinto shrines to protest. If gods are enshrined in nature, and worship of nature is the heart of Shinto, then the destruction of nature takes away the reason for Shinto's existence. If I were a Shinto believer, especially a priest, I would feel obligated to preserve what my faith is about. This however is Western logic. What seems a very obvious paradox to me might not be a contradiction at all to a Japanese. I began to question a wide range of persons, hoping to shed some light on this problem.

▲▲

"Aren't you disgusted about all this?" I asked a citizen of Gokurakuji, working on his newly set-up field below the golf course under construction. I expected him to be heartbroken. "No, it's all right. The golf company treats us well. They invited everyone in this neighborhood who supported the construction, by leas-

Photographs by Stephan Köhler

The New God is called Money, and it is enshrined in an Earth Mover.

comes to worship. So I feel that some gods are quite happy if they are moved from the mountaintop to a better spot. A better spot means a place accessible by modern man, where more people come to pray. It's hard to make a general judgement. Some gods are glad when moved, others aren't. The moving ceremony of a god to a new site should take place at 2 o'clock in the morning, in total darkness and quiet. But nowadays we don't do that. Humans are scared in the dark." Even though Katoh's posture was bent, I was sure he would not mind the darkness, but probably his younger helpers would. He continued: "Untouched nature? Its disappearance will definitely influence the souls of humans. Just listen to the difference in sound between a wild creek jumping from rock to rock, and the same water running over concrete brackets."

▲▲

"We are praying for smooth construction, and that no one gets hurt. Next year in August we will open. The population has been very supportive. We have a 20-year leasing contract with them."

"What will you do if they don't renew the lease in twenty years? Attitudes might change. Did you make any agreements to remove the drainage pipes you inserted underground and all the concrete-shelled lakes and dams?"

"I am sure that we are not going to leave in twenty years, but.." Ohashi put on a generous face," ... we would give all these water directive installations as a present to the Gokuraguchi Mino community. The earth will be returned as a golf course, with drainage and lawns. We are not obligated to remove anything when returning the land we use."

▲▲

"The first-year students we take on tours to explore the wildlife in the creeks running off the hills behind the school. There are lots of little crabs and tiny fish. The second year students are asked to make a map of the area around our school, and the children in third year are taken to a kind of park with rare trees and plants," explains Kimiharu Koizumi, vice director of the elementary school in

ing their land, to a two-night, three-day trip to the Japan Seacoast. The shrine? Oh, we had a god-moving ceremony last week. The priest took good care of it."

▲▲

Matsui Koji is one of the few shrine carpenters left in Gifu. "The Shinto church is very conservative. Conservative not in respect to preserving pristine nature, but in respect to being loyal to the government. Whatever the ruling power says is correct. Loyalty to nature is secondary compared to this political tie."

I wondered what would happen if some powerful politician ordered the demolition of Mount Fuji. Maybe the Shinto priests might not object; they would just move the Fuji god, probably to a smaller mountain of similar shape.

"How many gods have been moved in Gifu during the last five years, due to construction?" I asked. "No one knows, because the communities don't have to ask the Jinja Cho, the main office of the Shinto church, for permission to move a god. They just do it and send in an announcement that a new shrine has been inaugurated, without having to say why." I was surprised at this answer. I thought there was a record for everything in Japan, including the deigraphic dynamics of gods.

▲▲

Aimiya Seishi, assistant to the senior Shinto priest in Mugegawa-cho Hachiman, Gifu-ken, says: "If it benefits the majority of people in an area, then it is perfectly alright to move gods. Rocks need to be cut to make a road, and golf courses help relax the hard-working Japanese..." The Hachiman shrine he attends does well because of the Mino Country Club. The local Jinja Committee about twenty years ago signed a "lease" renting out a couple of the holy mountains for ¥7 million a year. Of course the mountains won't look the same when they're returned. Behind the shrine countless lost golf balls are slowly being overgrown by moss.

▲▲

Katoh Masanao, 85 years old, lives in Takatomi-cho, Gifu-ken; his shrine, founded 1,200 years ago, is also surrounded by three golf courses. "I became a Shinto priest when I was 23 years old. Since then the world has changed drastically. When people were mostly farmers, not salarymen, they would climb any mountain to worship and pray for health and good harvests. Villagers carried up all the stones and timber to build a shrine. Now people's muscles are weak and they are short of time. Very, very few people go up to pray at the little shrines on mountaintops around villages. And a god is nothing, does not exist, if no one

Gokurakuji, Mino-shi. "When I visit Tokyo, after only a day I desperately long for the sight of a mountain or a forest. Those people on subways look awfully tired and burnt out. Children who grow up in the countryside, close to nature, have a much better chance to become well-balanced adults. I think people in the countryside have a warmer look in their eyes than hectic city people." The hills behind the school are going to be the Mino Gifu Golf course. Already now the water coming out of the black drainage pipes is red.

"What about what happens a hundred yards behind your school? Will it affect your principles of teaching?"

"I can't really say anything about that. If Mino Mayor Nishibu thinks it is correct to make a golf course, then of course it is the right thing to do. And the designers promised to have the balls shoot off in the opposite direction, away from us. So we don't have to fear any broken windows. But if the little crabs in the river die out and the fish as well, certainly I will have the children question and think about why, in terms that a six-year-old can understand."

"Also south of this town, the Mino administrators have had a group of mountains removed to make Tecno Park, an industrial zone. They hope to attract people to move to Mino. However, I have heard that the population of Japan will shrink drastically in the coming decades. For whom is all this being done?"

"I have wondered that too. Within the next five years, we will have to close five of our eleven classes. We are quite worried about what to do with the excess teachers."

▲▲

"Benefits from having a golf course? Tax income, that's practically the only gain for Mino City, and jobs for about a hundred people." I was pleased to hear this honest and unpretentious answer from Jun Kawano, who works in the planning department of Mino City Hall.

"Regarding the conflict of Shinto attitudes versus development interests, I have to say as an administrator that economic considerations have priority. As an individual, I would want to conserve as much nature as possible, especially for my kids, so they can see a real river, an untouched mountain." Kawano spoke slowly, choosing his words carefully. His husky voice gave evidence of the political pressure he lived under. Obviously the conflict between his role as administrator and his private life makes Kawano suffer. I wonder how long such vessels can hold before they crack.

▲▲

"The shrine itself is just a symbol made by humans to pray to. The spirit is an entity in itself, that resides in mountains, trees, rocks and rivers; nature, generally speaking." Nagahiro Fujita, a high ranking Shinto priest, serves in the Jinja Cho in Tokyo, the head office of all Shinto Shrines in Japan. "Of course the energy of a holy place diminishes as it is changed by humans. Therefore, we should intervene in nature only if absolutely necessary. For traffic safety, for example... then people will not have to fear ill-luck cast upon a community by an insulted god. Whether a golf course is a legitimate reason to cut into nature is very questionable. Japan has gone too far with its construction greed. We need to slow down and reevaluate our relationship to nature. There is definitely a conflict between the concepts of Shintoism and development interests. We from the Jinja Cho have hosted some symposiums on this topic and are beginning to speak out concerning environmental matters. There are no great results yet, but I will keep you posted."

▲▲

I went to look for the site to which the Ontake god had been transferred. Soon I found myself in the parking lot in front of the recently scandal-tainted Shimizu Kensetsu construction office. A tanned worker was taking his cigarette break in the dusty cabin of his dump truck.

"The new shrine is on that hill there in the middle of the golf course. You can't drive up there now. Too dangerous because of the construction. Check inside the office."

"Do you enjoy making this golf course?" I had to ask the question of this tired, weathered face. Calloused fingers had an iron grip on the small cigarette.

"No, it is just a job to make a living, nothing else. Toys for rich people."

I was not in the mood to ask for permission to visit a place meant for people to come anytime to pray. I just drove arbitrarily into the carefully labeled lanes. "Turn right for holes, 4, 5, 6. Turn left for holes 11, 12, 13... Drive carefully. Avoid accidents..." and of course many NO TRESPASSING signs in *kanji*, which I cannot read.

For a moment, looking at the newly planted hedges, little shrubs and trees, I thought, how pretty; what a cute park this will be. Nice to take a stroll. However, as I turned my head, my eyes sank into the thickly woven mat of vines, weeds, and trees on an untouched slope and I was reminded of where home really was. Those natural arrangements, made by hands we never see, had an elegance and power that made me embarrassed to have been lured even for a second by the Shimizu workers' planting act.

Finally, along a clean pebble path, I made my way up to the new god-site. The old wooden gate had been replaced by a sturdy concrete one, made for eternity. The original fence and holy stones were sitting in more or less the same positions they had been in before, no longer on a peak, however, but somewhere midway on a hill. I breathed the air, sensed without eyes and ears and got the impression that the god had not quite made the move. The place felt empty and sterile. Either the god had gotten stuck on the way, or preferred to stay at home on its original peak in Nagano Prefecture. The old location on the scarred hill had had an aura, a power field, even though surrounded by bulldozers. The new site might have such power 500 years from now.

▲▲

From my conversations I learned that Shintoism is not as integrated into Japanese souls as I had assumed. People get their new cars blessed; properties; earth gods are calmed before construction; and people buy all kinds of good luck and wealth-attracting charms at the New Year. Japan has all kinds of elaborate, bizarre festivals. How far does it reach? Probably many of these rituals

have become empty phrasing, similar to the decreasing attendance at services in Christian churches, the hypocrisy contrasting with the happy celebrations of Christmas and Easter.

The Shinto priests probably don't act, because they would have to realize that in an industrial society their voice does not have the same weight as it had in the old agricultural society. Especially in comparison with prewar times, when the Emperor was a god, Shinto has weakened. The priests themselves have become, in a way, a commodity, objects of the capricious moods of consumers. Some priests can be hired like actors, to perform a nice custom for money. The new god is money. The charm of corporate identification, being a Sony, Coca Cola or Golf Course man, is far more powerful than any attachment to rudimentary values. Of course, one does not have to be a Shinto believer to protect mountains and rivers in danger. The children I talked to don't think about mountain gods. They just want their mountains back.

Now, the holy stones, the stone fence are all moved and the *omiage* from the great trip have all been eaten. A source told me that this Gokurakuji Golf trip had been seasoned with fights. Those who had leased 100 acres refused to sit at the same table and eat the same food as those who had only contributed 10 acres. They wanted lobsters and caviar. Once you've sold one of your children you've sold them all. The act of selling out in one aspect of your life contaminates all other aspects. These people are sitting on a chute, which looked so promising at first, and are going spiritually down, with no exit from their clever ride.

By the way, if you're interested in golf, 900 members have already signed up, but 300 memberships are still available at the Mino Gifu Golf Club. The cost is ¥17 million, with a ¥1 million non-refundable deposit. For more information call 0575-35 0111. Ask for Mr. Ohashi or Mr. Okumura. ▲

ねがい……
ぼくは今の山をみるととてもかなしいでもそれに、川が油なんかでよごされたら、しあわ
せすんでいた魚たちもむそこには住めなくなります。山の木もきりられればもちられるほど空気よ
れていくばかりです。ぼくはゆるせません。あそら、こてよい地球のことをもっと大切にしていくべ
だと思います。　村下彰洸

MOUNTAIN FEET

Photographs by Stephan Köhler

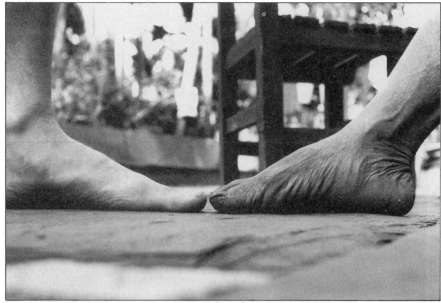

Two feet: German — asphalt walker / Rukai - Taiwan mountain walker

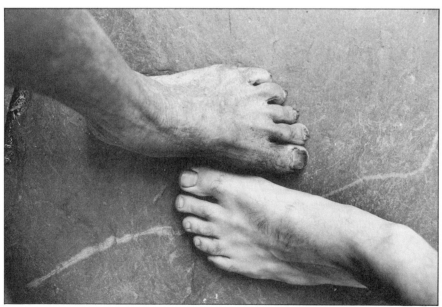

— Learn from those who know the earth. —

TONY HENDERSON

禅家曾説本
來空解脱必
君有飢同言
暑這方惟一
祇日持綱罟
伴漁翁

Kensu (Hsien-tzu) by Yōgetsu, late 15th century. Hsien-tzu, a legendary monk who was a popular subject among Ch'an and Zen painters, was said to be homeless, spending his days wandering along riverbanks eating shellfish (a practice forbidden by orthodox Buddhists). The poem translates: Zen believers say the origin of everything is emptiness. / An enlightened one like you — is there another? / Cold or hot, just one plain robe is enough. / Every day, carrying nets, you accompany fishermen.

Chuddy Cornfield was in a fix. He stood at the entrance to a Tokyo Zen temple but could not get himself to step over the threshold. Twenty-seven years old, more unshaven than bearded, curly brown hair and a lively gait — discontentedly married and mis-employed — there was a big hole in his life.

He had read a book about liberation and Zen Buddhism and one intriguing Zen sect temple was located near his apartment and he had noticed a long striding monk there, who, with one direct look, had caused some internal upset in Chuddy Cornfield.

Chuddy had noticed this fellow with the swinging walk over the previous months and had laughingly called him 'the mad monk,' for no particular reason, just something disturbing that aggravated. But now, Chuddy had a fear, somehow, of entering the temple grounds. A sense of suspension. It was as if he had to decide something important or be forever disappointed. This monk, who had the capacity to 'make people mad — on the inside,' was called Ei Fu.

When he had first arrived at the Obaku Zen sect temple of Ryugan-ji, or Dragon Eye Temple, in Meguro, once a village, today an integral part of modern Tokyo, the young monk Ei Fu had worn a sullen face. He did not show his frustration to the outside world, but in the temple he could not hide his feelings so well. Inside, he was churning.

As the first son of an Obaku Zen sect temple priest, Ei Fu had the responsibility of taking over the duties related to the family temple. While the rebellious side to Ei Fu's character was stubbornly against the formalities and orthodoxies of customary Zen ceremonies, there was something about the religious search and his own religious feeling that pulled him strongly.

After completing his eduction at the Buddhist University of Hanazono, Ei Fu had wanted to head for the mountains and seclusion but his Zen master, Mu-shin, who, unusually, dressed more like a farmer than a priest, had directed otherwise, saying, "Mountain is wine; for you, only tea — maybe wine later."

Mu-shin, meaning 'Spirit of Complete Emptiness,' had seen in Ei Fu's youthful earnestness a disequilibrium, caused by the simple things that make a young man thus mad. An unrelinquished burden in regard to woman; unreconciled relations with mother and father or once lover. These were held fast, as heavy recordings in his psyche. Mu-shin knew that these unresolved fragments would have plagued Ei Fu in the mountains to no intelligent release but in the city, well, there were opportunities for release when the pressure builds up and an answer is a need.

The acolyte was not ready for the mountains but he was earnestly sincere, which is both the best and the worst, bringing about either true life or spiritual captivity in one set form or another. So, he was ordered to Ryugan-ji.

Ei Fu's aging mentor at Ryugan-ji was energetic Yoshino-Sensei, who once taught primary school children in a rural area — for all of forty-five years — and had graduated to teach young men the ways of Zen after an encounter with the then young Zen monk Mu-shin.

On their first meeting Yoshino-Sensei told Ei Fu he did not believe in retirement so if Ei Fu found his quite dead carcase some morning not to give it second thought, just attend to the burial as if it were that of an old, if favoured, dog!

Ei Fu's duties were cleaning the temple, serving Yoshino-Sensei and any guests. Besides that, there was regular zazen, sitting meditation. It turned out to be a busy if straightforward life in regard to the externals. The internal experiences with zazen were a different matter.

While Yoshino-Sensei lived on long enough despite his unusual announcement and commanded respect, Ei Fu eventually became the power with the 'kyosaku' or warning stick that brought fear into the eyes of new students — such were his shouts and bangs of the stick during the Zen meditation sessions. No one dozed.

That came from his rough character, though Ei Fu presented the teaching in as ordinary a manner as Yoshino-Sensei, without talk, in action, in attending to the daily round. Ei Fu had come to terms with his wilder nature, the urgent sensuality of his twenties.

The most self-revealing period, for him, was in his third year at Ryugan-ji when he was hard put to stave off heavy depression and when he could hardly keep awake during his zazen sessions. All he could think of was the opposite gender, the most recently met female; the snack-shop lady who was so kind in her words as she looked at him with affection; the taut-muscled kerosene-delivery girl who came on Tuesdays. So much for 'emptying the mind of all thoughts,' which is the way of that form of Buddhist meditation. When he began to notice strong reveries surging through in his everyday activities, and found himself chatting too long with the ever curious and eager young ladies on visits to the temple, arriving there as part of their Tokyo sightseeing, something snapped inside.

The tension was too much and he confessed to bright-eyed Yoshino-Sensei, who immediately gave him ¥20,000 for a night out. "Go the full hog," he had said, "pick one that will take you to paradise — don't go for less. Don't go like a machine, go like a man, like a human, with warmth, with a sense of beauty. If you need more, come and see me again tomorrow evening."

Ei Fu could hardly believe his ears. He accepted the envelope — somehow a few of these were already prepared — he did notice there were other envelopes as well. "What shall I wear?" questioned a dazed Ei Fu with not a little instant practicality. "Not your robes, that's for sure," laughed wily old Yoshino-Sensei.

From that day Ei Fu got his smile back. He used three more envelopes and Yoshino-Sensei asked what was becoming of young men these days, in his day it would have taken at least five envelopes and he had put the remaining two in his kimono.

Ei Fu got permission to visit his own Zen master Mu-shin — the very same person that had caused Yoshino-Sensei to turn to that particular mystical path — but never did meet him for four more years because he had nothing important to say. All those years at Ryugan-ji and not a single query had come to him of worth to put to Mu-shin, but the energy was unblocked and a thousand-and-one new feelings and half-assembled questions did rise from his messy interior.

How Yoshino-Sensei gladdened at the sight of Ei Fu laughing and bawling out instructions in the zendo where the zazen training took place.

It was four years on from the days of the Red Light district excursions that Yoshino-Sensei's earthly life went out. A simple chill one autumn morning was the last kick of life that brought the happy old fellow to his final sleep. The last sound Yoshino-Sensei heard was the booming of the four-o-clock bell that was Ei Fu signalling for early morning prayers as the daily round went on into perpetuity.

Ei Fu did his duty as told but didn't dare do what he felt was most apt..... inscribing, "Here lies but an old dog," on Yoshino-Sensei's tomb. He did write a note to that effect to Zen master Mu-shin.

A reply was soon forthcoming. It read, 'To Ryugan-ji: Black flies buzz at dead dog's white teeth, man alone goes to meet the mountain."

It was not particularly addressed to Ei Fu, but to the Dragon Eye Temple inhabitants. Another old priest came to take over Ryugan-ji and Ei Fu wrapped his bowl and left for the mountain.

There was only one physical mountain that beckoned Ei Fu but it took some years to find that mountain and at first Ei Fu took to the pilgrim's trail as a mendicant monk in the old tradition. He begged his way from the high peaks of Northern Japan down to Nagano in the Japan Alps, then on to Omine-san in the Nara-Wakayama region where, one bright day, Ei Fu was met by two *Yamabushi*, the mountain ascetics of Japan.

They led him to a remote area and left him at a tangled path that had three directions and where they set him a question, pointing at the three paths.

"Do you progress into the past, the present or the future?" they asked. Ei Fu replied, "The present." The center path was indicated and the two Yamabushi walked back the way they had come.

He came across a village with a scattering of huts to the rear at the beginning of an uphill climb that led to severe crags. There were caves in the crags. These were the same caves that the Yamabushi Gongen — Mu-shin's own spiritual master — used in his years of relative solitude, before Gongen had realised that he was destined to share with others what he had learned and give orientation to his closer friends. Among these 'friends' and fellow travellers was the Zen monk Mu-shin — that was a decade ago.

This was something of a closed society among these friends who came from all callings and were not religious in the common sense, for it would be considered too strange that a Zen monk had a spiritual guide that was not of the official Zen lineage. But truth holds to no one container and travels diverse paths. A like striving had brought all these seekers together and they shared their endeavour with hearty sincerity.

Likewise, in Ei Fu's retreat, he too took up abode in those mountains, but chose an empty hut instead of a cave while making his arrangements in the same village.

That first night, with the wind howling, Ei Fu could hardly retain his joy. He felt he had come home. He felt everything he had experienced, including the years of confusion and utter sadness, all were worthwhile. Materially he had virtually nothing but on the other hand he had everything a man of few desires needs.

Life was simple. Mountain water was the perfect drink, made into a clear tea it was divine. Rice, a whole food, with mountain grown vegetables, gave good sustenance. All around was the abundance of nature, the stars at night in magnificent array, the brilliant moon, the changing shape of wind-chased cumulus or stormy nimbus. Ei Fu delighted in sunshine on rock, huge bole'd firs, insect life and bird song, streams and changing scenes with the changing seasons. He knew it all and was completely at home amongst it. There was something else. He

knew someone was there. He did not quite know what or who. It was not Zen master Mu-shin, but there was someone or something there, he was sure. It was the Yamabushi Gongen.

One night, as the wind rocked the little hut and creaked its roof, there was the rap of a staff on the door. Ei Fu hailed a welcome and slid the door aside.

There stood a tall man, not young and not old. A wisp of beard, a staff, deer skins hanging behind, prayer beads down to his navel, the lacquered cap typical of a celebrant Yamabushi and in his left hand a huge conch.

Ei Fu made a deep bow. The Yamabushi, fresh from his remote asceticism, held his height and said, "I must introduce you to your neighbours." With that he blew a mighty blast on the conch in a complex of notes that rode the wind down into the village. What a gathering that night. Ei Fu had never suspected such people existed, it was another world.

No tricks, no undue solemnity. A cask of saké was brought on a strong shoulder, and broken open with a wooden mallet by the door. Women from the village brought steaming rice and boxes of cooked foods, these were the men's wives mostly.

They drank from saké cups that held a good portion and drank to the good health of all devils, which Ei Fu immediately remonstrated on. But it was explained that to the Yamabushi — for these folk were mostly of that kin — their very role and duty was to tame devils and bring them to the civilized state that is beholden to Man. He heard songs of old Japan that night, songs of the mountain, of the adventures of the ancestors. The bamboo flute sang out with such penetrating tones, that Ei Fu went outside to sit on the wooden verandah, and wept enormous tears of gratitude.

Engrossed in the light and cloud play, he sensed there need be no restraint on tears for these were diamonds of revealed truth that his new companions had released in him.

It was three years later that Mu-shin paid his visit to Ei Fu's hut. Though unannounced, Ei Fu felt a visitor of some consequence was coming and even had the prescient confidence to give his place a general tidying, airing the spare mattress and putting fresh spring water in the kettle.

Ei Fu had just returned from his final flourish of setting the scene for this visitor,

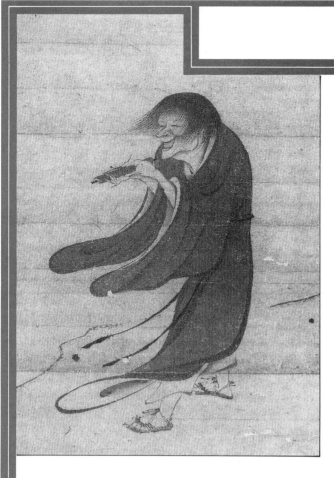

Kanzan (detail) by Reisai, 15th century, Daitōku Kinenbunko, Tokyo. Kanzan, the legendary mountain hermit of Ch'an Buddhism (usually depicted with his sidekick Jittoku), was named after his place of abode: Cold Mountain. Previous page: Lu Dong-bin "riding the dragon" by Sesson, 16th century, Yamato Bunkakan, Nara.

gathering mountain flowers that would only last an hour or two, and had thrown them into a slender pot, when a voice rang out.

"Is it in?" It was Mu-shin.

"Just come in!" answered Ei Fu. He laughed and slid open the door again to greet Mu-shin with a low bow, touching his head on the wooden floor planks.

Mu-shin did the same. They both rose, slowly, eying each other, their hearts brimming with emotion. The Zen master was tremendously encouraged at the sight of Ei Fu — what a man he had become and on Ei Fu's part, his master looked a little smaller somehow but as tough as a nut in his usual combat stance, as though confronting a band of ruffians.

Noting the whistling kettle and nought else but the tea caddy in sight, Mu-shin playfully remarked, "Have I come all this way for Uji tea?"

Ei Fu rejoined with, "It was always tea, between us, and tea will do us well today."

Mu-shin really did look a little crestfallen, such was the authority Ei Fu had gained. Aware of that slight alteration, Ei Fu made a flippant wager.

"I'll bet you a flagon you can't see over the abyss."

"How can I see over the abyss when it's filled?"

"What fills the abyss?"

"Nothing but life, life fills the abyss."

"Where flies this thing death then?"

"There is only life, life and more life!"

"What contains this life then?"

"The flagon, when it is emptied, contains life!"

"Whence goes the wine then?"

"Pour us the wine and I'll show it."

There was no hesitation between them. Gone was the old relationship of the one above and the one below. The dialogue ended with both laughing loudly. They laughed and laughed and each made the other laugh the more till the wooded glade rang with their merriment.

A conch was heard from the valley below, then another and the two men rose, still chortling and took a look down into the mountain's lower slopes. Not far off, down the path leading from the door, meandered a line of white robed figures and at least one of those figures was holding tightly onto a cask of saké. It was going to be one more night of celebration because another had returned.

Mu-shin did not stay more than a few weeks and soon after that brief visit Ei Fu moved into the cave. His stay there was not a long one. Enough to complete a series of exercises with those same Yamabushi who'd first knocked at his door in his early days on the mountain. It was a retreat for a group.

There were sufficient provisions in the cave for a month or so and plentiful mountain water. At the end of fourteen days, the Yamabushi left Ei Fu to it. From then on it was a tussle for the symbolic pearl of wisdom from the tenacious claws of the equally symbolic but no less real guardian dragons of the mountain.

There were descents into what people have called Hell. There were tribulations as old sites were revisited and fragments of the past recollected. Finally there was the ascent!

It was Ei Fu reborn in the present that gave instruction in zazen at Tokyo's Ryugan-ji as the monk had returned — to play his part in the esoteric endeavour — and to give his relief a furlough. In the meantime, neither Chuddy Cornfield nor Ei Fu knew nought of the other — and Gongen — he was joyfully dining with Mu-shin in the highest village on Omine, preparing himself for reconciliation with the big city — in a different role.

Chuddy caught sight of Ei Fu, striding between one smoothly drawn-aside sliding door and another. A brief glimpse, a merest glance. Next thing Chuddy knew he was amazedly listening to his shoes crunching up the neatly gravelled pathway, leading to a shaded entrance, guiding his way to the heart of the temple through the same sliding door that Ei Fu used. Chuddy knew the right phrase, "*Gomen kudasai,*" which brought Ei Fu, the not-so-mad monk, to the entrance. Smiling, he beckoned Chuddy — who stepped inside. ▲

THOSE FAMOUS TWIN PEAKS OF FUJI-SAN

F.J. LOGAN

These T-shirts are not T-shirts, my dear. Or at least not merely T-shirts. These are race T-shirts — hard-won, irreplaceable, priceless. Marathon races, forty-two point six kilometers. No, we cannot throw these T-shirts out, or even wash them. They are souvenirs from the land of pain, mementos dear as life itself. Yes, I know that doesn't make much sense. Please let me explain.

▲▲

It all began thirteen years ago in Edmonton, Alberta. My friend Rick and I were obese and serious junior professor types: bearded, bespectacled, and stern. We wore corduroy jackets with leather elbow patches, denim work shirts, knitted ties, and, although it was a struggle getting into them, Levis. We were pink stout little dumpling-men, bustling officiously about, panting and sweating, pop-eyed and dignified. Acutely conscious of our high calling, we often peered at students over the tops of our eyeglasses and waggled our eyebrows with quiet severity. Rick and I were serious educators. We had three degrees each, and three chins.

We had the high-colored, meaty, well-marbled look then much in vogue among Arts and Humanities gogues. It resulted mostly from gallons and gallons too much beer every night at the faculty club, and too little of anything remotely like exercise. For example, I was unable to climb the 48 steps to our second floor offices without pausing half-way for a five-minute breather. This inability, however, seemed to me regrettable but entirely normal; I was, after all, pushing thirty.

Rick, however, though two years my senior, could and did climb the 48 steps at one go. True, his jowls and forehead on these occasions would turn an alarming magenta, his glasses would fog up, and his legs would tremble. But he could do it, and I couldn't. He didn't have to zip up his Levis with a pair of pliers, and I did. He apparently still had some muscles left underneath there somewhere, and I didn't. I envied him his physical prowess.

One evening, however, Rick appeared at the faculty club, looking haggard. He fired up a Winston, gunned three drafts in quick succession, then sat, drawing skull-and-crossbones patterns with his pudgy forefinger in a slick of spilt beer. Finally he looked up and said, "I just came from the doctor's. Complete physical. Took an hour and a half."

"Why?" I asked. "You look okay to me."

"Life insurance." Rick snickered mirthlessly and chugged another beer.

"Well, how did it go?"

"Great. Wonderful. Said I'm in terrific shape —"

"I could have told you that."

"—terrific, *for a seventy year old man.*"

I felt an icy hand around my larded heart: if Rick was physically seventy, *how old was I?*

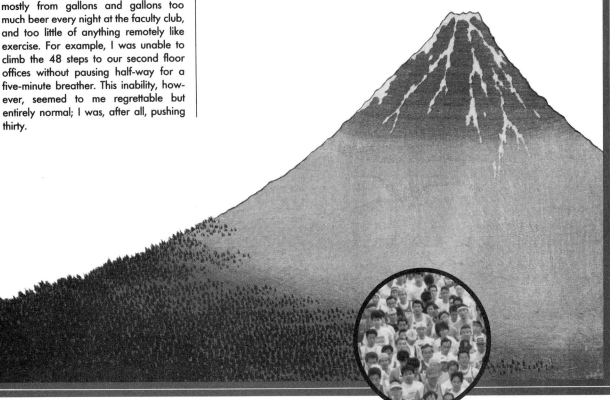

Well, somehow I quit smoking. I went on many diets. Then I quit drinking. I crept and trembled through the days, taking vitamins and avoiding drafts. I made a will. Then one day Ben, another portly friend, asked if I wanted to go running. Running! Why not just blow my heart out with a twelve-gauge? Was he, I asked, insane? The hockey rink, he said, once around. One lap, and one only. What was I afraid of? Or was it true, what everybody said, that I was a wimp?

Stung, I agreed. We waddled the lap. Next morning I felt as though I had been kicked and clubbed nearly to death. But two days later, under the lash of his scorn, I was back with Ben at the rink. And again, the following week. Soon it was Monday through Friday. Soon it was two laps, then three, then four. Thus all winter: two barely motile masses of juddering blubber, sweating and gasping and shin-sham-shimmying around and around. Then there came that glorious day in early spring when we achieved eight laps. Eight! Each lap was an eighth of a mile; we had run eight laps; ergo — hearty backslaps, fierce manly exultation — *we had run the mile!* And! We had done it in only twenty-two minutes.

We outfitted ourselves like the serious athletes we now were: $80 Nikes with soles like bright yellow waffles, colorful though constricting Bill Rogers track outfits, fearsomely complex nylon digital wristwatches by Seiko. As the weather warmed we began to run outside, slogging through the rich mud of the Saskatchewan river valley. I always carried a fistful of special high-energy runners' glucose tablets for the hills, and a can of illegal Mace for the animals. There were ferocious Rottweilers and Dobies along the trails, coursing leashless ahead of their doting owners ("Don't worry, Binky won't hurt you."), whole tribes of irascible porcupines, and, in the hollows, swarms of skunks, a high percentage of which were said to be rabid. We didn't care about the animals.

There was even a crazed neo-nazi regularly careering along the trails on his gigantic chestnut mare, intent upon trampling and intimidation. We didn't care about the Nazi. We kept steaming along — a mile, two, three. A year, two years. Quondam gobs of animated suet, we had gradually assumed the form of beings recognizably human.

Health! Sweet sleep, clear eyes, deep tans.

Strength! Lithe lats, mighty quads.

Stamina! Giant lungs, slow and stately pulses.

And I owed it all to running. One day we did five miles. "Hey," I said, in all innocence, *"How long is one of those marathons?"*

The next year I ran one, the first of seven.

Seven races, seven limping gimping finishes with subsequent sessions at the first-aid tent, seven character-building experiences: Achilles tendonitis, shinsplints, sunstroke, stress fractures, heat exhaustion, Morton's toe, hypothermia.

And seven T-shirts. By God, I wouldn't take a million dollars for these shirts, and that's a fact. There's not enough money in the world to buy them. Especially this last one, Kawaguchi-ko, 1985. Forty-two point six kilometers, and I was forty-two point six years old. The coincidence seemed to me somehow cosmic, portending great things. This, I felt, was to be my race; perhaps I would come in under three-thirty, thereby cancelling all the shame and pain of the first six. Kawaguchi-ko: I knew it would be special, and I was right. Look at that T-shirt — smell it. What do you smell? Fear, that's what. Agony and despair. Death, hell, and the grave. Sweet jesus, what I went through for this beauty! Seeing it, holding it, I'm right back there at the starting line. Me and four thousand others, milling in the icy mist beneath Mt. Fuji, killing time, waiting.

"Freezing our asses off — hey, buddy, the fuck's it gonna *do?* Clear up or get worse?" My interlocutor is a fat man, dressed as I am: no sweatsuit, no jacket, just a racing singlet and shorts. He is pitiful. His stomach is protruding from beneath his singlet, and he appears to be wearing some sort of halter-top support for his shapely breasts. And, though gross of torso, the man has pipestem arms and legs, deathly blue-white. His hands are stained with nicotine. His hair is thin, lank, oily. His face is like a burst red bag. I note the purple nose with its tracery of broken veins; and the complexion, nubbly-looking, with blotches; and the thick moist lips; and the small, deep-set, red-yellow-and-blue eyes nestled in their lavender pouches.

"Wonder'fieyoughtta wear the Gore-Tex," he muses aloud, and I stifle the urge to tell him it won't matter whether he wears his Gore-Tex or a moon suit or a ballerina outfit, because he won't get 500 meters before he cashes in. There is a saying among marathoners, that if you look about right then you're thirty pounds over; so, what if you *look* about seventy pounds *over?*

I am amused, contemptuous, but also faintly uneasy in this man's presence; there is, I feel, something horribly familiar about him. And suddenly I know what it is: *this man is me.* That is to say, he looks uncannily as I might well have, had I not cleaned up my act that decade previously. Looking at him I feel, pehaps, much as Dorian Gray felt on beholding his own loathsome portrait. There, I think, but for the grace of God...

"Nah," says my worser twin, "it's bad now but I think it's gonna clear. Don't wanna carry around alladat extra weighttada Gore-Tex." *Extra weight.* I think, but I let that one go too, and look up. There is the great cone of Fuji-san bulking enigmatically to the south. What will they send us, the mountain gods? I look down and around. Maybe four thousand lean and carefully turned out Japanese with here and there foreigners looming like gawky angular carrots in a tawny field. One ebullient man is dressed like a *samurai*, with plastic helmet and *katana*, but almost everyone else is in nylon jackets and pants. Many seem also to have bulky sweaters or sweatshirts on under the nylon. If the cold rain continues, these people will be relatively comfortable; if not, however, they will swelter. I think back to last year's race, to the blast-furnace horror that was Iwakuni — the lads decimated by heat exhaustion, twitching like fresh roadkill — and I make my decision: shorts and singlet, nothing more.

POW!

We're off!

Five minutes later we're still off, at least theoretically, while we bounce around, all bunched up and stymied in a freezing drizzle as the seeded runners streak off

into history and everyone else funnels at length onto the course.

Which is beautiful: twice around Lake Kawaguchi, the mountain our Great Spectator. Shivering, I drink in the view as we all begin to creep forward then finally pick up a bit of speed. Speed means exertion, and exertion means body heat, of which the running body can generate an amazing amount. I'm starting to relax, confident that my decision was the right one. Eggplant-hued and gasping, the fat man is long gone. I don't miss him. I seem to recall something about *doppelgangers*. The Germans believe, or did, that one encountered one's double as an immediate prelude to death. Nordic twaddle, of course, and the man resembles me hardly at all, but on this day of days I need no evil omens, however absurd. Because today I feel something — destiny? — and I know in my bones that this race will be special.

I'm nicely warmed up now, steaming slightly in the sleet. We're all strung out, so there's lots of room to maneuver and no danger of tripping over each other's feet. But what's this? We're bunching up again! Why? Can't see — oh, I don't believe it. A bus! A *bus* is angled across the course, blocking everyone, and once again we're all jammed together, squirming around and shouting at the driver and catching each other's elbows and shoulders as we try to outdo each other in rudeness of gesture to that hapless man.

Squirming, shouting, gesturing, and *freezing* — the sleet having sluiced away my healthy sweat and induced a fit of shivering — I hear a by-now familiar wheezing gasp, coming from behind.

"Hey! Asshole! Adainna a bus stop!"

Elbowing me aside, standing arms akimbo, booming his displeasure.

"Hey, dork! I'm freezin' myassoff!"

I regard the immensity of his buttocks and imagine them as globes of gooseflesh-stippled ice suddenly detaching themselves and crashing to the pavement. Trembling, I hug myself and wait, while a nasty little wind springs up, whipping sleet against my numb, blue flesh. My teeth are chattering uncontrollably. The bus driver, I notice, has managed to kill the engine twice, and appears to have mired his vehicle. In the cab — his *warm* cab — he is doing frantic and futile things. There go the windshield wipers, now the turn signals. Our lead runners

are by this time, I know, around the five K point and just hitting their pantherish strides.

"You son of a bitch!" The fat man turns to me. "Hey, buddy, the guy is one son of a bitch, idne? Just what we fuckin' need, fuckin' hypothermia, idnit? — Hey, looks like it finely moved, didnit?" I sprint around the bus and away, leaving the fat man for good, putting together three fast Ks, hoping to regain my body heat. Ah, here's the drinks table. Maybe they have Gator Ade or Pocari Sweat or something with sugar in it. Sugar means warmth.

But not this time. I'm just getting colder and colder, weaker and weaker. Well, nothing to do but slow down to six-minute Ks and tough it out. Maybe the mountain gods will smile, wind die down, the freezing rain stop, the sun come out. Maybe.

But maybe not. Half-way, and I admit that the weather is if anything deteriorating: the wind coming now in fitful gusts, the sky lowering, the lake lead-colored and whitecap-flecked. Fuji-san's a study in steely grays. And *I* am deteriorating, my legs nearly powerless and the cold moving in toward my heart. Flurries of Japanese ladies pad by, murmuring, *"Ganbatte kudasai."*

Well, I *am* doing my best, because I know this race will be special, but now, after a further 10K, the road seems to be moving of its own accord, snaking around alarmingly, and it's all I can do to retain my footing. Could be an earthquake. Strangely, the swarms of runners now steaming past and regarding me so intently seem oblivious to these pavement-convulsions. Well, it's their country, so they've probably developed quake-legs the way sailors develop sea-legs. These runners leave a wake of gentle words — advice, perhaps, which I for some reason cannot fathom — as they disappear around the bend, past the 30K marker.

Only two kilometers to go! Or is it *twenty* two?

Whatever, I must need a break, because here I am with my arms around a roadside tree, embracing it like a lover, my cheek against the rough gummy bark. I love this tree. It seems to pulse with private meaning. What is your wisdom, tree? I look down, my vision clears, and I behold its roots beneath my Nikes. Roots — of course! The message of the tree is Stasis. "Stay here with me," it seems to say. "Why puff and pant? Why

try so hard to *do* when you already *are*? Tarry awhile, and immerse yourself in Being. Strive to realize your personhood. Know thyself; that is the highest wisdom. Foolish mortal, what is your purpose? Are you running *from* or running *to*? Why do either, when you're already *there*, which is also *here*?"

Stunned by such profundity from a mere tree, I reel back, catching my heel on a root, sprawling upon a flat, slanted pink rock, depositing upon it five of a possible six bodily fluids, then rolling or feeling all Creation roll around me, then feeling nothing.

Still nothing.

Now nothing filigreed with blackness.

Now blackness, perfused with a certain viscous quiddity which on closer inspection reveals itself as a plenitude of half-frozen mud. Which I am loathe to leave. Lovely, rich, hospitable mud. Primal mud, first goddess. Ashes to ashes, mud to mud...

Time to go.

On the writhing road again, tacking and veering with some very special backfield moves — hello, what's this? Runners, but coming *toward* me! Three or six of them, all about eighty years old, and high above them those famous twin peaks of Fuji-san. What a sight! A cadre of ancients creaking gamely along, back toward the starting line! This is too much. This is too funny. Roaring and howling, doubled over, I watch them come abreast of me.

"Hey, Gramps! *Wrong way!* You. Are. Go. Ing..."

But perhaps I'm laughing too hard to make myself understood, beacuse they edge widely around and away, continuing as before, with undiminished absurdity. How could they be so stupid? How could anyone get turned around on a marathon course? How could...

A neuron fires, a tiny thought glimmers.

"Wait!" I shout. "Wait for me!" But the old-timers are nearly out of sight, out of earshot, and moving briskly. Incredibly, they are *gaining* on me — or seem to be.

143

They can't *really* be gaining on me, of course. Perhaps their speed is an optical illusion, or some sort of senile delusion on their part. To believe otherwise would be to believe that I am running dead last in a field of 4,000 — or, I think grimly, 3,999. The fat man, at least, is history.

Forty K! Great! I'm flashing right along now, resting only briefly at each tree, and thus probably recovering huge chunks of lost time, thinking only of the ineffable specialness of this race, and of the T-shirt waiting for me. But one thing is certain: no T-shirt for the fat man.

"Heyyyeee buddeedeedee." A strangled rasp of words, a rubbery purple diffuseness zooming and wowing in and out of relevance, a blackness expanding and contracting direly in the middle of the purple, from the blackness further fatman words, resonating in my throat with a vile synaesthetic tang to them like some hell-mulch of mothballs and tinfoil. "Heyyyeee, hellooo, anybody homomome? Listen buddy, don't look nowowow, but you are really fucked."

Blooming through the icy fog a raging flame of awareness: the fat man! Impossibly, my past has caught up with me! The fat man is here and can't be! Therefore he's a hallucination. But, he doesn't *smell* or *feel* like a hallucination, with his arms under mine — *as though I needed some kind of support!* — and his reeking beer-breath scorching my cheek, and his whiskers raking the back of my neck. Therefore the fat man is real — but a ringer! Suddenly I see it all, in a flash of insight: he's a ringer! My vile twin is himself a twin! *Of course:* he's been lurking here all day by the 40K marker, while his swinish simulcrum, who pretended to start the race, is by now no doubt roistering in some drinking-hell, roaring out the story of their evil prank. How could they *do* such a thing? And *why?* To discourage me, that's why — to psyche me out, to ruin my special race!

"Hah!" I scream, snapping my head back into his nose. "I'm onto you!"

"Ouch! Hey, no kidding, buddy, you better —"

"No T-shirt for you! Or your *brother.*"

I shake him off and leap at him puma-like, fangs bared, a spark of red murder in my otherwise frozen heart. But now his giant quadripartite hams appear to be gusting and billowing ahead of me, looming huge as the Fujis but seeming to diminish in the distance, although that's probably just a Doppler effect, or maybe a doppelganger effect, because I couldn't really be following *him* across the finish line, and then trailing around Linus-like in some numb fog roiled upon us from the flanks of the great gray cones, and deriving flashes of transcendental insight from these Primal Polarities above, nothing kaleidoscopic correspondencies below in the form of dualities which attenuate themselves before my eyes like strings of noumenal paper cut-out dolls, and feeling this Whatness of the Is wash through me, and grasping the ironically open-ended nature of this my vision quest, and dragging my metasymbolic T-shirt through proliferating multiplicities and mud for some indeterminate period of time, before feeling the hundred fatman hands upon me — *to despoil me of my prize* — and then hearing a horrid fatman hypothermurmur as blackening mystic flashes multiply and grow and intersect, while my phenomenal person battles the myriad murmurous muggermen, just before we all achieve benightenment.

▲ ▲

Now, my dear, do you understand? Now can you comprehend the preciousness of this T-shirt and all of them? As long as I have them, I can't forget. As long as I have them, I can spread them out like this and meditate upon their stains and stenches, read the message in their eloquent cuts and rips, recall their mute but luminous adjuration, so often in the past forgotten or ignored, to wit: don't ever, ever, ever even think about entering another god-dammed marathon. Besides, you never know, I may wear these T-shirts again. Don't laugh. I'd put one on right now and show you, if I could get it over my stomach. ▲

RICHARD EVANOFF

THE EMPOWERMENT OF MOUNTAINS

On New Year's Day a year or so ago I climbed a mountain near my house in western Tokyo to see the sunrise. Konpira-san is part of a chain of mountains that form the western boundary of the Kanto Plain. As I was climbing, I realized how difficult it is to keep up both American and Japanese customs — staying up late New Year's Eve with a bottle of champagne and getting up early New Year's Morn to see the sunrise from a mountaintop.

The sun wasn't up yet when I reached the summit, but the horizon was already bleeding with the colors of daybreak. Facing east I could see Tokyo rising up from the shadows. Skyscrapers came into focus on the distant horizon. The entire Kanto Plain began to fill in with buildings, highways, and railway lines. As the sky slowly grew brighter, the city itself seemed to be oozing up to the mountaintop-island I was standing on, slowly hardening into a scab of concrete and pavement. By nature I'm not misanthropic, but I'll admit that I was tempted by the thought of being able to pick off that scab in order to give the raw earth underneath a chance to heal in the open air. Looking out across Tokyo from the top of Konpira-san it was easy to see why in English we use the word "blight" to describe unchecked urban development. The mountains rimming Tokyo's western edge seemed to be containing the disease. But for how long?

I couldn't help wondering if civilization is a cancer that will eventually suck all the life out of its host organism and die with it.

Konpira-san is just one of many mountains in the Takao area of western Tokyo that have been threatened by development. About seventeen years ago a high school in Tokyo purchased part of the mountain for the purpose of building a new campus and sports complex. The plan was to dynamite a third of the mountain before the construction began. About 250,000 cubic meters of rock were to be removed, adding up to something like 45,000 eleven-ton truckloads over a five- to six-year period. The only thing that stood in the way of these plans was a 250-year old Shinto shrine that rested on the top of the mountain. The shrine is dedicated to Konpira, an alligator god who guards sailors and merchants. And it was at this shrine that the faith to move mountains confronted the faith to preserve them.

By Japanese law a shrine and the area surrounding it cannot be destroyed if the shrine is actively maintained. Mountains have always been regarded as sacred places in Japan, and the tradition of building shrines on top of them goes back a long way. Before the Meiji Period any "secular" use of mountain areas was tightly controlled. The custom of *iriai* (which literally means "to enter collec-

tively") regarded non-arable lands such as mountain forests, marshes, riverbeds, and bamboo groves as being owned in common by the villages located near them. Local people were permitted to enter these areas, but there were strict regulations on the use of resources. No one could collect more than their fair portion of edible plants, roots, firewood, and other forms of vegetation.

These days custom, tradition, law, and even the gods themselves rarely get in the way of development plans, especially when there's big money to be earned. The tension between profit-seeking developers and undeveloped areas can be dated from the 1870's when the Japanese government adopted a "modern" landholding system in which lands owned by the public under the old iriai system were confiscated and placed in the hands of private owners. The private owners could exploit the resources as they saw fit. Collusion between the government and development interests with regard to land policy has been going on ever since — one only need witness all the recent scandals involving politicians and construction firms for confirmation.

It came as no surprise, then, when the Hachioji City Government approved the plan to dynamite Konpira-san in 1984. In 1990 the Tokyo Metropolitan Government added its blessing, and the construction company Kumagai Gumi was

hired to begin blasting the mountain. When local citizens heard of the plan they decided to organize an opposition group, forming the Association to Protect the Nature of Takao and the Arakawa River on October 10, 1991. Under pressure from voters, the metropolitan government told the construction company that several conditions had to be met before Konpira-san could be dynamited, which included replanting endangered plants found on the mountain, assessing the impact of the project on local water supplies, and establishing an agreement with local residents.

The Shinto shrine on the top of Konpira-san had fallen into disuse, but in December 1991 the citizens group officially registered it with the national government. Many local residents, including a number of foreigners who live in the area, joined the newly formed shrine association. A Shinto priest, Tadamori Yamakoshi, was called in and began holding monthly rituals on the mountain. Construction was scheduled to begin on January 15, 1992 with the removal of the shrine, but since the shrine was now officially registered and in use, the dynamite couldn't touch it. The construction company wanted to move the shrine, but wasn't able to without the permission of the shrine association.

Festivals were held on the mountain throughout the following year, featuring traditional Japanese dance, magic shows, folk music, and singing. An archeological investigation revealed that the mountain had been the site of a medieval fortress. Moreover, a network of tunnels had been dug under the mountain during the Second World War, which were used for manufacturing and storing munitions. The historical significance of the mountain, both ancient and modern, lent weight to the arguments to save it. Lawyers on both sides of the issue and city officials wrangled over what should be done.

Matters were complicated when the builders put up a fence around the construction site, which impeded access to the shrine and trespassed on the property of a landowner who had refused to sell a wedge-shaped parcel of land to the developers. The school eventually redesigned its facilities around this wedge-shaped piece of land, but not before numerous attempts had been made to

persuade the landowner to sell through intimidation and character assassination. In addition to the cozy relations between politicians and construction firms already mentioned, it's interesting to note the connections that *yakuza* frequently have to development interests.

The threats (e.g., that his business would be ruined) and accusations (e.g., that he had numerous mistresses) did not scare off this particular landowner, but they did scare off a number of potential supporters of the Konpira citizens group. At first there were only a dozen or so members in the core group, and suspicions were aroused about our motives and tactics. We were frequently red-baited as "communists" who were opposed to "free enterprise" and the rights of owners to do whatever they damn well please with their own private property. In fact, a city councilor from the Communist Party was one of our few supporters in the Hachioji City government; the other parties were apparently more interested in representing a minority of corporate executives in faraway offices than the majority of citizens who actually live in the area. In our group itself, however, there were a variety of people with a variety of work, educational, and political backgrounds. In fact, many people in the group regarded themselves as conservatives — not in the sense of supporting the existing status quo and the ideology of unimpeded development, but in the sense of wanting to *conserve* local traditions, customs, landscapes, and environments. Steve Hesse, an environmental columnist for *The Japan Times* who is also active in the group, once told me he regards this usage of the term "conservative" as being the most appropriate. There is no reason why the pro-development politicos and corporate execs constantly rattling about economic and technological "progress" should be permitted to coopt the "conservative" label. The truly dangerous revolutionaries are not the Greens, but rather those "mainstream" business executives and political leaders who propose destroying both the environment and traditional social values in the name of progress and technology.

Despite initial misunderstandings about our group's purpose, the group began to grow. On October 10, 1992, just one year after the citizens group had been formed, more than 500 people showed

up for a rally on the top of the mountain. Empowerment for us was not the brute force of the bulldozer, but the inner strength that comes from fighting for a cause we believed in. And this inner strength wasn't purely personal, but was also collective, expressing itself in our solidarity with each other. We became a community. We got to know our neighbors. We were no longer isolated individuals living in separate box houses, going to our separate jobs in the morning, anonymously brushing elbows on the train, and returning home in the evening to those same separate boxes to sit in front of the T.V. for a few hours before starting the cycle all over again. We repudiated the whole logic of modernization that encourages isolation, competition, and the artificial sense of "community" created by the mass media.

Global capitalism disempowers people by making them more interested in the titillations of entertainment and consumer goods than in having democratic control over what's happening both in their communities and in the global environment; it promotes a weakened citizenry by making people dependent on political and economic elites whom they must beg "rights" from instead of giving them a sense of self-reliance and concern for others that equally emphasizes responsibilities.

As I see it, "people power" in Japan is as much about restoring traditional Japanese notions of responsibility and genuine cooperation among people as it is about democratic freedoms and rights. Japan is not one big homogenous group; such cultural overgeneralizations feed nationalistic stereotypes and do more harm than good. The primary dividing line is not between Japan and the West, but rather between those forces that support unimpeded development and economic growth and those forces that support ecologically sustainable lifestyles and societies.

▲▲

Since I have something of an interest in religion, I asked the Shinto priest, Yamakoshi-san, after one of the rituals on the mountain, "Where is God?"

"Where is God not?" he replied, touching the leaf of a nearby tree with his fingers. "God is right here, in every

leaf and flower. Everything that's alive has its *kami* — its own divine power."

In the modern way of thinking we cut the divine off from nature and regard God either as some kind of a supernatural being that lives apart from the world way up in "heaven" or as simply dead. Either way nature comes to be seen as nothing but brute matter, a source of raw materials and natural resources that humans regard as having only instrumental value. This view of nature has its origins in the rise of Western science and the Enlightenment tradition which takes as its root metaphor not "nature as organism" but rather "nature as machine." The rise of capitalism and the unleashing of technological forces in the Industrial Revolution contributed to the idea that the good life consists of producing more material goods and consuming more of nature's resources.

The humanistic idea that science and technology can insure infinite human progress remains the dominant paradigm in our society, despite the fact that the mechanistic worldview on which it is based has increasingly come under attack. Einstein's theory of relativity has replaced Newtonian mechanics and naive views of unlimited "progress" have foundered on the Second Law of Thermodynamics: the more "progress" we have, the faster we use up resources, the more quickly energy moves from an organized state to a disorganized state, and the sooner we approach entropy, i.e., death. In the long view of history, whatever conscious life forms succeed us will view modern civilization as nothing more than a *hanabi* (sparkler) that burned brightly and spectacularly before fizzling out into the black nothingness of night.

During the past few decades, however, a new organic worldview which emphasizes equilibrium and measured balance over infinite "upward progress" (i.e., "downward regress") has been struggling to be born. Ecologists have tried to replace the view that nature has only instrumental value with the view that nature also has intrinsic value. Moving beyond individual egotism and greed toward a sense of responsibility to others and to the planet is also a theme frequently found in ecological thinking (see, for example, Warwick Fox's new book

Richard Evanoff

Toward A Transpersonal Ecology). In days past, religion was the primary repository of this point of view. The Zen Buddhist sense of No-Self can also be taken as self without boundaries, self that is able to extend in compassion toward all sentient beings. The Shinto notion that all things are animated by *kami* means that all things must be regarded as sacred. In the West we hear the pagan Neoplatonist, Plotinus, speaking of Soul (the Greek *psyche*, which the American transcendentalist Ralph Waldo Emerson called Oversoul) as a divine presence that fills all things. Christian mystics fled institutionalized religion and society to find God in the wilderness. St. Francis was able to extend this love to all of creation, and to regard the sun, moon, water, and fire as his brothers and sisters. The problem is that we have ravaged our religious traditions as much as we have ravaged the environment. Instead of actively and creatively revitalizing our religions so that they speak to the problems of our times, we have either rejected them outright or gone off in search of new religio-mytho-symbolic universes to plunder (observe in native Americans, for example, the mostly negative reaction to non-natives who occupy sweat lodges and undertake vision quests). As a result of our own inability to recreate religious meaning, the religions we grew up with ossify at the level of dogma and supersition, and are left in the hands of charlatans and hucksters.

In many religious traditions, mountains have been regarded as symbols of transcendence, of experiencing a wider sense of Self. The mountain we climb is ourselves. There is the struggle to reach the top, a stripping away of physical and mental fat and flab, a honing of sensitivities. And the closer we climb toward the top, the closer we are moving towards the center where we not only "find ourselves," but where we also find God. If God is at the center of everything that exists, then God is also at the center of ourselves. By contemplatively looking within we confront all the dark terrors of our inner selves — all the hatred, greed, fear, and insecurity that traditional religion calls illusion and sin — but if we look carefully enough we will also find a divine spark of light struggling to become a mighty flame. We can either allow that flame to grow or we can extinguish it.

Why look for God in the faraway heavens, if God is already here with us? The problem is that most of us are no longer able to experience the world as sacred. In the West a mystical sense of the immanence of the divine has largely been lost. Instead of experiencing the divine within nature, within ourselves, and within other people, we have elevated God to the status of a majestic, omnipotent isolate king and disempowered everything else by regarding humanity as "totally depraved" and nature as nothing more than "brute matter." A sense of the sacredness of nature has

Why

also been lost in Japan, however, where "love of nature" often degenerates into sentimentalism and the attention of most people is directed toward acquiring ever more extravagant lifestyles. Despite Japan's professed "love of nature," the forces that would willingly dynamite a mountain such as Konpira-san in the name of "technology and progress" are all too strong in Japanese society. We need to preserve these mountains precisely because they help us recover a sense of the sacredness of ourselves and nature. Mountains are where we go to meet God face-to-face, to hear the still small voice within, to be transfigured.

▲▲

How can we bring this sense of empowerment, that we experience on the tops of mountains, back with us into the valleys? Do we remain on the mountaintops? Do we build shrines on them so we can bask in the light of our own transfigurations? Or do we return? Do we come back down out of the mountains with a new vision, a new spirit of compassion and love? Are we able to become boddhisattvas and suffering servants, turning our backs on the highest heavens in order to descend once again to the valleys of greed and destruction? Just as degenerate religion splits God off from creation, so we too have split the world into sacred and secular domains. We split nature off from humanity and see the two in opposition to each other, with no possibility of rapprochement. We allow the mountains to be sacred; we have transformative experiences on their summits; but forget about redeeming the rest of the world.

In "Good, Wild, Sacred," an article which appeared in *CoEvolution Quarterly* before the magazine changed its name to *Whole Earth Review*, Gary Snyder marvels at the pockets of ancient climax forest that surround Shinto shrines in Japan, made possible by the fact that the land on which they are built cannot be destroyed. In the same article, however, Snyder also describes how a range of hills ten miles south of Kobe was leveled to supply the earth to create the artificial "New Island" in Kobe harbor. It took a full twelve years for the dirt to be carried from the hills to the harbor, and when the work was finished the leveled area was

Why climb a mountain?

Look! a mountain there.

I don't climb mountain.
Mountain climbs me.

Mountain is myself.
I climb on myself.

There is no mountain
nor myself.
Something
moves up and down
in the air.

Nanao Sakaki

From Break the Mirror,
North Point, 1987

used for a housing development. Evidently no shrines had been built on the tops of these mountains. "In the industrial world, it's not that 'nothing is sacred,'" Synder writes, "it's that the sacred is sacred and that's *all* that's sacred."

If we begin to regard everything that exists as holy, then all of the land in the valley is holy too — all the plains and forests and coastlines and wetlands. Why regard the stones on the mountains as holy and the stones of the valley as expendable? Aren't we able to hear both types singing to us, to see the sacredness of each with our inner eye? Why do we allow ourselves to have self-righteous feelings of spirituality on the summits of mountains if we aren't willing to roll up our shirt sleeves once we return to the

valleys, and create a society that stands in genuine harmony with nature instead of constantly trying to dominate it? Why do we retreat to nature in order to escape from civilization, instead of directly confronting the system that makes us want to escape in the first place? Why do we fight to keep the mountains "holy" but tolerate an economic system that openly admits to being based on greed and the unlimited pursuit of opulence?

The "environmental crisis" is not some future apocalyptic event. It is already *here*. The question is not how much longer can we go on with our overconsumptive lifestyles before the situation gets "really serious." The situation already *is* really serious. People are *already* dying from pollution; our quality of life has *already* deteriorated; the lines of battle over the future control and use of resources are *already* being drawn. The only way we can continue to believe in the "rightness" of our present social system is by closing our eyes to all the poverty, crime, drugs, homelessness, sexual abuse, racism, violence, and ecological devastation it has already generated. If this is the best that our present capitalistic system can do with all its wondrous technology, then it's time for a change.

In the case of Konpira-san, the local citizens group finally won. On May 21, 1993 the school that had planned to dynamite the mountain formally abandoned the project. The presence of the shrine, the historical significance of the mountain, and the inability to reach an agreement with local residents were cited as reasons. The Konpira issue provides a small but significant example of local citizens taking power back into their own hands, instead of leaving it in the hands of government officials and business leaders. Unfortunately, however, the citizens movement is a mere David standing before the Goliath of industry and government bureaucracy. In Zushi, for example, local citizens have roundly rejected plans for the U.S. government to build military housing on forested land, by democratically electing an anti-development local government. Japan's national government nonetheless supports the plan to build the housing, and has bulldozed over Zushi's local government by giving permission for construction to begin.

Whose democracy is the U.S. military and Japan's national government presuming to defend and uphold?

In Takao we face similar pressures. Konpira-san has been saved, but the construction company hired to dynamite the mountain still has plans to develop the forested area south of Takao by building a golf course and condominiums to house 20,000 people. There are also plans to build a spaghetti-style interchange and a tunnel through Mt. Takao to provide an exit ramp for the *Ken-o-do*, a proposed loopway that would connect the outlying areas of Tokyo. Not only would plant and animal life be destroyed, but the people who live in the area would also face more traffic jams, loss of scenery, and a degraded environment. Nonetheless, powerful business interests stand behind these projects, and the national government stands behind them as well. Only the local residents stand opposed.

Konpira-san is one of the first mountains a traveler sees when heading west out of Tokyo. The mountains extend south to Tanzawa, north to Okutama, and west to Mt. Fuji, and many of these areas are under threat of development. Mountains are already being flattened to make housing projects. Despite Japan's refusal to import foreign agricultural products, on the grounds that it needs to maintain food self-sufficiency, valuable farmland is increasingly being paved over by development projects. The proposed linear motor car (Maglev) will cut a swath of ecological destruction through these mountains all the way from Kofu to Tokyo. The propaganda supporting all this development claims that more houses and faster train service will help to improve our overall "quality of life." Certainly those who stand to profit from these development projects will be richer than before, but the rest of us will have to contend with even more congestion, even higher land prices, and ever-shrinking housing space. More development will not improve our quality of life, but only help to make Tokyo eventually look like something out of *Bladerunner*.

I've been hiking through a lot of these mountains, trying to travel as extensively in my own area as Thoreau did in Concord. I keep a record of all the paths I've been on and figure there are enough trails in

Natsuyama (Ohara, summer) Komatsu Hitoshi, 1957, Shiga Museum of Modern Art

these mountains to keep me busy for the rest of my life. Like Thoreau, I believe that we need to stand momentarily outside of civilization if we are to really come to a true understanding of ourselves. We each have a wild untamed part of ourselves that can't be imprisoned in office buildings and straightjacketed in business suits. Like the sages and desert saints of old, the wilderness is where we go to conquer the demons within us and hopefully also to meet the divine. Mountains can empower us, they can transform us. And that same power can be used to transform the world.

Walking home one evening recently, I saw the sun slipping down behind Konpira-san. The mountain was still there, just like it's been for ages and just like I hope it'll be for a long time to come. The sun was a nimbus of gold behind it; the entire horizon was bathed in the light of dusk. The divine is here with us, the earth and everything in it is sacred.   ▲

MOUNTAINS OF THE MIND

ROBERT BRADY

Everyone knows that the mind becomes extremely mountainous only a few steps in from the coast. The creatures that reside in this uncharted area on our mental maps are seldom seen by others, yet are common to us all; still, they can be a hazard to the solitary explorer who is not prepared to confront the unbelievable in his hinterland as he wends his way into the nether regions, from which few return unchanged. Hermits, poets and other explorers of these fastnesses are well acquainted with the species of the inward realms, and are even known on occasion to have these creatures eating out of their hands. But these nether fauna can never be completely tamed; and what would the outer reaches be, without their inner complement of native wildlife? Between ourselves, however, we can only use

metaphoric nomenclature to speak of these denizens we harbor in common, the names we call them imparting no description of their morphology, coloring or way of life. These are not crude and dispensable beings, but highly developed and specialized life forms essential to our spiritual ecology (psychological and religious taxonomy notwithstanding). And there are many more such beings that have no names; yet we all know very well in ourselves of at least the presence of these creatures, who have at times poked their heads out of the thick undergrowth that adorns the verge of each of us: they are all part of the vastness of the experience when, in the world outside, we see a mountain and its wilds, that call to us as like to like; to climb such a peak and view the world from its summit is to do so as well within ourselves, to view at one remove the panoramas that we are. And in so ascending we metaphorically surmount the wilderness within, survive vicarious passage to the summits of ourselves, to a clearer light, a cleaner wind. And we take this knowledge with us on our return to the narrow lowlands where we spend our daily lives as habitants of seeming mountainous islands, surrounded by seas of intercourse teeming with creatures that thrive in the depths of the apparent distance between us, those sometimes stormy, sometimes tranquil seas of relation that are as much illusion as the real world; for as each mountain is aware, at the foundation we are all connected. ●

Cairn, Kuju Range, Kyushu: John Einarsen